The Science
of Secrecy

The Science of Secrecy

THE SECRET HISTORY OF
CODES AND CODEBREAKING

Fourth Estate • London

First published in Great Britain in 2000 by
Fourth Estate Limited
6 Salem Road
London W2 4BU
www.4thestate.co.uk

1 3 5 7 9 10 8 6 4 2

A catalogue record for this book is available from the British Library.
ISBN 1-84115-435-0

Typeset by Type Technique, London W1
Designed by Robert Updegraff
Printed in Great Britain by Biddles Ltd, Guildford & Kings Lynn

The urge to discover secrets is deeply ingrained in human nature; even the least curious mind is roused by the promise of sharing knowledge withheld from others. Some are fortunate enough to find a job which consists in the solution of mysteries, but most of us are driven to sublimate this urge by the solving of artificial puzzles devised for our entertainment. Detective stories or crossword puzzles cater for the majority; the solution of secret codes may be the pursuit of a few.

John Chadwick
The Decipherment of Linear B

Contents

Introduction

FOR THOUSANDS OF YEARS, kings, queens and generals have relied on efficient communication in order to govern their countries and command their armies. At the same time they have all been aware of the consequences of their messages falling into the wrong hands, revealing precious secrets to rival nations and betraying vital information to opposing forces. It was the threat of enemy interception that motivated the development of codes and ciphers – techniques for disguising a message so that only the intended recipient can read it.

The desire for secrecy has led nation states to establish codemaking departments, responsible for ensuring the security of communications by inventing and implementing the best possible codes. At the same time, enemy codebreakers have attempted to break these codes and steal secrets. Codebreakers are linguistic alchemists, a mystical tribe attempting to conjure sensible words out of meaningless symbols. The history of codes and ciphers is the story of the centuries-old battle between codemakers and codebreakers, an intellectual arms race that has had a dramatic impact on the course of history.

When I attempted to describe the history of codes and codebreaking in the Channel 4 TV series *The Science of Secrecy*, it was clear from the outset that I would be able to give just an outline of a few of the most important historical events. Television is a remarkably powerful medium, reaching millions of people, but its weakness is its inability to provide the details of a subject. Often, the most exciting aspects of a subject are to be found in its scientific and historical details. The aim of this book is to explore more deeply the subjects covered in the TV series, each chapter corresponding to one episode from the series. To achieve this, I have used many examples and anecdotes from my first book on codes and codebreaking, *The Code Book*.

This book, like the TV series, has two main objectives. The first is to chart the evolution of codes. 'Evolution' is a wholly appropriate term, because the development of codes can be viewed as an evolutionary struggle. A code is constantly under attack from codebreakers. When the codebreakers have developed a new weapon that reveals a code's weakness, that code is no longer useful. It either becomes extinct or it evolves into a new, stronger code. In turn, this new code thrives only until the codebreakers identify its weakness, and so on. This is analogous to the situation facing, for example, a strain of infectious bacteria. The bacteria live, thrive and survive until doctors discover an antibiotic that exposes a weakness in the bacteria and kills them. The bacteria are forced to evolve to outwit the antibiotic, and, if successful, they will thrive once again and re-establish themselves. The bacteria are continually forced to evolve in order to survive the onslaught of new antibiotics.

The ongoing battle between codemakers and codebreakers has inspired a whole series of brillliant scientific breakthroughs. The codemakers have continually striven to construct ever-stronger codes for defending communications, while the codebreakers have continually invented more ingenious methods for attacking them. In their efforts to destroy or preserve secrecy, both sides have drawn upon a diverse range of disciplines and technologies — from mathematics to linguistics, from information theory to quantum theory. In return, codemakers and codebreakers have enriched these subjects, and their work has accelerated technological development, most notably in the case of the modern computer.

History is punctuated with codes. They have decided the outcomes of battles and led to the deaths of kings and queens. I have therefore been able to call upon stories of political intrigue and tales of life and death to illustrate the key turning points in the evolutionary development of codes. The history of codes is so inordinately rich that I have been forced to leave out many fascinating stories, which in turn means that my account is not definitive. If you would like to find out more about your favourite tale or your favourite codebreaker, please refer to the list of further reading at the end of the book.

After describing the evolution of codes and their impact on history, the book's second objective is to demonstrate how codes are more relevant today than ever before. As information becomes an increasingly valuable commodity, and as the communications revolution changes society, so the process of encoding messages, known as encryption, is coming to play a crucial role in everyday life. Nowadays our phone calls bounce off satellites and our e-mails pass through various computers, and both forms of communication can be intercepted with ease, jeopardising our privacy. Similarly, as more and more business is conducted over the Internet, safeguards must be put in place to protect companies and their clients. Encryption is the only way to protect our privacy and guarantee the success of the digital marketplace. The science of secret communication, otherwise known as cryptography, will provide the locks and keys of the Information Age.

The epilogue covers an aspect of cryptography that was barely touched upon in the television series, a dilemma that results from the strength and widespread availability of today's encryption systems. Like the majority of technologies, cryptography is a double-edged sword. On the positive side, it can now guarantee the privacy of ordinary citizens and enable businesses to conduct e-commerce. On the negative side, it can provide criminals with the tools required to avoid surveillance. For decades, the police have used wire-taps to gather evidence against criminals, but the development of ultra-strong codes threatens to undermine the value of wire-taps. Consequently, the forces of law and order are lobbying governments to restrict the public use of cryptography. At the same time, civil libertarians are pressing for the widespread use of cryptography in order to protect the privacy of the individual, and arguing alongside them are businesses, which require strong cryptography to guarantee the security of Internet transactions. The question is, which do we value more — our privacy and a thriving economy or an effective police force? Or is there a compromise?

Before concluding this introduction, I must mention a problem that faces any author who tackles the subject of cryptography. By its very nature, research into codes and ciphers is often conducted behind closed doors. This is illustrated by the fact that many of the heroes in this book never gained recognition for their work during their lifetimes because their contribution could not be publicly acknowledged while their invention was still of diplomatic or military value. Today, organisations such as GCHQ and America's National Security Agency continue to conduct classified research into cryptography, which means that their breakthroughs remain secret and the individuals who make them remain anonymous. There is a great deal more going on, of which neither I nor any other science writer is aware. The science of secrecy is indeed a secret science.

CHAPTER ONE

The Cipher of Mary Queen of Scots

The birth of cryptography, the substitution cipher and frequency analysis

O N THE MORNING of Saturday 15 October 1586, Queen Mary entered the crowded courtroom at Fotheringhay Castle. Years of imprisonment and the onset of rheumatism had taken their toll, yet she remained dignified, composed and indisputably regal. Assisted by her physician, she made her way past the judges, officials and spectators, and approached the throne that stood halfway along the long, narrow chamber. Mary had assumed that the throne was a gesture of respect towards her, but she was mistaken. The throne symbolised the absent Queen Elizabeth, Mary's enemy and prosecutor. Mary was gently guided away from the throne and over to the opposite side of the room, towards the defendant's seat, a crimson velvet chair.

Mary Queen of Scots was on trial for treason. She had been accused of plotting to assassinate Queen Elizabeth in order to take the English crown for herself. Sir Francis Walsingham, Elizabeth's principal private secretary, had already arrested the other conspirators, extracted confessions, and executed them. Now he planned to prove that Mary was at the heart of the plot, and was therefore equally culpable and equally deserving of death.

Walsingham knew that before he could have Mary executed he would have to convince Queen Elizabeth of her guilt. Although Elizabeth despised Mary, she had several reasons for being reluctant to see her put to death. First, Mary was a Scottish queen, and many questioned whether an English court had the authority to execute a foreign head of state. Second, executing Mary might establish an awkward precedent – if the state is allowed to kill one queen, then perhaps rebels might have fewer qualms about killing another, namely Elizabeth. Third, Elizabeth and Mary were relatives, and their blood tie made Elizabeth all the more squeamish about ordering her execution. In short, Elizabeth would sanction Mary's execution only if Walsingham could prove beyond any hint of doubt that she had been part of the assassination plot.

The conspirators were a group of young English Catholic noblemen intent on removing Elizabeth, a Protestant, and replacing her with Mary, a fellow Catholic. It was apparent to the court that Mary was a figurehead for the conspirators, but it was not clear that she had actually given her blessing to the conspiracy. In fact, Mary had authorised the plot. The challenge for Walsingham was to demonstrate a palpable link between Mary and the plotters.

Mary Queen of Scots

On the morning of her trial, Mary sat alone in the dock, dressed in sorrowful black velvet. In cases of treason the accused was forbidden counsel and was not permitted to call witnesses. Mary was not even allowed secretaries to help her prepare her case. However, her plight was not hopeless because she had been careful to ensure that all her correspondence with the conspirators had been written in cipher. The cipher turned her words into a meaningless series of symbols, and Mary believed that even if Walsingham had captured the letters, he could have no idea of the meaning of the words within them. If their contents were a mystery, then the letters could not be used as evidence against her. However, this all depended on the assumption that her cipher had not been broken.

Unfortunately for Mary, Walsingham was not merely Elizabeth's principal private secretary, he was also England's spymaster. In fact, he was the father of the English secret service. He had intercepted Mary's letters to the plotters, and he knew exactly who might be capable of deciphering them. Thomas Phelippes was the nation's foremost expert on breaking codes. For years he had been deciphering messages sent by those who plotted against Queen Elizabeth, thereby providing the evidence needed to condemn them. If he could decipher the incriminating letters between Mary and the conspirators, then her death would be inevitable. On the other hand, if Mary's cipher was strong enough to conceal her secrets, then there was a chance she might survive. Not for the first time, a life hung on the strength of a cipher.

The Evolution of Secret Writing

Some of the earliest accounts of secret writing date back to Herodotus, 'the Father of History' according to the Roman philosopher and statesman Cicero. In *The Histories*, Herodotus chronicled the conflicts between Greece and Persia in the fifth century BC, which he viewed as a confrontation between freedom and slavery, between the independent Greek states and the oppressive Persians. Herodotus believed that it was the art of secret writing that had saved Greece from being conquered by Xerxes, King of Kings, the despotic leader of the Persians.

The long-running feud between Greece and Persia reached a crisis soon after Xerxes began constructing a city at Persepolis, the new capital for his kingdom. Tributes and gifts arrived from all over the empire and neighbouring states, with the notable exceptions of Athens and Sparta. Determined to avenge this insolence, Xerxes began mobilising a force, declaring that, 'We shall extend the empire of Persia such that its boundaries will be God's own sky, so the sun will not look down upon any land beyond the boundaries of what is our own.' He spent the next five years secretly assembling the greatest fighting force in history, and then, in 480 BC, he was ready to launch a surprise attack.

However, the Persian military build-up had been witnessed by Demaratus, a Greek who had been expelled from his homeland and lived in the Persian city of Susa. Despite being exiled he still felt some loyalty to Greece, so he decided to send a message to warn the Spartans of Xerxes' invasion plan. The challenge was how to dispatch the message without it being intercepted by the Persian guards. Herodotus wrote:

> As the danger of discovery was great, there was only one way in which he could contrive to get the message through: this was by scraping the wax off a pair of wooden folding tablets, writing on the wood underneath what Xerxes intended to do, and then covering the message over with wax again. In this way the tablets, being apparently blank, would cause no trouble with the guards along the road. When the message reached its destination, no one was able to guess the secret, until, as I understand, Cleomenes' daughter Gorgo, who was the wife of Leonidas, divined and told the others that if they scraped the wax off, they would find something written on the wood underneath. This was done; the message was revealed and read, and afterwards passed on to the other Greeks.

As a result of this warning, the hitherto defenceless Greeks began to arm themselves. Profits from the state-owned silver mines, which were usually shared among the citizens, were instead diverted to the navy for the construction of two hundred warships.

Xerxes had lost the vital element of surprise, and on 23 September 480 BC, when the Persian fleet approached the Bay of Salamis near Athens, the Greeks were prepared. Although Xerxes believed he had trapped the Greek navy, the Greeks were deliberately enticing the Persian ships to enter the bay. The Greeks knew that their ships, smaller and fewer in number, would have been destroyed in the open sea, but they realised that within the confines of the bay they might outmanoeuvre the Persians. As the wind changed direction the Persians found themselves being blown into the bay, forced into an engagement on Greek terms. The Persian princess Artemisia became surrounded on three sides and attempted to head back out to sea, only to ram one of her own ships. Panic ensued, more Persian ships collided, and the Greeks launched a full-blooded onslaught. Within a day the formidable forces of Persia had been humbled.

Demaratus' strategy for secret communication relied on simply hiding the message. Herodotus also recounted another incident in which concealment was sufficient to secure the safe passage of a message. He chronicled the story of Histaiaeus, who wanted to encourage Aristagoras of Miletus to revolt against the Persian king. To convey his instructions securely, Histaiaeus shaved the head of his messenger, wrote the message on his scalp, and then waited for the hair to regrow. This was clearly a period of history that tolerated a certain lack of urgency. The messenger, apparently carrying nothing contentious, could travel without being harassed. Upon arriving at his destination he then shaved his head and pointed it at the intended recipient.

Secret communication achieved by hiding the existence of a message is known as *steganography*, derived from the Greek words *steganos*, meaning 'covered', and *graphein*, meaning 'to write'. In the two thousand years since Herodotus, various forms of steganography have been used throughout the world. For example, the ancient Chinese wrote messages on fine silk that was scrunched into a tiny ball and covered in wax, which the messenger would then swallow. In the sixteenth century, the Italian scientist Giovanni Porta described how to conceal a message within a hard-boiled egg by making an ink from a mixture of one ounce of alum and a pint of vinegar, which is then used to write on the shell. The solution penetrates the porous shell and leaves a message on the surface of the hardened egg albumen, which can be read only when the shell is removed. Steganography also includes the practice of writing in invisible ink. As far back as the first century AD, Pliny the Elder explained how the 'milk' of the thithymallus plant could be used as invisible ink. Although it is transparent after drying, gentle heating chars the ink and turns it brown. Many organic fluids behave in a similar way because they are rich in carbon and therefore char easily. Indeed, it is not unknown for modern spies who have run out of standard-issue invisible ink to improvise by using their own urine.

The longevity of steganography illustrates that it certainly offers a modicum of security, but it does suffer from a fundamental weakness. If the messenger is searched and the message is found, then the contents of the secret communication are revealed at once. Interception of the message immediately compromises all security. A thorough guard might routinely search any person crossing a border, scraping any wax tablets, heating blank sheets of paper, shelling boiled eggs, shaving people's heads, and so on, and inevitably there will be occasions when the message is discovered.

Hence, in parallel with the development of steganography, there was the evolution of *cryptography*, derived from the Greek word *kryptos*, meaning 'hidden'. The aim of cryptography is not to hide the existence of a message but rather to hide its meaning, a process known as *encryption*. To render a message unintelligible, it is scrambled according to a particular protocol which is agreed beforehand between the sender and the intended recipient. Thus the recipient can reverse the scrambling protocol and make the message comprehensible. The advantage of cryptography is that if the enemy intercepts an encrypted message, then the message is unreadable. Without knowing the scrambling protocol, the enemy should find it difficult – if not impossible – to recreate the original message from the encrypted text.

Although cryptography and steganography are independent, it is possible to both scramble and hide a message to maximise security. For example, the microdot is a form of steganography that became popular during the Second World War. German agents in Latin America would photographically shrink a page of text down to a dot less than a millimetre in diameter, and then hide this microdot on top of a full stop in an apparently innocuous letter. The first microdot to be spotted by the FBI was in 1941, following a tip-off that the Americans should look for a tiny gleam from the surface of a letter, indicative of smooth film. Thereafter the Americans could read the contents of most intercepted microdots, except when the German agents had taken the extra precaution of scrambling their message before reducing it. In such cases of cryptography combined with steganography, the

Americans were sometimes able to intercept and block communications, but they were prevented from gaining any new information about German spying activity. Of the two branches of secret communication, cryptography is the more powerful because of this ability to prevent information from falling into enemy hands.

In turn, cryptography itself can be divided into two branches, known as *transposition* and *substitution*. In transposition, the letters of a message are simply rearranged, effectively generating an anagram. For very short messages, such as a single word, this method is relatively insecure because there are only a limited number of ways of rearranging a handful of letters. For example, three letters can be arranged in only six different ways, e.g. **cow cwo ocw owc wco woc**. However, as the number of letters gradually increases, the number of possible arrangements rapidly explodes, making it impossible to get back to the original message unless the exact scrambling process is known. **For example, consider this short sentence.** It contains just 35 letters, and yet there are more than 50,000,000,000,000,000,000,000,000,000,000,000 distinct ways to arrange them. If one person could check one arrangement per second, and if all the people in the world worked night and day, it would still take more than a thousand times the lifetime of the universe to check all the arrangements.

A random transposition of letters seems to offer a very high level of security because it would be impractical for an enemy interceptor to unscramble even a short sentence. But there is a drawback. Such transposition effectively generates an incredibly difficult anagram, and if the letters are randomly jumbled, with neither rhyme nor reason, then unscrambling the anagram is impossible for the intended recipient as well as an enemy interceptor. In order for transposition to be effective, the rearrangement of letters needs to follow a straightforward system, one that has been previously agreed by sender and receiver, but kept secret from the enemy. For example, schoolchildren sometimes send messages using the 'rail fence' transposition, in which the message is written with alternate letters on separate upper and lower lines. The sequence of letters on the lower line is then tagged on at the end of the sequence on the upper line to create the final encrypted message. For example:

THY SECRET IS THY PRISONER; IF THOU LET IT GO, THOU ART A PRISONER TO IT

↓

T Y E R T S H P I O E I T O L T T O H U R A R S N R O T
H S C E I T Y R S N R F H U E I G T O A T P I O E T I

↓

TYERTSHPIOEITOLTTOHURARSNROTHSCEITYRSNRFHUEIGTOATPIOETI

The receiver can recover the message by simply reversing the process. There are various other forms of systematic transposition, including the three-line rail fence cipher, in which the message is first written on three separate lines instead of two. Alternatively, one could swap each pair of letters so that the first and second letters switch places, the third and fourth letters switch places, and so on.

The alternative to transposition is substitution. One of the earliest descriptions of encryption by substitution appears in the *Kāma-sūtra*, a text written in the fourth century AD by the Brahmin scholar Vātsyāyana, but based on manuscripts dating back to the fourth century BC. The *Kāma-sūtra* recommends that women should study sixty-four arts, such as cooking, dressing, massage and the preparation of perfumes. The list also includes some less obvious arts, namely conjuring, chess,

THE SCYTALE: CIPHER ON A STICK

The first ever military cryptographic device, the Spartan *scytale*, dating back to the fifth century BC, demonstrates a form of transposition. The scytale is a wooden staff around which a strip of leather or parchment is wound. The sender writes the message (**SEND MORE TROOPS . . .**) along the length of the scytale, and then unwinds the strip, which now appears to carry a list of meaningless letters (**S, T, S, F, . . .**). The message has been scrambled. The messenger would take the leather strip, and, as a steganographic twist, he might disguise it as a belt with the letters facing the inside. To recover the message, the receiver simply wraps the leather strip around a scytale of the same diameter as the one used by the sender.

In 404 BC Lysander of Sparta was confronted by a messenger, bloody and battered, one of only five to have survived the arduous journey from Persia. The messenger handed his belt to Lysander, who wound it around his scytale to learn that Pharnabazus of Persia was planning to attack him. Thanks to the scytale, Lysander was prepared for the attack and repulsed it.

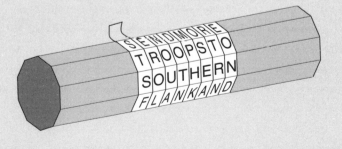

bookbinding and carpentry. Number 45 on the list is *mlecchita-vikalpā*, the art of secret writing, advocated for helping women to conceal details of their liaisons. One of the recommended techniques is to pair letters of the alphabet at random, and then substitute each letter in the original message with its partner. If we apply the principle to the Roman alphabet, we could pair letters as follows:

A	D	H	I	K	M	O	R	S	U	W	Y	Z
↕	↕	↕	↕	↕	↕	↕	↕	↕	↕	↕	↕	↕
V	X	B	G	J	C	Q	L	N	E	F	P	T

Then, instead of **meet at midnight**, the sender would write **CUUZ VZ CGXSGIBZ**. This form of secret writing is called a substitution cipher because each letter in the original text is substituted for a different symbol, thus acting in a complementary way to the transposition cipher. In transposition each letter retains its identity but changes its position, whereas in substitution each letter changes its identity but retains its position.

The first documented use of a substitution cipher for military purposes appears in Julius Caesar's *Gallic Wars*. Caesar describes how he sent a message to Cicero, who was besieged and on the verge of surrendering. The substitution replaced Roman letters with Greek letters, rendering the message unintelligible to the enemy. Caesar described the dramatic delivery of the message:

> The messenger was instructed, if he could not approach, to hurl a spear, with the letter fastened to the thong, inside the entrenchment of the camp. Fearing danger, the Gaul discharged the spear, as he had been instructed. By chance it stuck fast in the tower, and for two days was not sighted by our troops; on the third day it was sighted by a soldier, taken down, and delivered to Cicero. He read it through and then recited it at a parade of the troops, bringing the greatest rejoicing to all.

Caesar used secret writing so frequently that Valerius Probus wrote an entire treatise on his ciphers, which unfortunately has not survived. However, thanks to Suetonius' *Lives of the Caesars LVI*, written in the second century AD, we do have a detailed description of one of the types of substitution cipher used by Julius Caesar. He simply replaced each letter in the message with the letter that is three places further down the alphabet. Cryptographers often think in terms of the *plain alphabet*, the alphabet used to write the original message, and the *cipher alphabet*, the letters that are substituted in place of the plain letters. When the plain alphabet is placed above the cipher alphabet, as shown in Figure 1, it is clear that the cipher alphabet has been shifted by three places, and hence

Plain alphabet	a b c d e f g h i j k l m n o p q r s t u v w x y z
Cipher alphabet	D E F G H I J K L M N O P Q R S T U V W X Y Z A B C

Plaintext	v e n i, v i d i, v i c i
Ciphertext	Y H Q L, Y L G L, Y L F L

Figure 1 *The Caesar cipher applied to a short message. The Caesar cipher is based on a cipher alphabet that is shifted a certain number of places (in this case three) relative to the plain alphabet. The convention in cryptography is to write the plain alphabet in lower-case letters, and the cipher alphabet in capitals. Similarly, the original message, the plaintext, is written in lower case, and the encrypted message, the ciphertext, is written in capitals.*

FROM CAESAR CIPHER TO JULIAN CALENDAR

Gaius Julius Caesar, to give him his full name, is the best-known personage in the long history of the Roman world. He was a tall, noble figure, one of the greatest generals of all time, a noted orator and a great reformer. The Caesar cipher is just one of the many ways in which his name lives on as part of our language. For example, *Caesarean section* is the name given to an operation for delivering a baby through an incision in the abdomen and uterus, for legend has it that this was how Julius Caesar (or perhaps one of his ancestors) was born. *Caesarean* can also mean an imperialist, reflecting Caesar's dictatorial approach to leadership and his empire-building ambitions, the former quality leading to his assassination by the conspirators Brutus and Cassius in 44 BC. Similarly, his name is the inspiration for the German *Kaiser* and Russian *tsar*, both meaning 'great ruler'.

Less politically relevant, but equally enduring, the Romans renamed the month of Quintilis (in which he was born) in his honour, and we still call it July. The Julian calendar, with twelve months, was introduced by Julius Caesar in 45 BC to replace the old Roman calendar, which with its ten months was failing to keep step with the seasons. He also introduced the leap day, an extra day added to the end of the second month every four years. Despite these refinements, the Julian calendar does not quite keep pace with the seasons, for the Earth takes just a little less than the average Julian year of 365.25 days to complete one orbit of the Sun (we now use the Gregorian calendar). Nevertheless, it is still in use in some Eastern Orthodox Christian countries.

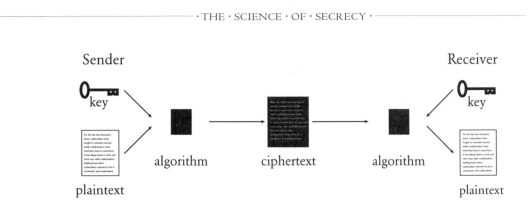

Figure 2 To encrypt a plaintext message, the sender passes it through an encryption algorithm. The algorithm is a general system for encryption, and needs to be specified exactly by selecting a key. Applying the key and algorithm together to a plaintext generates the encrypted message, or ciphertext. The ciphertext may be intercepted by an enemy while it is being transmitted to the receiver, but the enemy should not be able to decipher the message. However, the receiver, who knows both the key and the algorithm used by the sender, is able to turn the ciphertext back into the plaintext message.

this form of substitution is often called the *Caesar shift cipher*, or simply the Caesar cipher. A cipher is the name given to any form of cryptographic substitution in which each letter is replaced by another letter or symbol.

Although Suetonius mentions only a Caesar shift of three places, it is clear that by using any shift between 1 and 25 places it is possible to generate 25 distinct ciphers. In fact, if we do not restrict ourselves to shifting the alphabet but instead permit the cipher alphabet to be any rearrangement of the plain alphabet, then we can generate an even greater number of distinct ciphers. There are over 400,000,000,000,000,000,000,000,000 such rearrangements, and therefore the same number of distinct ciphers.

Each distinct cipher can be considered in terms of an *algorithm*, which is a general encrypting method, and a *key*, which specifies the exact details of a particular encryption. In this case, the algorithm involves substituting each letter in the plain alphabet with a letter from a cipher alphabet, and the cipher alphabet is allowed to consist of any rearrangement of the plain alphabet. The key defines the exact cipher alphabet to be used for a particular encryption. The relationship between the algorithm and the key is illustrated in Figure 2.

An enemy studying an intercepted scrambled message may have a strong suspicion of the algorithm, but would not know the exact key. For example, they may well suspect that each letter in the plaintext has been replaced by a different letter according to a cipher alphabet, but they are unlikely to know which particular cipher alphabet has been used. If the cipher alphabet, the key, is kept a closely guarded secret between the sender and receiver, then the enemy cannot decipher the intercepted message. The significance of the key, as opposed to the algorithm, is an enduring principle of cryptography. It was definitively stated in 1883 by the Dutch linguist Auguste Kerckhoffs in his book *La Cryptographie militaire*. Kerckhoffs's Principle states that 'the security of a cryptosystem must not depend on keeping secret the crypto-algorithm. The security depends only on keeping secret the key.'

In addition to keeping the key secret, a secure cipher system must also have a wide range of potential keys. For example, if the sender uses the Caesar shift cipher to encrypt a message, then encryption is relatively weak because there are only 25 potential keys. From the enemy's point of view, if they intercept the message and suspect that the algorithm being used is the Caesar shift, then they merely have to check the 25 possibilities. However, if the sender uses the more general substitution algorithm, which permits the cipher alphabet to be any rearrangement of the plain alphabet, then there are 400,000,000,000,000,000,000,000,000 possible keys from which to choose. One such is shown in Figure 3. From the enemy's point of view, if the message is intercepted and the algorithm is known, there is still the horrendous task of checking all possible keys. If an enemy agent were able to check one of the 400,000,000,000,000,000,000,000,000 possible keys every second, it would take roughly a billion times the lifetime of the universe to check them all and decipher the message.

The beauty of this type of cipher is that it is easy to implement, but provides a high level of security. It is easy for the sender to define the key, which consists merely of stating the order of the 26 letters in the rearranged cipher alphabet, and yet it is effectively impossible for the enemy to check all possible keys by the so-called brute-force attack. The simplicity of the key is important because the sender and receiver have to share knowledge of the key, and the simpler the key, the less the chance of a misunderstanding.

| Plain alphabet | a b c d e f g h i j k l m n o p q r s t u v w x y z |
| Cipher alphabet | J L P A W I Q B C T R Z Y D S K E G F X H U O N V M |

| Plaintext | e t t u, b r u t e ? |
| Ciphertext | W X X H, L G H X W ? |

Figure 3 *An example of the general substitution algorithm, in which each letter in the plaintext is substituted with another letter according to a key. The key is defined by the cipher alphabet, which can be any rearrangement of the plain alphabet.*

In fact, an even simpler key is possible if the sender is prepared to accept a slight reduction in the number of potential keys. Instead of randomly rearranging the plain alphabet to achieve the cipher alphabet, the sender chooses a *keyword* or *keyphrase*. For example, to use **JULIUS CAESAR** as a keyphrase, begin by removing any spaces and repeated letters (**JULISCAER**), and then use this as the beginning of the jumbled cipher alphabet. The remainder of the cipher alphabet is merely the remaining letters of the alphabet, in their correct order, starting with the letter following the last letter in the keyphrase. Hence, the cipher alphabet would read as follows.

Plain alphabet   a b c d e f g h i j k l m n o p q r s t u v w x y z
Cipher alphabet   J U L I S C A E R T V W X Y Z B D F G H K M N O P Q

The advantage of building a cipher alphabet in this way is that it is easy to memorise the keyword or keyphrase, and hence the cipher alphabet. This is important because if the sender has to keep the cipher alphabet on a piece of paper, the enemy might capture the paper, discover the key, and read any communications that have been encrypted with it. However, if the key can be committed to memory it is less likely to fall into enemy hands. Clearly the number of cipher alphabets generated by keyphrases is smaller than the number of cipher alphabets generated without restriction, but the number is still immense, and it would be effectively impossible for the enemy to unscramble a captured message by testing all possible keyphrases.

This simplicity and strength meant that the substitution cipher dominated cryptography throughout the first millennium AD. Codemakers had evolved a system for guaranteeing secure communication, so there was no need for further development — without necessity, there was no need for further invention. The onus had fallen upon the codebreakers, those who were attempting to crack the substitution cipher. Was there any way for an enemy interceptor to unravel an encrypted message? Many ancient scholars considered that the substitution cipher was unbreakable, thanks to the gigantic number of possible keys, and for centuries this seemed to be true. However, codebreakers would eventually find a shortcut to the process of exhaustively searching all keys. Instead of taking billions of years to crack a cipher, the shortcut could reveal the message in a matter of minutes. The breakthrough occurred in the East, and required a brilliant combination of linguistics, statistics and religious devotion.

The Arab Cryptanalysts

At the age of about forty, Muhammad began regularly visiting an isolated cave on Mount Hira just outside Mecca. This was a retreat, a place for prayer, meditation and contemplation. It was during a period of deep reflection, around AD 610, that he was visited by the archangel Gabriel, who proclaimed that Muhammad was to be the messenger of God. This was the first of a series of revelations which continued until Muhammad died some twenty years later. The revelations were recorded by various scribes during the Prophet's life, but only as fragments, and it was left to Abū Bakr, the first caliph of Islam, to gather them together into a single text. The work was continued by Umar, the second caliph, and his daughter Hafsa, and was eventually completed by Uthmān, the third caliph. Each revelation became one of the 114 chapters of the Koran.

The ruling caliph was responsible for carrying on the work of the Prophet, upholding his teachings and spreading his word. Between the appointment of Abū Bakr in 632 and the death of the fourth caliph, Alī, in 661, Islam spread until half of the known world was under Muslim rule. Then in 750, after a century of consolidation, the start of the Abbasid caliphate (or dynasty) heralded the golden age of Islamic civilisation. The arts and sciences flourished in equal measure. Islamic craftsmen bequeathed us magnificent paintings, ornate carvings and the most elaborate textiles in history, while the legacy of Islamic scientists is evident from the number of Arabic words that pepper the lexicon of modern science, words such as *algebra*, *alkaline* and *zenith*.

The richness of Islamic culture was to a large part the product of a wealthy and peaceful society. The Abbasid caliphs were less interested than their predecessors in conquest, and instead concentrated on establishing an organised and affluent society. Lower taxes encouraged businesses to grow and gave rise to greater commerce and industry, while strict laws reduced corruption and protected the citizens. All of this relied on an effective system of administration, and in turn the administrators relied on secure communication achieved through the use of encryption. As well as encrypting sensitive affairs of state, it is documented that officials protected tax records, demonstrating a widespread and routine use of cryptography. Further evidence comes from many administrative manuals, such as the tenth-century *Adab al-Kuttāb* ('The Secretaries' Manual'), which include sections devoted to cryptography.

The administrators usually employed a cipher alphabet which was simply a rearrangement of the plain alphabet, as described earlier, but they also used cipher alphabets that contained other types of symbol. For example, **a** in the plain alphabet might be replaced by **#** in the cipher alphabet, **b** might be replaced by **+**, and so on. The *monoalphabetic substitution cipher* is the general name given to any substitution cipher in which the cipher alphabet consists of either letters or symbols, or a mix of both. All the substitution ciphers we have met so far fall into this general category.

Had the Arabs merely been familiar with the use of the monoalphabetic substitution cipher, they would not warrant a significant mention in any history of cryptography. However, in addition to employing ciphers, the Arab scholars were also capable of destroying them. It was they who invented *cryptanalysis*, the science of unscrambling a message without knowledge of the key. While the cryptographer develops new methods of secret writing, it is the cryptanalyst who struggles to find weaknesses in these methods in order to break into secret messages. Arabian cryptanalysts succeeded in finding a method for breaking the monoalphabetic substitution cipher, a cipher that had remained invulnerable for several centuries.

Cryptanalysis could not be invented until a civilisation had reached a sufficiently sophisticated level of scholarship in several disciplines, including mathematics, statistics and linguistics. The Muslim civilisation provided an ideal cradle for cryptanalysis, because Islam demands justice in all spheres of human activity, and achieving this requires knowledge, or *ilm*. Every Muslim is obliged to pursue knowledge in all its forms, and the economic success of the Abbasid caliphate meant that scholars had the time, money and materials required to fulfil their duty. They endeavoured to acquire the knowledge of previous civilisations by obtaining Egyptian, Babylonian, Indian, Chinese, Farsi, Syriac, Armenian, Hebrew and Roman texts and translating them into Arabic. In 815, the Caliph al-Ma'mūn established in Baghdad the Bait al-Hikmah ('House of Wisdom'), a library and centre for translation.

At the same time as acquiring knowledge, the Islamic civilisation was able to disperse it because it had procured the art of paper-making from the Chinese. The manufacture of paper gave rise to the profession of *warraqīn*, or 'those who handle paper', human photocopying machines who copied manuscripts and supplied the burgeoning publishing industry. At its peak, tens of thousands of books were published every year, and in just one suburb of Baghdad there were over a hundred bookshops. As well as such classics as *Tales from the Thousand and One Nights*, these bookshops also sold textbooks on every imaginable subject and helped to support the most literate and learned society in the world.

In addition to a greater understanding of secular subjects, the invention of cryptanalysis also depended on the growth of religious scholarship. At major theological schools established in Basra, Kufa and Baghdad, theologians scrutinised the revelations of Muhammad as contained in the Koran. The theologians were interested in establishing the chronology of the revelations, which they did by counting the frequencies of words contained in each revelation. The theory was that certain words had evolved relatively recently, and hence if a revelation contained a high number of these newer words, this would indicate that it came later in the chronology. Theologians also studied the *Hadith*, which consists of the Prophet's daily utterances. They tried to demonstrate that each statement was indeed attributable to Muhammad. This was done by studying the etymology of words and the structure of sentences, to test whether particular texts were consistent with the linguistic patterns of the Prophet.

Significantly, the religious scholars did not stop their scrutiny at the level of words. They also analysed individual letters, and in particular they discovered that some letters are more common than others. The letters **a** and **l** are the commonest in Arabic, partly because of the definite article **al-**, whereas the letter **j** appears only a tenth as frequently. This apparently innocuous observation would lead to the first great breakthrough in cryptanalysis.

Although it is not known who first realised that the variation in the frequencies of letters could be exploited in order to break ciphers, the earliest known description of the technique is by the ninth-century scientist Abū Yūsuf Ya'qūb ibn Is-hāq ibn as-Sabbāh ibn 'omrān ibn Ismaīl al-Kindī. Known as 'the philosopher of the Arabs', al-Kindī was the author of 290 books on medicine, astronomy, mathematics, linguistics and music. His greatest treatise, which was rediscovered only in 1987 in the Sulaimaniyyah Ottoman Archive in Istanbul, is entitled *A Manuscript on Deciphering Cryptographic Messages* (see box overleaf). Although it contains detailed discussions on statistics, Arabic phonetics and Arabic syntax, al-Kindī's revolutionary system of cryptanalysis is encapsulated in two short paragraphs:

> One way to solve an encrypted message, if we know its language, is to find a different plaintext of the same language long enough to fill one sheet or so, and then we count the occurrences of each letter. We call the most frequently occurring letter the 'first', the next most occurring letter the 'second', the following most occurring letter the 'third', and so on, until we account for all the different letters in the plaintext sample.
>
> Then we look at the ciphertext we want to solve and we also classify its symbols. We find the most occurring symbol and change it to the form of the 'first' letter of the plaintext sample, the next most common symbol is changed to the form of the 'second' letter, and

the following most common symbol is changed to the form of the 'third' letter, and so on, until we account for all symbols of the cryptogram we want to solve.

Al-Kindī's explanation is easier to explain in terms of the English alphabet. First of all, it is necessary to study a lengthy piece of normal English text, perhaps several, in order to establish the average frequency of each letter of the alphabet. In English, **e** is the commonest letter, followed by **t**, then **a**, and so on, as given in Table 1. Next, examine the ciphertext in question, and work out the frequency of each letter. If the commonest letter in the ciphertext is, for example, **J**, then it would seem likely that this is a substitute for **e**. And if the second commonest letter in the ciphertext is **P**, then this is probably a substitute for **t**, and so on. Al-Kindī's technique, known as *frequency analysis*, shows that it is unnecessary to check each of the billions of potential keys. Instead, it is possible to reveal the contents of a scrambled message simply by analysing the frequency of the characters in the ciphertext.

However, it is not possible to apply al-Kindī's recipe for cryptanalysis unconditionally because the standard list of frequencies in Table 1 is only an average, and it will not correspond exactly to the frequencies of every text. For example, a brief message discussing the effect of the atmosphere on the movement of striped quadrupeds in Africa would not yield to straightforward frequency analysis: 'From Zanzibar to Zambia and Zaire, ozone zones make zebras run zany zigzags.' In general, short texts are likely to deviate significantly from the standard frequencies, and if there are less than a hundred letters, then decipherment will be difficult. On the other hand, longer texts are more likely to follow the standard frequencies.

Table 1 *This table of standard frequencies is based on passages taken from newspapers and novels, and the total sample was 100,362 alphabetic characters. The table was compiled by H. Beker and F. Piper, and originally published in* Cipher Systems: The Protection of Communication.

Letter	Percentage	Letter	Percentage	Letter	Percentage
a	8.2	j	0.2	s	6.3
b	1.5	k	0.8	t	9.1
c	2.8	l	4.0	u	2.8
d	4.3	m	2.4	v	1.0
e	12.7	n	6.7	w	2.4
f	2.2	o	7.5	x	0.2
g	2.0	p	1.9	y	2.0
h	6.1	q	0.1	z	0.1
i	7.0	r	6.0		

THE HOUSE OF WISDOM

This is the front page of al-Kindī's *A Manuscript on Deciphering Cryptographic Messages*, containing the oldest known description of cryptanalysis by frequency analysis. It also contains the first known discussion of statistics, an integral part of his approach to codebreaking. Al-Kindī conducted his research on cryptanalysis while he was director of the House of Wisdom, a combined library and research centre built in AD 815 in Baghdad. The library acquired books from all over the world; translation therefore took up much of its resources.

Furthermore, some of the foreign texts needed to be decrypted. Encryption suggested that the passages in question were highly significant. It is likely that part of al-Kindī's motivation for writing a treatise on cryptanalysis was to enable the House of Wisdom to gain access to encrypted secrets.

THE STRANGE CASE OF THE MISSING 'E'

Although the frequencies of letters in long texts generally follow the standard frequencies, there are some outstanding exceptions. In 1969 the French author Georges Perec (pictured below) wrote *La Disparition*, a 200-page novel that did not use words that contain the letter **e**. Doubly remarkable is the fact that the English novelist and critic Gilbert Adair succeeded in translating *La Disparition* into English, while still following Perec's shunning of the letter **e**. Such writings, in which one or more particular letters are avoided, are known as *lipograms*. Here is the opening paragraph from Adair's translation, entitled *A Void*:

Today, by radio, and also on giant hoardings, a rabbi, an admiral notorious for his links to masonry, a trio of cardinals, a trio, too, of insignificant politicians (bought and paid for by a rich and corrupt Anglo-Canadian banking corporation), inform us all of how our country now risks dying of starvation. A rumour, that's my initial thought as I switch off my radio, a rumour or possibly a hoax. Propaganda, I murmur anxiously – as though, just by saying so, I might allay my doubts – typical politicians' propaganda. But public opinion gradually absorbs it as a fact. Individuals start strutting around with stout clubs. 'Food, glorious food!' is a common cry (occasionally sung to Bart's music), with ordinary hard-working folk harassing officials, both local and national, and cursing capitalists and captains of industry. Cops shrink from going out on night shift. In Mâcon a mob storms a municipal building. In Rocadamour ruffians rob a hangar full of foodstuffs, pillaging tons of tuna fish, milk and cocoa, and also a vast quantity of corn – all of it, alas, totally unfit for human consumption. Without fuss or ado, and naturally without any sort of trial, an indignant crowd hangs 26 solicitors on a hastily built scaffold in front of Nancy's law courts (this Nancy is a town, not a woman) and ransacks a local journal, a disgusting right-wing rag that is siding against it. Up and down this land of ours looting has brought docks, shops and farms to a virtual standstill.

Having described the first tool of cryptanalysis, I shall continue by giving an example of how frequency analysis is used to decipher a ciphertext. I have avoided peppering the whole book with examples of cryptanalysis, but with frequency analysis I make an exception because it is the primary cryptanalytic tool. Furthermore, the example that follows provides insight into the modus operandi of the cryptanalyst. Although frequency analysis requires logical thinking, you will see that it also demands guile, intuition, flexibility and guesswork.

Cryptanalysing a Ciphertext

PCQ   VMJYPD   LBYK   LYSO   KBXBJXWXV   BXV   ZCJPO   EYPD
KBXBJYUXJ   LBJOO   KCPK.   CP   LBO   LBCMKXPV   XPV   IYJKL   PYDBL,
QBOP   KBO   BXV   OPVOV   LBO   LXRO   CI   SX'XJMI,   KBO   JCKO   XPV
EYKKOV   LBO   DJCMPV   ZOICJO   BYS,   KXUYPD: 'DJOXL   EYPD,   ICJ   X
LBCMKXPV   XPV   CPO   PYBLK   Y   BXNO   ZOOP   JOACMPLYPD   LC   UCM   LBO
IXZROK   CI   FXKL   XDOK   XPV   LBO   RODOPVK   CI   XPAYOPL   EYPDK.   SXU   Y   SXEO
KC   ZCRV   XK   LC   AJXNO   X   IXNCMJ   CI   UCMJ   SXGOKLU?'

OFYRCDMO, LXROK IJCS LBO LBCMKXPV XPV CPO PYDBLK

Imagine that we have intercepted this scrambled message. The challenge is to decipher it. We know that the text is in English, and that it has been scrambled according to a monoalphabetic substitution cipher, but we have no idea of the key. Searching all possible keys is impractical, so we must apply frequency analysis. What follows is a step-by-step guide to cryptanalysing this ciphertext.

The immediate reaction of any cryptanalyst upon seeing such a ciphertext is to analyse the frequency of all the letters, which results in Table 2. Not surprisingly, the letters vary in their frequency. The question is, can we identify what any of them represent, based on their frequencies? The ciphertext is relatively short, so we cannot slavishly apply frequency analysis. For example, it would be naive to assume that the eighth most frequent letter in the ciphertext, **Y**, represents the eighth most frequent letter in English, **h**. An unquestioning application of frequency analysis would soon lead to complete gibberish. For example, the first word **PCQ** would be deciphered as **aov**.

However, we can begin by focusing attention on the only three letters that appear more than thirty times in the ciphertext, namely **O**, **X** and **P**. It is fairly safe to assume that the commonest letters in the ciphertext probably represent the commonest letters

Table 2 *Frequency analysis of enciphered message.*

Letter	Frequency		Letter	Frequency	
	Occurrences	Percentage		Occurrences	Percentage
A	3	0.9	N	3	0.9
B	25	7.4	O	38	11.2
C	27	8.0	P	31	9.2
D	14	4.1	Q	2	0.6
E	5	1.5	R	6	1.8
F	2	0.6	S	7	2.1
G	1	0.3	T	0	0.0
H	0	0.0	U	6	1.8
I	11	3.3	V	18	5.3
J	18	5.3	W	1	0.3
K	26	7.7	X	34	10.1
L	25	7.4	Y	19	5.6
M	11	3.3	Z	5	1.5

in the English alphabet, but not necessarily in the right order. In other words, we cannot be sure that **O** = **e**, **X** = **t**, and **P** = **a**, but we can make the tentative assumption that:

O = **e**, **t** or **a**;   **X** = **e**, **t** or **a**;   **P** = **e**, **t** or **a**.

In order to proceed with confidence, and pin down the identity of the three commonest letters, **O**, **X** and **P**, we need a more subtle form of frequency analysis. Instead of simply counting the frequency of the three letters, we can focus on how often they appear next to all the other letters. For example, does the letter **O** appear before or after several other letters, or does it tend to neighbour just a few special letters? Answering this question will be a good indication of whether **O** represents a vowel or a consonant. If **O** represents a vowel it should appear before and after most of the other letters, whereas if it represents a consonant it will tend to avoid many of the other letters. For example, the letter **e** can appear before and after virtually every other letter, but the letter **t** is rarely seen before or after **b**, **d**, **g**, **j**, **k**, **m**, **q** or **v**.

The table opposite takes the three commonest letters in the ciphertext, **O**, **X** and **P**, and lists how frequently each appears before or after every letter. For example, **O** appears before **A** on 1 occasion, but never appears immediately after it, giving a total of 1 in the first position. The letter **O** neighbours the majority of letters, and there are only 7 that it avoids completely, represented by the 7 zeros in the **O** row.

The letter **X** is equally sociable, because it too neighbours most of the letters, and avoids only 8 of them. However, the letter **P** is much less friendly. It tends to lurk around just a few letters, and avoids 15 of them. This evidence suggests that **O** and **X** represent vowels, while **P** represents a consonant.

	A	B	C	D	E	F	G	H	I	J	K	L	M	N	O	P	Q	R	S	T	U	V	W	X	Y	Z
O	1	9	0	3	1	1	1	0	1	4	6	0	1	2	2	8	0	4	1	0	0	3	0	1	1	2
X	0	7	0	1	1	1	1	0	2	4	6	3	0	3	1	9	0	2	4	0	3	3	2	0	0	1
P	1	0	5	6	0	0	0	0	0	1	1	2	2	0	8	0	0	0	0	0	0	0	1	10	9	0

Now we must ask ourselves which vowels are represented by **O** and **X**. They are probably **e** and **a**, the two most popular vowels in the English language, but does **O** = **e** and **X** = **a**, or does **O** = **a** and **X** = **e**? An interesting feature in the ciphertext is that the combination **OO** appears twice, whereas **XX** does not appear at all. Since the letters **ee** appear far more often than **aa** in plaintext English, it is likely that **O** = **e** and **X** = **a**.

At this point, we have confidently identified two of the letters in the ciphertext. Our conclusion that **X** = **a** is supported by the fact that **X** appears on its own in the ciphertext, and **a** is one of only two English words that consist of a single letter. The only other letter that appears on its own in the ciphertext is **Y**, and it seems highly likely that this represents the only other one-letter English word, which is **i**. Focusing on words with only one letter is a standard cryptanalytic trick, but here it works only because this ciphertext still has spaces between the words. Often, a cryptographer will remove all the spaces to make it harder for an enemy interceptor to unscramble the message.

Although we have spaces between words, the following trick would also work where the ciphertext has been merged into a single string of characters. The trick allows us to spot the letter **h**, once we have already identified the letter **e**. In the English language, the letter **h** frequently goes before the letter **e** (as in **the**, **then**, **they**, etc.), but rarely after **e**. The table below shows how frequently the **O**, which we think represents **e**, precedes or follows all the other letters in the ciphertext. The table suggests that **B** represents **h**, because it appears before **O** on 9 occasions, but it never goes after it. No other letter in the table has such an asymmetric relationship with **O**.

	A	B	C	D	E	F	G	H	I	J	K	L	M	N	O	P	Q	R	S	T	U	V	W	X	Y	Z
After **O**	1	0	0	1	0	1	0	0	1	0	4	0	0	0	2	5	0	0	0	0	0	2	0	1	0	0
Before **O**	0	9	0	2	1	0	1	0	0	4	2	0	1	2	2	3	0	4	1	0	0	1	0	0	1	2

Each letter in the English language has its own unique personality, which includes its frequency and its relation to other letters. It is this personality that allows us to establish the true identity of a letter, even when it has been disguised by monoalphabetic substitution.

We have now confidently established four letters, **O = e**, **X = a**, **Y = i** and **B = h**, and we can begin to replace some of the letters in the ciphertext with their plaintext equivalents. I shall stick to the convention of keeping ciphertext letters in upper case, while putting plaintext letters in lower case. This will help to distinguish between those letters we still have to identify, and those that have already been established.

> PCQ   VMJiPD   LhiK   LiSe   KhahJaWaV   haV   ZCJPe   EiPD
> KhahJiUaJ   LhJee   KCPK.   CP   Lhe   LhCMKaPV   aPV   IiJKL   PiDhL,
> QheP   Khe   haV   ePVeV   Lhe   LaRe   CI   Sa'aJMI,   Khe   JCKe   aPV
> EiKKev   Lhe   DJCMPV   ZeICJe   hiS,   KaUiPD: 'DJeaL   EiPD,   ICJ   a
> LhCMKaPV   aPV   CPe   PiDhLK   i   haNe   ZeeP   JeACMPLiPD   LC   UCM   Lhe
> IaZReK   CI   FaKL   aDeK   aPV   Lhe   ReDePVK   CI   aPAiePL   EiPDK.   SaU   i   SaEe
> KC   ZCRV   aK   LC   AJaNe   a   IaNCMJ   CI   UCMJ   SaGeKLU?'

>   eFiRCDMe,   LaReK   IJCS   Lhe   LhCMKaPV   aPV   CPe   PiDhLK

This simple step helps us to identify several other letters, because we can guess some of the words in the ciphertext. For example, the most common three-letter words in English are **the** and **and**, and these are relatively easy to spot — **Lhe**, which appears six times, and **aPV**, which appears five times. Hence, **L** probably represents **t**, **P** probably represents **n**, and **V** probably represents **d**. We can now replace these letters in the ciphertext with their true values:

> nCQ   dMJinD   thiK   tiSe   KhahJaWad   had   ZCJne   EinD
> KhahJiUaJ   thJee   KCnK.   Cn   the   thCMKand   and   IiJKt   niDht,
> Qhen   Khe   had   ended   the   taRe   CI   Sa'aJMI,   Khe   JCKe   and
> EiKKed   the   DJCMnd   ZeICJe   hiS,   KaUinD: 'DJeat   EinD,   ICJ   a
> thCMKand   and   Cne   niDhtK   i   haNe   Zeen   JeACMntinD   tC   UCM   the
> IaZReK   CI   FaKt   aDeK   and   the   ReDendK   CI   anAient   EinDK.   SaU   i   SaEe
> KC   ZCRd   aK   tC   AJaNe   a   IaNCMJ   CI   UCMJ   SaGeKtU?'

>   eFiRCDMe,   taReK   IJCS   the   thCMKand   and   Cne   niDhtK

Once a few letters have been established, cryptanalysis progresses very rapidly. For example, the word at the beginning of the second sentence is **Cn**. Every word has a vowel in it, so **C** must be a vowel. There are only two vowels that remain to be identified, **u** and **o**; **u** does not fit, so **C** must represent **o**. We also have the word **Khe**, which implies that **K** represents either **t** or **s**. But we already know that **L = t**, so it becomes clear that **K = s**. Having identified these two letters, we insert them into the ciphertext, and there appears the phrase **thoMsand and one niDhts**. A sensible guess for this would be **thousand and one nights**, and it seems likely that the final line is telling us that this is a passage from *Tales from the Thousand and One Nights*. This implies that **M = u, I = f, J = r, D = g, R = l** and **S = m**.

We could continue trying to establish other letters by guessing other words, but instead let us have a look at what we now know about the plain alphabet and cipher alphabet. These two alphabets form the key, and they were used by the cryptographer in order to perform the substitution that scrambled the message. Already, by identifying the true values of letters in the ciphertext, we have effectively been working out the details of the cipher alphabet. A summary of our achievements so far is given in the plain and cipher alphabets below.

Plain alphabet   a b c d e f g h i j k l m n o p q r s t u v w x y z
Cipher alphabet   X – – V O I D B Y – – R S P C – – J K L M – – – – –

By examining the partial cipher alphabet, we can complete the cryptanalysis. The sequence **VOIDBY** in the cipher alphabet suggests that the cryptographer has chosen a keyphrase as the basis for the key. Some guesswork is enough to suggest the keyphrase might be **A VOID BY GEORGES PEREC**, which is reduced to **AVOIDBYGERSPC** after removing spaces and repetitions. Thereafter, the letters continue in alphabetical order, omitting any that have already appeared in the keyphrase.

Plain alphabet   a b c d e f g h i j k l m n o p q r s t u v w x y z
Cipher alphabet   X Z A V O I D B Y G E R S P C F H J K L M N Q T U W

In this particular case the cryptographer took the unusual step of not starting the keyphrase at the beginning of the cipher alphabet, but rather starting it three letters in. This is possibly because the keyphrase begins with the letter **A**, and the cryptographer wanted to avoid encrypting **a** as **A**.

At last, having established the complete cipher alphabet, we can unscramble the entire ciphertext, and the cryptanalysis is complete.

> Now during this time Shahrazad had borne King Shahriyar three sons. On the thousand and first night, when she had ended the tale of Ma'aruf, she rose and kissed the ground before him, saying: 'Great King, for a thousand and one nights I have been recounting to you the fables of past ages and the legends of ancient kings. May I make so bold as to crave a favour of your majesty?'
>
> Epilogue, *Tales from the Thousand and One Nights*

Renaissance in the West

Between AD 800 and 1200, Arab scholars enjoyed a vigorous period of intellectual achievement. At the same time, Europe was firmly stuck in the Dark Ages. While al-Kindī was describing the invention of cryptanalysis, Europeans were still struggling with the basics of cryptography. The only European institutions to encourage the study of secret writing were the monasteries, where monks would study the Bible in search of hidden meanings, a fascination that has persisted through to modern times.

Medieval monks were intrigued by the fact that the Old Testament contained deliberate and obvious examples of cryptography. For example, the Old Testament includes pieces of text encrypted with *atbash*, a traditional form of Hebrew substitution cipher. Atbash involves taking each letter, noting the number of places it is from the beginning of the alphabet, and replacing it with a letter that is an equal number of places from the end of the alphabet. In English this would mean that **a**, at the beginning of the alphabet, is replaced by **Z**, at the end of the alphabet, **b** is replaced by **Y**, and so on. The term atbash itself hints at the substitution it describes, because it consists of the first letter of the Hebrew alphabet, *aleph*, followed by the last letter, *taw*, and then there is the second letter, *beth*, followed by the second-to-last letter, *shin*. An example of atbash appears in Jeremiah 25: 26 and 51: 41, where 'Babel' is replaced by the word 'Sheshach'; the first letter of Babel is *beth*, the second letter of the Hebrew alphabet, and this is replaced by *shin*, the second-to-last letter; the second letter of Babel is also *beth*, and so it too is replaced by *shin*; and the last letter of Babel is *lamed*, the twelfth letter of the Hebrew alphabet, and this is replaced by *kaph*, the twelfth-to-last letter.

Atbash and other similar Biblical ciphers were probably intended to add mystery rather than to conceal meaning, but they were enough to spark an interest in serious cryptography. European monks began to rediscover old substitution ciphers, they invented new ones, and, in due course, they helped to reintroduce cryptography into Western civilisation. The first known European book to describe the use of cryptography was written in the thirteenth century by the English Franciscan monk and polymath Roger Bacon. *Epistle on the Secret Works of Art and the Nullity of Magic* included seven methods for keeping messages secret, and cautioned: 'A man is crazy who writes a secret in any other way than one which will conceal it from the vulgar.'

By the fourteenth century the use of cryptography had become increasingly widespread, with alchemists and scientists using it to keep their discoveries secret. Although better known for his literary achievements, Geoffrey Chaucer was also an astronomer and a cryptographer, and he is responsible for one of the most famous examples of early European encryption. In his *Treatise on the Astrolabe* he provided some additional notes, entitled 'The Equatorie of the Planetis', which included several encrypted paragraphs. Chaucer's encryption replaced plaintext letters with symbols, for example b with δ. A ciphertext consisting of strange symbols rather than letters may at first sight seem more complicated, but it is essentially equivalent to the traditional letter-for-letter substitution. The process of encryption and the level of security are exactly the same.

By the fifteenth century, European cryptography was a burgeoning industry. The revival in the arts, sciences and scholarship during the Renaissance nurtured the capacity for cryptography, while an explosion in political machinations offered ample motivation for secret communication. Italy, in particular, provided the ideal environment for cryptography. As well as being at the heart of the Renaissance, it consisted of independent city states, each trying to outmanoeuvre the others. Diplomacy flourished, and each state would send ambassadors to the courts of the others. Each ambassador received messages from his respective head of state, describing details of the foreign policy he was to implement. In response, each ambassador would send back any information that he had gleaned. Clearly there was a great incentive to encrypt communications in both directions, so states established cipher offices, and every ambassador had a cipher secretary.

At the same time that cryptography was becoming a routine diplomatic tool, the science of cryptanalysis was beginning to emerge in the West. Diplomats had only just familiarised themselves with the skills needed to establish secure communications,

and already there were individuals attempting to breach this security. It is quite probable that cryptanalysis was independently discovered in Europe, but there is also the
possibility that it was introduced from the Arab world. Islamic discoveries in science
and mathematics strongly influenced the rebirth of science in Europe, and cryptanalysis might have been part of the imported knowledge.

Arguably the first great European cryptanalyst was Giovanni Soro, appointed as
Venetian cipher secretary in 1506. Soro's reputation was known throughout Italy,
and friendly states would send intercepted messages to Venice for cryptanalysis.
Even the Vatican, probably the second most active centre of cryptanalysis, would
send Soro seemingly impenetrable messages that had fallen into its hands. In 1526
Pope Clement VII sent him two encrypted messages, and both were returned having been successfully cryptanalysed. And when one of the Pope's own encrypted
messages was captured by the Florentines, the Pope sent a copy to Soro in the
hope that he would be reassured that it was unbreakable. Soro claimed that he
could not break the Pope's cipher, implying that the Florentines would also be
unable to decipher it. However, this may have been a ploy to lull the Vatican cryptographers into a false sense of security – Soro might have been reluctant to point
out the weaknesses of the Papal cipher, because this would only have encouraged
the Vatican to switch to a more secure cipher, one that Soro might not have been
able to break.

Elsewhere in Europe, other courts were also beginning to employ skilled cryptanalysts, such as Philibert Babou, cryptanalyst to King Francis I of France. Babou
gained a reputation for being incredibly persistent, working day and night and perse-
vering for weeks on end in order to crack an intercepted message. Unfortunately for
Babou, this gave the king ample opportunity to carry on a long-term affair with
Babou's wife. Towards the end of the sixteenth century the French consolidated their
codebreaking prowess with the arrival of François Viète, who took particular pleas-
ure in cracking Spanish ciphers. Spain's cryptographers, who appear to have been
naive compared with their rivals elsewhere in Europe, could not believe it when they
discovered that their messages were transparent to the French. King Philip II of
Spain went as far as petitioning the Vatican, claiming that the only explanation for
Viète's cryptanalysis was that he was an 'archfiend in league with the devil'. Philip
argued that Viète should be tried before a Cardinal's Court for his demonic deeds;
but the Pope, who was aware that his own cryptanalysts had been reading Spanish
ciphers for years, rejected the Spanish petition. News of the petition soon reached

cipher experts in various countries, and Spanish cryptographers became the laughing stock of Europe.

The Spanish embarrassment was symptomatic of the state of the battle between cryptographers and cryptanalysts. This was a period of transition, with cryptographers still relying on the monoalphabetic substitution cipher, while cryptanalysts were beginning to use frequency analysis to break it. Those yet to discover the power of frequency analysis continued to trust monoalphabetic substitution, ignorant of the extent to which cryptanalysts such as Soro, Babou and Viète were able to read their messages.

Meanwhile, countries that were alert to the weakness of the straightforward monoalphabetic substitution cipher were anxious to develop a better cipher, something that would protect their own nation's messages from being unscrambled by enemy cryptanalysts. One of the simplest improvements to the security of the monoalphabetic substitution cipher was the introduction of *nulls*, symbols or letters that were not substitutes for actual letters, merely blanks that represented nothing. For example, one could substitute each plain letter with a number between 1 and 99, which would leave 73 numbers that represent nothing, and these could be randomly sprinkled throughout the ciphertext with varying frequencies. The nulls would pose no problem to the intended recipient, who would know that they were to be ignored. However, the nulls would baffle an enemy interceptor because they would confuse an attack by frequency analysis. An equally simple development was that cryptographers would sometimes deliberately misspell words before encrypting the message. **Thys haz thi ifekkt off diztaughting thi ballans off frikwenseas** – making it harder for the cryptanalyst to apply frequency analysis. However, the intended recipient, who knows the key, can unscramble the message and then deal with the bad, but not unintelligible, spelling.

Another attempt to shore up the monoalphabetic substitution cipher involved the introduction of codewords. The term *code* has a very broad meaning in everyday language, and it is often used to describe any method for communicating in secret. However, it actually has a very specific meaning and applies only to a certain form of substitution. So far we have concentrated on the idea of a substitution cipher, whereby each letter is replaced by a different letter, number or symbol. But it is also possible to have substitution at a much higher level whereby each word is represented by another word or symbol – and this would be a code. For example:

assassinate	= D	general	= Σ	immediately	= 08
blackmail	= P	king	= Ω	today	= 73
capture	= J	minister	= ψ	tonight	= 28
protect	= Z	prince	= θ	tomorrow	= 43

Plain message = **assassinate the king tonight**
Encoded message = D–Ω–28

Technically, a *code* is defined as substitution at the level of words or phrases, whereas a *cipher* is defined as substitution at the level of letters. Hence the term *encipher* means to scramble a message using a cipher, while *encode* means to scramble a message using a code. Similarly, the term *decipher* applies to unscrambling an enciphered message, and *decode* to unscrambling an encoded message. The terms *encrypt* and *decrypt* are more general, and cover scrambling and unscrambling with respect to both codes and ciphers. Figure 4 presents a brief summary of definitions. In general, I shall keep to these definitions, but when the sense is clear I might use a term such as 'codebreaking' to describe a process that is really 'cipher breaking' – the latter phrase might be technically accurate, but the former phrase is widely accepted.

At first sight, codes seem to offer more security than ciphers because words are much less vulnerable to frequency analysis than are letters. To decipher a monoalphabetic cipher you need only identify the true value of each of the 26 characters, whereas to decipher a code you need to identify the true value of hundreds or even thousands of codewords. However, if we examine codes in more detail, we see that they suffer from two major practical failings when compared with ciphers. First,

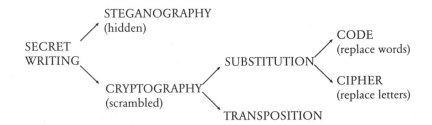

Figure 4 The science of secret writing and its main branches.

once the sender and receiver have agreed upon the 26 letters in the cipher alphabet (the key) they can encipher any message, but to achieve the same level of flexibility using a code they would need to go through the painstaking task of defining a code-word for every one of the thousands of possible plaintext words. The codebook would consist of hundreds of pages, and would look something like a dictionary. In other words, compiling a codebook is a major task, and carrying it around is a major inconvenience.

Second, the consequences of having a codebook captured by the enemy are devastating. Immediately, all previously encoded messages would become transparent to the enemy. It would be necessary to go through the painstaking process of having to compile an entirely new codebook, and then this hefty new tome would have to be distributed to everyone in the communications network, which might mean securely transporting it to every ambassador in every state. In comparison, if the enemy succeeds in capturing a cipher key, then it is relatively easy to compile a new cipher alphabet of 26 letters, which can be memorised and easily distributed.

Even in the sixteenth century, cryptographers appreciated the inherent weaknesses of codes, and instead relied largely on ciphers, or sometimes *nomenclators*. A nomenclator is a system of encryption that relies on a cipher alphabet, which is used to encrypt the majority of a message, and a limited list of codewords. For example, a nomenclator might consist of a front page containing the cipher alphabet, and then a second page containing a list of codewords. Despite the addition of codewords, a nomenclator is not much more secure than a straightforward cipher, because the bulk of a message can be deciphered using frequency analysis, and the remaining encoded words can be guessed from the context.

As well as coping with the introduction of the nomenclator, the best cryptanalysts were also capable of dealing with badly spelt messages and the presence of nulls. In short, they were able to break the majority of encrypted messages. Their skills provided a steady flow of discovered secrets which influenced the decisions of their masters and mistresses, thereby affecting Europe's history at critical moments.

Nowhere is the impact of cryptanalysis more dramatically illustrated than in the case of Mary Queen of Scots. The outcome of her trial depended wholly on the battle between her codemakers and Queen Elizabeth's codebreakers. Mary was one of the most significant figures of the sixteenth century – Queen of Scotland, Queen of France, pretender to the English throne – yet her fate would be decided by a slip of paper, the message it bore, and whether or not that message could be deciphered.

The Babington Plot

On 24 November 1542 the English forces of Henry VIII demolished the Scottish army at the Battle of Solway Moss. It appeared that Henry was on the verge of conquering Scotland and stealing the crown of King James V. After the battle the distraught Scottish king suffered a complete mental and physical breakdown, and withdrew to the palace at Falkland. Even the birth of a daughter, Mary, just two weeks later could not revive the ailing king. It was as if he had been waiting for news of an heir so that he could die in peace, safe in the knowledge that he had done his duty. Just a week after Mary's birth, King James V, still only thirty years old, died. The baby princess had become Mary Queen of Scots.

Mary was born prematurely, and initially there was considerable concern that she would not survive. Rumours in England suggested that the baby had died, but this was merely wishful thinking at the English court, which was keen to hear any news that might destabilise Scotland. In fact, Mary soon grew strong and healthy, and at the age of nine months, on 9 September 1543, she was crowned in the chapel of Stirling Castle, surrounded by three earls, bearing on her behalf the royal crown, sceptre and sword.

The fact that Queen Mary was so young offered Scotland a respite from English incursions. It would have been deemed unchivalrous had Henry VIII attempted to invade the country of a recently dead king, now under the rule of an infant queen. Instead, the English king decided on a policy of wooing Mary in the hope of arranging a marriage between her and his son Edward, thereby uniting the two nations under a Tudor sovereign. He began his manoeuvring by releasing the Scottish nobles captured at Solway Moss, on the condition that they campaign in favour of a union with England.

However, after considering Henry's offer, the Scottish court rejected it in favour of a marriage to Francis, the dauphin of France. Scotland was choosing to ally itself with a fellow Roman Catholic nation, a decision which pleased Mary's mother, Mary of Guise, whose own marriage with James V had been intended to cement the relationship between Scotland and France. Mary and Francis were still children, but the plan for the future was that they would eventually marry, and Francis would ascend the throne of France with Mary as his queen, thereby uniting Scotland and France. In the meantime, France would defend Scotland against any English onslaught.

The promise of protection was reassuring, particularly as Henry VIII had switched from diplomacy to intimidation in order to persuade the Scots that his own son was a more worthy groom for Mary. His forces committed acts of piracy, destroyed crops, burned villages, and attacked towns and cities along the border. This 'rough wooing', as it was known, continued even after Henry's death in 1547. Under the auspices of his son, King Edward VI (the would-be suitor), the attacks culminated in the Battle of Pinkie Cleugh, at which the Scottish army was routed. As a result of this slaughter it was decided that, for her own safety, Mary should leave for France, beyond the reach of the English threat, where she could prepare for her marriage to Francis. On 7 August 1548, at the age of six, she set sail for the port of Roscoff.

Mary's first few years at the French court would be the most idyllic time of her life. She was surrounded by luxury, protected from harm, and she grew to love her future husband, the dauphin. At the age of sixteen they married, and the following year Francis and Mary became King and Queen of France. Everything seemed set for her triumphant return to Scotland, until her husband, who had always suffered from poor health, fell gravely ill. An ear infection that he had nursed since a child had worsened, the inflammation spread towards his brain, and an abscess began to develop. In 1560, within a year of being crowned, Francis was dead and Mary was widowed.

From this time onwards Mary's life would be repeatedly struck by tragedy. She returned to Scotland in 1561, where she discovered a transformed nation. During her long absence Mary had confirmed her Catholic faith, while her Scottish sub-jects had increasingly moved towards the Protestant church. Mary tolerated the wishes of the majority and at first reigned with relative success, but in 1565 she married her cousin, Henry Stuart, the Earl of Darnley, an act that led to a spiral of decline. Darnley was a vicious and brutal man whose ruthless greed for power lost Mary the loyalty of the Scottish nobles. The following year Mary witnessed for her-self the full horror of her husband's barbaric nature when he murdered David Riccio, her secretary, in front of her. It became clear to everyone that for the sake of Scotland it was necessary to get rid of Darnley. Historians debate whether it was Mary or the Scottish nobles who instigated the plot, but on the night of 9 February 1567, Darnley's house was blown up and, as he attempted to escape, he was strangled. The only good to come from the marriage was a son and heir, James.

Mary's next marriage, to James Hepburn, the Fourth Earl of Bothwell, was hardly more successful. By the summer of 1567 the Protestant Scottish nobles had become completely disillusioned with their Catholic Queen, and they exiled Bothwell and imprisoned Mary, forcing her to abdicate in favour of her fourteen-month-old son, James VI, while her half-brother, the Earl of Moray, acted as regent. The next year Mary escaped from her prison, gathered an army of six thousand royalists, and made a final attempt to regain her crown. Her soldiers confronted the regent's army at the small village of Langside, near Glasgow, and Mary witnessed the battle from a nearby hilltop. Although her troops were greater in number, they lacked discipline, and Mary watched as they were torn apart. When defeat was inevitable, she

THE TUDOR DYNASTY

The defeat of Richard III at Bosworth Field on 22 August 1485 by Henry Tudor marked the end of the thirty-year power struggle between the rival Houses of York and Lancaster that came to be known as the Wars of the Roses. It ushered in a rather more stable period in English history and established a new ruling dynasty, the House of Tudor, which gave England five sovereigns: Henry VII, as Henry Tudor became; his son, Henry VIII, and Henry VIII's three children: Edward VI, Mary and Elizabeth I. Henry Tudor had Lancastrian roots. His grandfather, Owen Tudor, had married Henry VI's widow, Catherine of Valois, while his mother, Margaret Beaufort, was the great-granddaughter of John of Gaunt, son of Edward III. The two rival houses were joined when Henry married Elizabeth, daughter of Edward IV and heiress of the House of York. The union was symbolised by the Tudor

ELIZABETH I

MARY Queen of Scots

rose, which superimposed the red rose of Lancaster upon the white rose of York.

In the 1530s Henry VIII split from the Roman Catholic Church over the issue of his divorce from Catherine of Aragon, who had failed to produce the male heir Henry desired; the English Reformation and the establishment of the Anglican Church were completed during the reign of Elizabeth I. The lack of male heirs to Henry, after the death at the age of sixteen of his only son Edward VI, and the rift between Protestants and Catholics were to overshadow the question of royal succession. The Catholics looked to Mary Queen of Scots as their figurehead. Mary, of the Scottish House of Stuart, was also a great-granddaughter of Henry VII, and thus posed a threat to Elizabeth's hold on the English crown.

fled. Ideally she would have headed east to the coast, and then on to France, but this would have meant crossing territory loyal to her half-brother, so instead she headed south to England, where she hoped that her cousin Queen Elizabeth I would provide refuge.

Mary had made a terrible misjudgement. Elizabeth offered Mary nothing more than another prison. The official reason for her arrest was in connection with the murder of Darnley, but the true reason was that Mary posed a threat to Elizabeth,

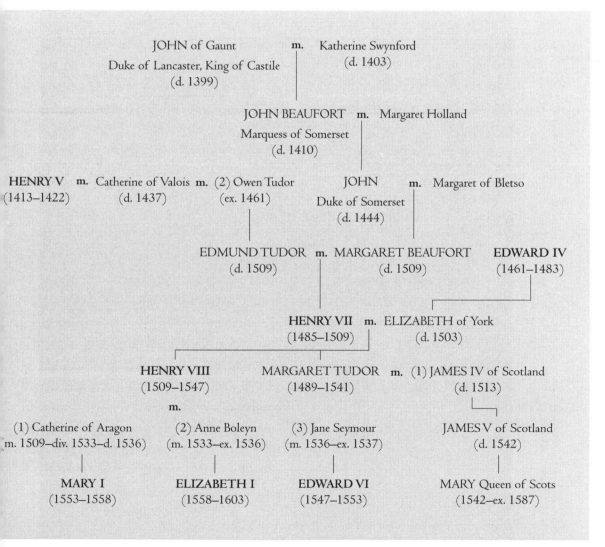

because English Catholics considered Mary to be the true queen of England. Through her grandmother, Margaret Tudor, the elder sister of Henry VIII, Mary did indeed have a claim to the throne, but Henry's last surviving offspring, Elizabeth I, would seem to have a prior claim. However, according to the Catholics, Elizabeth was illegitimate because she was the daughter of Anne Boleyn, Henry's second wife after he had divorced Catherine of Aragon in defiance of the Pope. English Catholics did not recognise Henry VIII's divorce, did not acknowledge his ensuing marriage to Anne Boleyn, and certainly did not accept their daughter Elizabeth as Queen. Catholics saw Elizabeth as a 'bastard usurper'.

Mary was imprisoned in a series of castles and manors. Although Elizabeth thought of her as one of the most dangerous figures in England, many Englishmen admitted that they admired her gracious manner, her obvious intelligence and her great beauty. William Cecil, Elizabeth's Great Minister, commented on 'her cunning and sugared entertainment of all men', and Nicholas White, Cecil's emissary, made a similar observation: 'She hath withal an alluring grace, a pretty Scotch accent, and a searching wit, clouded with mildness.' But as each year passed, her appearance waned, her health deteriorated and she began to lose hope. Her jailer, Sir Amyas Paulet, a Puritan, was immune to her charms, and treated her with increasing harshness.

By 1586, after eighteen years of imprisonment, she had lost all her privileges. She was confined to Chartley Hall in Staffordshire, and was no longer allowed to take the waters at Buxton, which had previously helped to alleviate her frequent illnesses. On her last visit to Buxton she used a diamond to inscribe a message on a window-pane: 'Buxton, whose warm waters have made thy name famous, perchance I shall visit thee no more – Farewell.' It appears that she suspected that she was about to lose what little freedom she had.

Mary's growing sorrow was compounded by the actions of her nineteen-year-old son, King James VI of Scotland. She had always hoped that one day she would escape and return to Scotland to share power with her son, whom she had not seen since he was one year old. However, James felt no such affection for his mother. He had been brought up by Mary's enemies, who had taught James that his mother had murdered his father in order to marry her lover. James despised her, and feared that if she returned then she might seize his crown. His hatred of Mary was demonstrated by the fact that he had no qualms in seeking a marriage with Elizabeth I, the woman responsible for his mother's imprisonment (and who was also thirty years his senior). Elizabeth declined the offer.

Mary wrote to her son in an attempt to win him over, but her letters never reached the Scottish border. By this stage Mary was more isolated then ever before: all her outgoing letters were confiscated, and any incoming correspondence was kept by her jailer. Mary's morale was at its lowest, but it was under these severe and desperate circumstances that, on 6 January 1586, she received an astonishing package of letters.

The letters were from Mary's supporters on the Continent, and they had been smuggled into her prison by Gilbert Gifford, a Catholic who had left England in 1577 and trained as a priest at the English College in Rome. On his return to England in 1585, apparently keen to serve Mary, he immediately approached the French Embassy in London, where a pile of correspondence had accumulated. The Embassy had known that if they forwarded the letters by the formal route, Mary would never see them. However, Gifford claimed that he could smuggle the letters into Chartley Hall, and sure enough he lived up to his word. This delivery was the first of many, and Gifford began a career as a courier, not only passing messages to Mary but also collecting her replies. He had a rather cunning way of sneaking letters into Chartley Hall. He took the messages to a local brewer, who wrapped them in a leather packet, which was then hidden inside a hollow bung used to seal a barrel of beer. The brewer would deliver the barrel to Chartley Hall, whereupon one of Mary's servants would open the bung and take the contents to the Queen of Scots. The process worked equally well for getting messages out of Chartley Hall.

Meanwhile, unknown to Mary, a plan to rescue her was being hatched in the taverns of London. At the centre of the plot was Anthony Babington, aged just twenty-four but already well known in the city as a handsome, charming and witty bon viveur. What his many admiring contemporaries failed to appreciate was that Babington deeply resented the establishment, which had persecuted him, his family and his faith. The state's anti-Catholic policies had reached new heights of terror, with Catholic priests being accused of treason, and anybody caught harbouring them punished by the rack, mutilation and disembowelling while still alive. The Catholic mass was officially banned, and families who remained loyal to the Pope were forced to pay crippling taxes. Babington's animosity was fuelled by the death of Lord Darcy, his great-grandfather, who was beheaded for his involvement in the Pilgrimage of Grace, a Catholic uprising against Henry VIII.

The conspiracy began one evening in March 1586, when Babington and six confidants gathered in The Plough, an inn outside Temple Bar. As the historian Philip

Caraman observed, 'He drew to himself by the force of his exceptional charm and personality many young Catholic gentlemen of his own standing, gallant, adventurous and daring in defence of the Catholic faith in its day of stress; and ready for any arduous enterprise whatsoever that might advance the common Catholic cause.' Over the next few months an ambitious plan emerged to free Mary Queen of Scots, assassinate Queen Elizabeth, and incite a rebellion supported by an invasion from abroad.

The conspirators were agreed that the Babington Plot, as it became known, could not proceed without the blessing of Mary, but there was no apparent way to communicate with her. Then, on 6 July 1586, Gifford arrived on Babington's doorstep. He delivered a letter from Mary, explaining that she had heard about Babington via her supporters in Paris, and looked forward to hearing from him. In reply, Babington compiled a detailed letter in which he outlined his scheme, including a reference to the excommunication of Elizabeth by Pope Pius V in 1570, which he believed legitimised her assassination.

> Myself with ten gentlemen and a hundred of our followers will undertake the delivery of your royal person from the hands of your enemies. For the dispatch of the usurper, from the obedience of whom we are by the excommunication of her made free, there be six noble gentlemen, all my private friends, who for the zeal they bear to the Catholic cause and your Majesty's service will undertake that tragical execution.

As before, Gifford used his trick of concealing the message in the bung of a beer barrel in order to sneak it past Mary's guards. This can be considered a form of steganography, because the letter was being hidden. As an extra precaution Babington enciphered his letter so that even if it was intercepted by Mary's jailer, it would be indecipherable and the plot would not be uncovered. He used a cipher which was not a simple monoalphabetic substitution, but rather a nomenclator (see box).

Gifford was still a youth, even younger than Babington, yet he conducted his deliveries with confidence and guile. His aliases, such as Mr Colerdin, Pietro and Cornelys, enabled him to travel the country without suspicion, and his contacts within the Catholic community provided him with a series of safe houses between London and Chartley Hall. However, unknown to Babington, as Gifford travelled to Chartley Hall, he made a detour. Although Gifford was apparently acting as an agent for Mary, he was actually a double agent. Back in 1585, before his return to

England, Gifford had written to Sir Francis Walsingham, principal private secretary to Queen Elizabeth, offering his services. Gifford realised that his Catholic background would provide the perfect mask for infiltrating plots against Queen Elizabeth. In the letter to Walsingham, he wrote, 'I have heard of the work you do and I want to serve you. I have no scruples and no fear of danger. Whatever you order me to do I will accomplish.'

Walsingham was Elizabeth's most ruthless minister. He was a Machiavellian figure, a spymaster who was responsible for the security of the monarch. He had inherited a small network of spies which he rapidly expanded into the Continent, where many of the plots against Elizabeth were being hatched. After his death it was discovered that he had been receiving regular reports from twelve locations in France, nine in Germany, four in Italy, four in Spain and three in the Low Countries, as well as having informants in Constantinople, Algiers and Tripoli.

MARY'S NOMENCLATOR

a	b	c	d	e	f	g	h	i	k	l	m	n	o	p	q	r	s	t	u	x	y	z

Nulles   Dowbleth

and	for	with	that	if	but	where	as	of	the	from	by

so	not	when	there	this	in	wich	is	what	say	me	my	wyrt

send	lře	receave	bearer	I	pray	you	Mte	your	name	myne

The nomenclator of Mary Queen of Scots consisted of a cipher alphabet and codewords. There were 23 symbols that were to be substituted for the letters of the alphabet (excluding j, v and w), along with 35 symbols representing words or phrases. In addition, there were four nulls (ff. ⌐ . ⌐ . d.) and a symbol σ which signified that the next symbol represented a double letter ('dowbleth').

Walsingham recruited Gifford as a spy, and in fact it was Walsingham who ordered Gifford to approach the French Embassy and offer himself as a courier. Each time Gifford collected a message to or from Mary, he would first take it to Walsingham. The vigilant spymaster would then pass it to his counterfeiters, who would break the seal on each letter, make a copy, and then reseal the original letter with an identical stamp before handing it back to Gifford. The apparently untouched letter would then be delivered to Mary or her correspondents, who remained oblivious to what was going on.

When Gifford handed Walsingham the letter from Babington to Mary, the first objective was to decipher it. Walsingham had originally encountered codes and ciphers while reading a book written by the Italian mathematician and cryptographer Girolamo Cardano (who, incidentally, proposed a form of writing for the blind based on touch, a precursor to Braille). Cardano's book aroused Walsingham's interest, but it was a decipherment by the Flemish cryptanalyst Philip van Marnix that really convinced him of the wisdom of having a codebreaker at his disposal. In 1577 Philip of Spain was using ciphers to correspond with his half-brother and fellow Catholic Don John of Austria, who was in control of much

Sir Francis Walsingham was the most influential figure at Elizabeth's court for nearly two decades. The queen respected his genius and integrity but did not always heed his advice, and in matters of foreign policy he often acted on his own initiative. Elizabeth, perhaps fearing his power, paid him poorly and he died in 1590 in debt and poverty.

of the Netherlands. Philip's letter described a plan to invade England, but it was intercepted by William of Orange, who passed it to Marnix, his cipher secretary. Marnix deciphered the plan, and William passed the information to Daniel Rogers, an English agent working on the Continent, who in turn warned Walsingham of the invasion. The English reinforced their defences, which was enough to deter the invasion attempt.

Now fully aware of the value of cryptanalysis, Walsingham established a cipher school in London and employed Thomas Phelippes as his cipher secretary, a man 'of low stature, slender every way, dark yellow haired on the head, and clear yellow bearded, eaten in the face with smallpox, of short sight, thirty years of age by appearance'.

Phelippes was a linguist who could speak French, Italian, Spanish, Latin and German, and, more importantly, he was one of Europe's finest cryptanalysts.

Upon receiving the message to Mary, Phelippes devoured it. He was a master of frequency analysis, and it would be merely a matter of time before he found a solution. He established the frequency of each character, and tentatively proposed values for those that appeared most often. When a particular approach hinted at absurdity, he would backtrack and try alternative substitutions. Gradually he would identify the nulls – the cryptographic red herrings – and put them to one side. Eventually all that remained was the handful of codewords, whose meaning could be guessed from the context.

When Phelippes deciphered Babington's message to Mary, which clearly proposed the assassination of Elizabeth, he immediately forwarded the damning text to his master. At this point Walsingham could have pounced on Babington, but he wanted more than the execution of a handful of rebels. He bided his time in the hope that Mary would reply and authorise the plot, thereby incriminating herself. Walsingham had long wished for the death of Mary Queen of Scots, but he was aware of Elizabeth's reluctance to execute her cousin. However, if he could prove that Mary was endorsing an attempt on the life of Elizabeth, then surely his queen would permit the execution of her Catholic rival. Walsingham's hopes were soon fulfilled.

On 17 July Mary replied to Babington, effectively signing her own death warrant. She explicitly wrote about the 'design', showing particular concern that she should be released simultaneously with, or before, Elizabeth's assassination, otherwise news might reach her jailer, who might then murder her. Before reaching Babington, the letter made the usual detour to Phelippes. Having cryptanalysed the earlier message, he deciphered this one with ease, read its contents, and marked it with a 'Π' – the sign of the gallows.

Walsingham had all the evidence he needed to arrest Mary and Babington, but still he was not satisfied. To destroy the conspiracy completely he needed the names of all those involved. He asked Phelippes to forge a postscript to Mary's letter which would entice Babington to name names. The postscript (shown overleaf) can be deciphered using Mary's nomenclator to reveal the following plaintext:

> I would be glad to know the names and qualities of the six gentlemen which are to accomplish
> the designment; for it may be that I shall be able, upon knowledge of the parties, to give you
> some further advice necessary to be followed therein, as also from time to time particularly how
> you proceed: and as soon as you may, for the same purpose, who be already, and how far
> everyone is privy hereunto.

The cipher of Mary Queen of Scots clearly demonstrates that weak encryption can be worse than no encryption at all. Both Mary and Babington wrote explicitly about their intentions because they believed that their communications were secure, whereas if they had been communicating without encryption they would have referred to their plan in a more discreet manner. Furthermore, their faith in their cipher made them particularly vulnerable to accepting Phelippes's forgery. Sender and receiver often have such confidence in the strength of their cipher that they consider it impossible for the enemy to mimic the cipher and insert forged text. The correct use of a strong cipher is a clear boon to sender and receiver, but the misuse of a weak cipher can generate a very false sense of security.

Soon after receiving the message and its postscript, Babington needed to go abroad to organise the invasion, and had to register at Walsingham's department in order to acquire a passport. This would have been an ideal time to capture the traitor, but the bureaucrat who was manning the office, John Scudamore, was not expecting the most wanted traitor in England to turn up at his door. Scudamore, with no support to hand, took the unsuspecting Babington to a nearby tavern, stalling for time while his assistant organised a group of soldiers. A short while later a note arrived at the tavern informing Scudamore that it was time for the arrest. Babington, however, caught sight of it. He casually said that he would pay for the beer and meal and rose to his feet, leaving his sword and coat at the table, implying that he would return in an instant. Instead, he slipped out of the back door and escaped, first to St John's Wood and then on to Harrow. He attempted to disguise himself, cutting his hair short and

The postscript added by Thomas Phelippes to Mary's message. It can be deciphered by referring to Mary's nomenclator. One of Phelippes's additional talents was as a forger, and it was said that he had the ability 'to write any man's hand, if he had once seen it, as if the man himself had writ it'.

staining his skin with walnut juice to mask his aristocratic background. He managed to elude capture for ten days, but by 15 August Babington and his six colleagues had all been captured and brought to London. Church bells across the city rang out in triumph. Their executions were horrid in the extreme. In the words of the Elizabethan historian William Camden, 'they were all cut down, their privities were cut off, bowelled alive and seeing, and quartered'.

Meanwhile, on 11 August, Mary Queen of Scots and her entourage had been allowed the exceptional privilege of riding in the grounds of Chartley Hall. As Mary crossed the moors she spied some horsemen approaching, and immediately thought that they must be Babington's men coming to rescue her. It soon became clear that these men had come to arrest her, not lead her to freedom. Mary had been implicated in the Babington Plot and was charged under the Act of Association, an Act of Parliament passed in 1584 specifically designed to convict anybody who was part of a conspiracy against Elizabeth.

The trial was held in Fotheringhay Castle, a bleak, miserable place in the middle of the featureless fens of East Anglia. It began on Wednesday 15 October, in front of two chief justices, four other judges, the Lord Chancellor, the Lord Treasurer, Walsingham, and various earls, knights and barons. At the back of the courtroom there was space for spectators, such as local villagers and the servants of the commissioners, all eager to see the humiliated Scottish queen beg forgiveness and plead for her life. However, Mary remained dignified and composed throughout the trial. Her main defence was to deny any connection with Babington. 'Can I be responsible for the criminal projects of a few desperate men', she proclaimed, 'which they planned without my knowledge or participation?' Her statement had little impact in the face of the evidence against her.

Mary and Babington had relied on a cipher to keep their plans secret, but they lived during a period when cryptography was being weakened by advances in cryptanalysis. Although their cipher would have been sufficient protection against the prying eyes of an amateur, it stood no chance against an expert in frequency analysis. In the spectators' gallery sat Phelippes, quietly watching the presentation of the evidence that he had conjured from the enciphered letters.

The trial went into a second day, and Mary continued to deny any knowledge of the Babington Plot. When the trial finished, she left the judges to decide her fate, pardoning them in advance for the inevitable decision. Ten days later, the Star Chamber met in Westminster and concluded that Mary had been guilty of 'compassing and imagining since June 1st matters tending to the death and destruction of the Queen of England'. They recommended the death penalty, and Elizabeth signed the death warrant.

THE EXECUTION OF MARY QUEEN OF SCOTS

Richard Wingfield, in his *Narration of the Last Days of the Queen of Scots*, described Mary's final moments in the following words:

Then she laide herself upon the blocke most quietlie, & stretching out her armes & legges cryed out In manus tuas domine three or foure times, & at the laste while one of the executioners held her slightlie with one of his handes, the other gave two strokes with an axe before he cutt of her head, & yet lefte a little gristle behinde at which time she made verie small noyse & stirred not any parte of herself from the place where she laye . . . Her lipps stirred up & downe almost a quarter of an hower after her head was cutt of. Then one of her executioners plucking of her garters espied her little dogge which was crept under her clothes which could not be gotten forth but with force & afterwardes could not depart from her dead corpse, but came and laye betweene her head & shoulders a thing dilligently noted.

On 8 February 1587, in the Great Hall of Fotheringhay Castle, an audience of three hundred gathered to watch the beheading. Walsingham was determined to minimise Mary's influence as a martyr, and he ordered the block, Mary's clothing, and everything else relating to the execution to be burned afterwards in order to avoid the creation of any holy relics. He also planned a lavish funeral procession for his son-in-law, Sir Philip Sidney, to take place the following week. Sidney, a popular and heroic figure, had died fighting Catholics in the Netherlands, and Walsingham believed that a magnificent parade in his honour would dampen sympathy for Mary. However, Mary was equally determined that her final appearance should be a defiant gesture, an opportunity to reaffirm her Catholic faith and inspire her followers.

While the Dean of Peterborough led the prayers, Mary spoke aloud her own prayers for the salvation of the English Catholic Church, for her son and for Elizabeth. With her family motto, 'In my end is my beginning', in her mind, she composed herself and approached the block. The executioners requested her forgiveness, and she replied, 'I forgive you with all my heart, for now I hope you shall make an end of all my troubles.'

CHAPTER TWO

Le Chiffre Indéchiffrable

The invention of the Vigenère cipher, and why cryptographers
seldom get credit for their breakthroughs

FOR CENTURIES, the simple monoalphabetic substitution cipher had been
sufficient to ensure secrecy. The subsequent development of frequency analysis, first in the Arab world and then in Europe, destroyed its security. The
execution of Mary Queen of Scots was a tragic illustration of the weaknesses of
monoalphabetic substitution, and in the battle between cryptographers and cryptanalysts it was clear that the cryptanalysts had gained the upper hand. Anybody
sending an encrypted message had to accept that an expert enemy codebreaker
might intercept and decipher their most precious secrets.

The onus was clearly on the cryptographers to concoct a new, stronger cipher,
something that could outwit the cryptanalysts. Although this cipher would not
emerge until the end of the sixteenth century, its origins can be traced back to the
fifteenth-century Florentine polymath Leon Battista Alberti.

Sometime in the 1460s, Alberti was wandering through the gardens of the
Vatican when he bumped into his friend Leonardo Dato, the pontifical secretary,
who began chatting to him about some of the finer points of cryptography. This
casual conversation prompted Alberti to write an essay on the subject, outlining
what he believed to be a new form of cipher. At the time, all substitution ciphers
required a single cipher alphabet for encrypting each message. However, Alberti
proposed using two or more cipher alphabets, and switching between them during
encipherment, thereby confusing potential cryptanalysts.

Plain alphabet	a b c d e f g h i j k l m n o p q r s t u v w x y z
Cipher alphabet 1	F Z B V K I X A Y M E P L S D H J O R G N Q C U T W
Cipher alphabet 2	G O X B F W T H Q I L A P Z J D E S V Y C R K U H N

For example, here we have two possible cipher alphabets, and we could encrypt a message by alternating between them. To encrypt the message **hello**, we would encrypt the first letter according to the first cipher alphabet, so that **h** becomes **A**, but we would encrypt the second letter according to the second cipher alphabet, so that **e** becomes **F**. To encrypt the third letter we return to the first cipher alphabet, and to encrypt the fourth letter we return to the second alphabet. This means that the first **l** is enciphered as **P**, but the second **l** is enciphered as **A**. The final letter, **o**,

LEON BATTISTA ALBERTI – RENAISSANCE MAN

Born in 1404 in Genoa, Leon Battista Alberti was one of the leading figures of the Renaissance – humanist, painter, composer, poet, musician and philosopher, as well as the author of the first scientific analysis of perspective, a treatise on the housefly and a eulogy for his dog. He is probably best known as an architect, and was inspired by the Classical Roman architect Vitruvius. Roman Classicism is evident in his own designs, among them Rome's first Trevi Fountain, and many

churches including San Francesca at Rimini and Santa Maria Novella at Florence, where he worked from 1428. His *De re aedificatoria* ('On Architecture') was the first book on architecture to be printed, and acted as a catalyst for the transition from medieval Gothic to Renaissance design. Like Leonardo da Vinci, who followed him half a century later, Alberti's catholic interests made him what we think of now as a 'Renaissance man'.

is enciphered according to the first cipher alphabet and becomes **D**. The complete ciphertext reads **AFPAD**. The crucial advantage of Alberti's system is that the same letter in the plaintext does not necessarily appear as the same letter in the ciphertext, so the repeated **l** in **hello** is enciphered differently in each case. Similarly, the repeated **A** in the ciphertext represents a different plaintext letter in each case, first **h** and then **l**.

Although he had hit upon the most significant breakthrough in encryption for over a thousand years, Alberti failed to develop his concept into a fully formed system of encryption. That task fell to a diverse group of intellectuals who built on his initial idea. First came Johannes Trithemius, a German abbot born in 1462, then Giovanni Porta, an Italian scientist born in 1535, and finally Blaise de Vigenère, a French diplomat born in 1523. Vigenère became acquainted with the writings of Alberti, Trithemius and Porta when, at the age of twenty-six, he was sent to Rome on a two-year diplomatic mission. Initially, his interest in

Blaise de Vigenère

cryptography was purely practical and was linked to his diplomatic work. At the age of thirty-nine, Vigenère decided that he had accumulated enough money to abandon his career and concentrate on a life of study. It was only then that he examined in detail the ideas of Alberti, Trithemius and Porta, weaving them into a coherent and powerful new cipher.

Although Alberti, Trithemius and Porta all made vital contributions, the cipher is known as the Vigenère cipher in honour of the man who developed it into its final form. The strength of the Vigenère cipher lies in its use of not one, but 26 distinct cipher alphabets to encrypt a message. The first step in encipherment is to draw up a so-called Vigenère square, as shown in Table 3 (overleaf): a plaintext alphabet followed by 26 cipher alphabets, each shifted by one letter with respect to the previous alphabet. Hence, row 1 represents a cipher alphabet with a Caesar shift of 1, which means that it could be used to implement a Caesar shift cipher in which every letter of the plaintext is replaced by the letter one place farther on in the alphabet.

Table 3 *A Vigenère square.*

Plain	a b c d e f g h i j k l m n o p q r s t u v w x y z
1	B C D E F G H I J K L M N O P Q R S T U V W X Y Z A
2	C D E F G H I J K L M N O P Q R S T U V W X Y Z A B
3	D E F G H I J K L M N O P Q R S T U V W X Y Z A B C
4	E F G H I J K L M N O P Q R S T U V W X Y Z A B C D
5	F G H I J K L M N O P Q R S T U V W X Y Z A B C D E
6	G H I J K L M N O P Q R S T U V W X Y Z A B C D E F
7	H I J K L M N O P Q R S T U V W X Y Z A B C D E F G
8	I J K L M N O P Q R S T U V W X Y Z A B C D E F G H
9	J K L M N O P Q R S T U V W X Y Z A B C D E F G H I
10	K L M N O P Q R S T U V W X Y Z A B C D E F G H I J
11	L M N O P Q R S T U V W X Y Z A B C D E F G H I J K
12	M N O P Q R S T U V W X Y Z A B C D E F G H I J K L
13	N O P Q R S T U V W X Y Z A B C D E F G H I J K L M
14	O P Q R S T U V W X Y Z A B C D E F G H I J K L M N
15	P Q R S T U V W X Y Z A B C D E F G H I J K L M N O
16	Q R S T U V W X Y Z A B C D E F G H I J K L M N O P
17	R S T U V W X Y Z A B C D E F G H I J K L M N O P Q
18	S T U V W X Y Z A B C D E F G H I J K L M N O P Q R
19	T U V W X Y Z A B C D E F G H I J K L M N O P Q R S
20	U V W X Y Z A B C D E F G H I J K L M N O P Q R S T
21	V W X Y Z A B C D E F G H I J K L M N O P Q R S T U
22	W X Y Z A B C D E F G H I J K L M N O P Q R S T U V
23	X Y Z A B C D E F G H I J K L M N O P Q R S T U V W
24	Y Z A B C D E F G H I J K L M N O P Q R S T U V W X
25	Z A B C D E F G H I J K L M N O P Q R S T U V W X Y
26	A B C D E F G H I J K L M N O P Q R S T U V W X Y Z

Similarly, row 2 represents a cipher alphabet with a Caesar shift of 2, and so on. The top row of the square, in lower case, represents the plaintext letters. You could encipher each plaintext letter according to any one of the 26 cipher alphabets. For example, if cipher alphabet number 2 is used, then the letter **a** is enciphered as **C**, but if cipher alphabet number 12 is used, then **a** is enciphered as **M**.

If the sender were to use just one of the cipher alphabets to encipher an entire message, this would effectively be a simple Caesar cipher, which would be a very weak form of encryption, easily deciphered by an enemy interceptor. However, in the Vigenère cipher a different row of the Vigenère square (a different cipher alphabet) is used to encrypt different letters of the message. In other words, the sender might encrypt the first letter according to row 5, the second according to row 14, the third according to row 21, and so on.

To unscramble the message, the intended receiver needs to know which row of the Vigenère square has been used to encipher each letter, so there must be an agreed system of switching between rows. This is achieved by using a keyword. To illustrate how a keyword is used with the Vigenère square to encrypt a short message, let us encipher **divert troops to east ridge**, using the keyword **WHITE**. First of all, the keyword is spelt out above the message, and repeated over and over again so that each letter in the message is associated with a letter from the keyword. The ciphertext is then generated as follows. To encrypt the first letter, **d**, begin by identifying the key letter above it, **W**, which in turn defines a particular row in the Vigenère square. The row beginning with **W**, row 22, is the cipher alphabet that will be used to find the substitute letter for the plaintext **d**. We look to see where the column headed by **d** intersects the row beginning with **W**, which turns out to be at the letter **Z**. Consequently, the letter **d** in the plaintext is represented by **Z** in the ciphertext.

Keyword	W H I T E W H I T E W H I T E W H I T E W H I
Plaintext	d i v e r t t r o o p s t o e a s t r i d g e
Ciphertext	Z P D X V P A Z H S L Z B H I W Z B K M Z N M

To encipher the second letter of the message, **i**, the process is repeated. The key letter above **i** is **H**, so it is encrypted via a different row in the Vigenère square: the **H** row (row 7) which is a new cipher alphabet. To encrypt **i**, we look to see where the column headed by **i** intersects the row beginning with **H**, which turns out to be at the letter **P**. Consequently, the letter **i** in the plaintext is represented by **P** in the ciphertext. Each letter of the keyword indicates a particular cipher alphabet within the Vigenère square, and because the keyword contains five letters, the sender encrypts the message by cycling through five rows of the Vigenère square. The fifth letter of the message is enciphered according to the fifth letter of the keyword, **E**, but to encipher the sixth letter of the message we have to return to the first letter of the keyword. A longer keyword, or perhaps a keyphrase, would bring more rows into the encryption process and increase the complexity of the cipher. Table 4 (overleaf) shows a Vigenère square in which are highlighted the five rows (i.e. the five cipher alphabets) defined by the keyword **WHITE**.

The great advantage of the Vigenère cipher is that it is impregnable to the frequency analysis described in Chapter 1. For example, a cryptanalyst applying frequency analysis to a piece of ciphertext would usually begin by identifying the most common letter in the ciphertext, which in this case is Z, and then assume that this represents the most common letter in English, e. In fact, the letter Z represents three different letters, d, r and s, but not e. This is clearly a problem for the cryptanalyst. The fact that a letter which appears several times in the ciphertext can represent a different plaintext letter on each occasion generates tremendous ambiguity for the cryptanalyst. Equally confusing is the fact that a letter which appears several times

Table 4 *A Vigenère square with the rows defined by the keyword* **WHITE** *highlighted. Encryption is achieved by switching between the five highlighted cipher alphabets, defined by* **W**, **H**, **I**, **T** *and* **E**.

Plain	a	b	c	d	e	f	g	h	i	j	k	l	m	n	o	p	q	r	s	t	u	v	w	x	y	z
1	B	C	D	E	F	G	H	I	J	K	L	M	N	O	P	Q	R	S	T	U	V	W	X	Y	Z	A
2	C	D	E	F	G	H	I	J	K	L	M	N	O	P	Q	R	S	T	U	V	W	X	Y	Z	A	B
3	D	E	F	G	H	I	J	K	L	M	N	O	P	Q	R	S	T	U	V	W	X	Y	Z	A	B	C
4	E	F	G	H	I	J	K	L	M	N	O	P	Q	R	S	T	U	V	W	X	Y	Z	A	B	C	D
5	F	G	H	I	J	K	L	M	N	O	P	Q	R	S	T	U	V	W	X	Y	Z	A	B	C	D	E
6	G	H	I	J	K	L	M	N	O	P	Q	R	S	T	U	V	W	X	Y	Z	A	B	C	D	E	F
7	H	I	J	K	L	M	N	O	P	Q	R	S	T	U	V	W	X	Y	Z	A	B	C	D	E	F	G
8	I	J	K	L	M	N	O	P	Q	R	S	T	U	V	W	X	Y	Z	A	B	C	D	E	F	G	H
9	J	K	L	M	N	O	P	Q	R	S	T	U	V	W	X	Y	Z	A	B	C	D	E	F	G	H	I
10	K	L	M	N	O	P	Q	R	S	T	U	V	W	X	Y	Z	A	B	C	D	E	F	G	H	I	J
11	L	M	N	O	P	Q	R	S	T	U	V	W	X	Y	Z	A	B	C	D	E	F	G	H	I	J	K
12	M	N	O	P	Q	R	S	T	U	V	W	X	Y	Z	A	B	C	D	E	F	G	H	I	J	K	L
13	N	O	P	Q	R	S	T	U	V	W	X	Y	Z	A	B	C	D	E	F	G	H	I	J	K	L	M
14	O	P	Q	R	S	T	U	V	W	X	Y	Z	A	B	C	D	E	F	G	H	I	J	K	L	M	N
15	P	Q	R	S	T	U	V	W	X	Y	Z	A	B	C	D	E	F	G	H	I	J	K	L	M	N	O
16	Q	R	S	T	U	V	W	X	Y	Z	A	B	C	D	E	F	G	H	I	J	K	L	M	N	O	P
17	R	S	T	U	V	W	X	Y	Z	A	B	C	D	E	F	G	H	I	J	K	L	M	N	O	P	Q
18	S	T	U	V	W	X	Y	Z	A	B	C	D	E	F	G	H	I	J	K	L	M	N	O	P	Q	R
19	T	U	V	W	X	Y	Z	A	B	C	D	E	F	G	H	I	J	K	L	M	N	O	P	Q	R	S
20	U	V	W	X	Y	Z	A	B	C	D	E	F	G	H	I	J	K	L	M	N	O	P	Q	R	S	T
21	V	W	X	Y	Z	A	B	C	D	E	F	G	H	I	J	K	L	M	N	O	P	Q	R	S	T	U
22	W	X	Y	Z	A	B	C	D	E	F	G	H	I	J	K	L	M	N	O	P	Q	R	S	T	U	V
23	X	Y	Z	A	B	C	D	E	F	G	H	I	J	K	L	M	N	O	P	Q	R	S	T	U	V	W
24	Y	Z	A	B	C	D	E	F	G	H	I	J	K	L	M	N	O	P	Q	R	S	T	U	V	W	X
25	Z	A	B	C	D	E	F	G	H	I	J	K	L	M	N	O	P	Q	R	S	T	U	V	W	X	Y
26	A	B	C	D	E	F	G	H	I	J	K	L	M	N	O	P	Q	R	S	T	U	V	W	X	Y	Z

in the plaintext can be represented by different letters in the ciphertext. For example, the letter **o** is repeated in **troops**, but it is substituted by two different letters — the **oo** is enciphered as **HS**.

As well as being invulnerable to frequency analysis, the Vigenère cipher has an enormous number of keys. The sender and receiver can agree on any word in the dictionary, any combination of words, or even fabricate words. A cryptanalyst would be unable to crack the message by searching all possible keys because the number of options is simply too great.

Vigenère's work culminated in his *Traicté des chiffres* ('A Treatise on Secret Writing'), published in 1586. Ironically, this was the same year that Thomas Phelippes was breaking the cipher of Mary Queen of Scots. If only Mary's secretary had known about the Vigenère cipher, Mary's messages to Babington would have baffled Phelippes, and her life might have been saved.

Previous forms of cipher were called monoalphabetic substitution ciphers because they used only one cipher alphabet per message. In contrast, the Vigenère cipher belongs to a class of cipher known as *polyalphabetic*, a name that reflects the fact that the cipher employs several cipher alphabets per message.

Because of its strength and its guarantee of security, it would seem natural that the Vigenère cipher would be rapidly adopted by cipher secretaries around Europe. Surely they would be relieved to have access, once again, to a secure form of encryption? On the contrary, cipher secretaries seem to have spurned the Vigenère cipher. This apparently flawless system would remain largely neglected for the next two centuries, mainly because encrypting and decrypting were such complex processes.

In any case, for many seventeenth-century purposes, the monoalphabetic substitution cipher was perfectly adequate. If you wanted to ensure that your servant was unable to read your private correspondence, or if you wanted to protect your diary from the prying eyes of your spouse, then the old-fashioned type of cipher was quite sufficient. Monoalphabetic substitution was quick, easy to use and secure against people unschooled in cryptanalysis. In fact, the simple monoalphabetic substitution cipher endured in various forms for many centuries (see box overleaf).

For more serious applications, such as military and government communications, where security was paramount, the straightforward monoalphabetic cipher was clearly inadequate. Professional cryptographers in combat with professional cryptanalysts needed something better, yet they were still reluctant to adopt the polyalphabetic cipher because of its complexity. Military communications, in particular, required speed and simplicity; a diplomatic office might be sending and receiving hundreds of messages each day, so time was of the essence. Consequently, cryptographers searched for an intermediate cipher, one that was harder to crack than a straightforward monoalphabetic cipher, but one that was simpler to implement than a polyalphabetic cipher.

The various candidates included the remarkably effective *homophonic substitution cipher*. Here, each letter is replaced with a variety of substitutes, the number of potential substitutes being proportional to the frequency of the letter. For example, the letter **a** accounts for roughly 8 per cent of all letters in written English, and so we would assign eight symbols to represent it. Each time **a** appeared in the plaintext it would be replaced in the ciphertext by one of the eight symbols chosen at

THE PIGPEN CIPHER

The pigpen cipher is a monoalphabetic substitution cipher that was used by Freemasons in the 1700s to keep their records private, and is still sometimes used by schoolchildren. It may have got its name from the resemblance of its grid to a farmyard enclosure for pigs. The cipher does not substitute one letter for another, rather it substitutes each letter for a symbol according to the following scheme.

To encrypt a particular letter, find its position in one of the four grids, then sketch that portion of the grid to represent that letter. Hence:

$$a = \lrcorner, \quad b = \sqcup, \quad \ldots, \quad z = \wedge$$

If you know the key, the pigpen cipher is easy to decipher. If not, it can be broken by:

Table 5 *An example of a homophonic substitution cipher. The top row represents the plain alphabet, while the numbers below represent the cipher alphabet, with several options for frequently occurring letters.*

a	b	c	d	e	f	g	h	i	j	k	l	m	n	o	p	q	r	s	t	u	v	w	x	y	z
09	48	13	01	14	10	06	23	32	15	04	26	22	18	00	38	94	29	11	17	08	34	60	28	21	02
12	81	41	03	16	31	25	39	70			37	27	58	05	95			35	19	20	61		89		52
33		62	45	24			50	73			51		59	07				40	36	30	63				
47			79	44			56	83			84		66	54				42	76	43					
53				46			65	88					71	72				77	86	49					
67				55			68	93					91	90				80	96	69					
78				57										99					75						
92				64															85						
				74															97						
				82																					
				87																					
				98																					

random, so that by the end of the encipherment each symbol would constitute roughly 1 per cent of the enciphered text. By comparison, the letter **b** accounts for only 2 per cent of all letters, and so we would assign only two symbols to represent it. Each time **b** appeared in the plaintext, either of the two symbols could be chosen, and by the end of the encipherment each symbol would also constitute roughly 1 per cent of the enciphered text. This process of allotting varying numbers of symbols to act as substitutes for each letter continues throughout the alphabet, until we get to **z**, which is so rare that it has only one symbol to act as a substitute. In the example given in Table 5, the substitutes in the cipher alphabet happen to be two-digit numbers, and there are between one and twelve substitutes for each letter in the plain alphabet, depending on each letter's relative abundance.

We can think of all the two-digit numbers that correspond to the plaintext letter **a** as effectively representing the same sound in the ciphertext, namely the sound of the letter **a** — hence the origin of the term 'homophonic substitution', *homos* meaning 'same' and *phonos* meaning 'sound' in Greek. The point of offering several substitution options for popular letters is to balance out the frequencies of symbols in the ciphertext. If we enciphered a message using the cipher alphabet in Table 5, then every number would constitute roughly 1 per cent of the entire text. If no symbol appeared more frequently than any other, then this would seem to defy any potential attack via frequency analysis. Perfect security? Not quite.

The ciphertext still contains many subtle clues for the clever cryptanalyst. As we saw in Chapter 1, each letter in the English language has its own personality, defined according to its relationship with all the other letters, and these traits can still be discerned even if the encryption is by homophonic substitution. In English the most extreme example of a letter with a distinct personality is the letter **q**, which is only followed by one letter, namely **u** (the small number of exceptions are words imported from other languages, mainly Arabic). If we were attempting to decipher a ciphertext, we might begin by noting that **q** is a rare letter, and is therefore likely to be represented by just one symbol, and we know that **u**, which accounts for roughly 3 per cent of all letters, is probably represented by three symbols. So, if we find a symbol in the ciphertext that is only ever followed by three particular symbols, then it would be sensible to assume that the first symbol represents **q** and the other three symbols represent **u**. Other letters are harder to spot, but are also betrayed by their relationships to one another. Although the homophonic cipher is breakable, it is much more secure than a straightforward monoalphabetic cipher.

A homophonic cipher might seem similar to a polyalphabetic cipher inasmuch as each plaintext letter can be enciphered in many ways, but there is a crucial difference, and the homophonic cipher is in fact a type of monoalphabetic cipher. In the homophonic cipher in Table 5, the letter **a** can be represented by any of eight numbers. Significantly, these eight numbers represent only the letter **a**. In other words, a plaintext letter can be represented by several symbols, but each symbol can only represent one letter. In a polyalphabetic cipher, a plaintext letter will also be represented by different symbols, but, even more confusingly, these symbols will represent different letters during the course of an encipherment.

Perhaps the fundamental reason why the homophonic cipher is considered monoalphabetic is that once the cipher alphabet has been established, it remains constant throughout the process of encryption. The fact that the cipher alphabet contains several options for encrypting each letter is irrelevant. In contrast, a cryptographer who is using a polyalphabetic cipher must continually switch between distinctly different cipher alphabets during the process of encryption.

The Black Chambers

Reinforcing the monoalphabetic cipher by adding homophones might have been sufficient during the 1600s, but by the 1700s cryptanalysis was becoming industrialised, with teams of government cryptanalysts working together to crack many of the most complex monoalphabetic ciphers. Each European power had its own so-called Black Chamber, a nerve centre for deciphering messages and gathering intelligence. The most celebrated, disciplined and efficient Black Chamber was the Geheime Kabinets-Kanzlei in Vienna.

It operated according to a rigorous timetable, because it was vital that its nefarious activities should not interrupt the smooth running of the postal service. Letters which were supposed to be delivered to embassies in Vienna were first routed via the Black Chamber, arriving at 7 a.m. Secretaries melted seals, and a team of stenographers worked in parallel to make copies of the letters. If necessary, a language specialist would take responsibility for duplicating unusual scripts. Within three hours the letters had been resealed in their envelopes and returned to the central post office so that they could be delivered to their intended destination. Mail merely in transit through Austria would arrive at the Black Chamber at 10 a.m., and mail leaving Viennese embassies for destinations outside Austria would arrive at 4 p.m. All these letters would also be copied before being allowed to continue on their journey. Each day a hundred letters would filter through the Viennese Black Chamber.

The copies were passed to the cryptanalysts, who sat in little kiosks, ready to tease out the meanings of the messages. As well as supplying the emperors of Austria with invaluable intelligence, the Viennese Black Chamber sold the information it harvested to other powers in Europe. In 1774 an arrangement was made with Abbot Georgel, the secretary at the French Embassy, which gave him access to a twice-weekly package of information in exchange for 1,000 ducats. He then sent these letters, which contained the supposedly secret plans of various monarchs, straight to Louis XV in Paris.

The Black Chambers were effectively making all forms of monoalphabetic cipher insecure. Confronted with such professional cryptanalytic opposition, cryptographers were at last forced to adopt the more complex but more secure Vigenère cipher. Gradually, cipher secretaries began to switch to using polyalphabetic ciphers. In addition to more effective cryptanalysis, there was another pressure that was encouraging the move towards securer forms of encryption: the development of the telegraph, and the need to protect telegrams from interception and decipherment.

Although the electric telegraph, together with the ensuing telecommunications revolution, appeared in the nineteenth century, its origins can be traced back to 1753. An anonymous letter in a Scottish magazine described how a message could be sent across large distances by connecting the sender and receiver with twenty-six cables, one for each letter of the alphabet. The sender could then spell out the message by sending pulses of electricity along each wire. For example, to spell out **hello**, the sender would begin by sending a signal down the **h** wire, then one down the **e** wire, and so on. The receiver would somehow sense the electrical current emerging from each wire and read the message. However, this 'expeditious method of conveying intelligence', as the inventor called it, was never constructed, because there were several technical obstacles that had to be overcome.

For example, engineers needed a sufficiently sensitive system for detecting electrical signals. In England, Charles Wheatstone and William Fothergill Cooke built detectors from magnetised needles, which would be deflected in the presence of an incoming electric current. By 1839 the Wheatstone–Cooke system was being used to send messages between railway stations in West Drayton and Paddington, a distance of 29 km. The reputation of the telegraph and its remarkable speed of communication soon spread, and nothing did more to popularise its power than the birth of Queen Victoria's second son, Prince Alfred, at Windsor on 6 August 1844. News of the birth was telegraphed to London, and within the hour *The Times* was on the streets announcing the news. It credited the technology that had enabled this feat, mentioning that it was 'indebted to the extraordinary power of the Electro-Magnetic Telegraph'. The following year, the telegraph gained further fame when it helped capture John Tawell, who had murdered his mistress in Slough and attempted to escape by jumping onto a London-bound train. The local police telegraphed Tawell's description to London, and he was arrested as soon as he arrived at Paddington.

Meanwhile, in America, Samuel Morse had just built his first telegraph line running for 60 km between Baltimore and Washington. Morse used an electromagnet to enhance the signal, so that when it arrived at the receiver's end it was strong enough to make a series of dots and dashes on a strip of paper. He also developed the now familiar Morse code for translating each letter of the alphabet into dots and dashes (see box). To complete his system he designed a sounder, so that the receiver would hear each letter as a series of audible dots and dashes.

SAMUEL MORSE AND THE ELECTRIC TELEGRAPH

Samuel Morse

Electrical telegraphy originated in a chance meeting between a physician and a portrait painter on the packet-ship *Sully* returning from Le Havre to New York in 1832. The physician was Charles Thomas Jackson and the painter was Samuel Finley Breese Morse, the first president of the National Academy of Design in New York. Jackson, on his way back from studying an outbreak of cholera in Vienna, would later abandon medicine for geology. Morse's career too would take a sharp turn. On board ship the two men had discussed the phenomena of electricity and magnetism, subjects that were familiar to Morse from his college days at Yale. Five years later, he turned the ideas that emerged from that conversation into a working electric telegraph. In 1836, the same year that Cooke and Wheatstone patented their telegraph in Britain, Morse, unfamiliar with their work, filed for a US patent. That year he demonstrated his system to Congress, from which he obtained $30,000 of funding in 1843 to construct the first operational telegraph line in America, between Washington and Baltimore. On 24 May 1844, using a simple spring-loaded device of his own design (the Morse key), Morse transmitted the first message on his line: 'What hath God wrought?' He developed the Morse code, shown here in its later international version, for telegraphists to use.

Symbol	Code	Symbol	Code	Symbol	Code
A	· —	P	· — — ·	5	· · · · ·
B	— · · ·	Q	— — · —	6	— · · · ·
C	— · — ·	R	· — ·	7	— — · · ·
D	— · ·	S	· · ·	8	— — — · ·
E	·	T	—	9	— — — — ·
F	· · — ·	U	· · —	0	— — — — —
G	— — ·	V	· · · —	full stop	· — · — · —
H	· · · ·	W	· — —	comma	— — · · — —
I	· ·	X	— · · —	question mark	· · — — · ·
J	· — — —	Y	— · — —	colon	— — — · · ·
K	— · —	Z	— — · ·	semicolon	— · — · — ·
L	· — · ·	1	· — — — —	hyphen	— · · · · —
M	— —	2	· · — — —	slash	— · · — ·
N	— ·	3	· · · — —	quotation mark	· — · · — ·
O	— — —	4	· · · · —		

Back in Europe, Morse's system gradually overtook Wheatstone and Cooke's in popularity, and in 1851 a European form of Morse code, which included accented letters, was adopted throughout the Continent. As each year passed, Morse code and the telegraph had an increasing influence on the world, enabling the police to capture more criminals, helping newspapers to gather the very latest news, allowing distant companies to make instantaneous deals and providing countries with the means to communicate with far-flung parts of their empires.

However, guarding these often sensitive communications was a major concern. The Morse code itself is not a form of cryptography because there is no concealment of the message: the dots and dashes are merely a convenient way to represent letters for the telegraphic medium. Morse code is effectively nothing more than an alternative alphabet. The problem of security arose primarily because anyone wanting to send a message would have to deliver it to a Morse code operator, who would then have to read it in order to transmit it. The telegraph operators had access to every message, and hence there was a risk that one company might bribe an operator in order to gain access to a rival's communications. This problem was outlined in an article on telegraphy published in 1853 in England's *Quarterly Review*:

> Means should also be taken to obviate one great objection, at present felt with respect to sending private communications by telegraph – the violation of all secrecy – for in any case half-a-dozen people must be cognisant of every word addressed by one person to another. The clerks of the English Telegraph Company are sworn to secrecy, but we often write things that it would be intolerable to see strangers read before our eyes. This is a grievous fault in the telegraph, and it must be remedied by some means or other.

The solution was to encipher a message before handing it to the telegraph operator. The operator would then turn the ciphertext into Morse code before transmitting it. As well as preventing the operators from seeing sensitive material, encryption also stymied the efforts of any spy who might be tapping the telegraph wire. The polyalphabetic Vigenère cipher was clearly the best way to ensure secrecy for important business communications. It was considered unbreakable, and became known as *le chiffre indéchiffrable*. Cryptographers had, for the time being at least, a clear lead over the cryptanalysts.

Mr Babbage Versus the Vigenère Cipher

The most intriguing figure in nineteenth-century cryptanalysis is Charles Babbage, the eccentric British genius best known for developing the blueprint for the modern computer. He was born in 1791, the son of Benjamin Babbage, a wealthy London banker. When Charles married without his father's permission, he no longer had access to the Babbage fortune, but he still had enough money to be financially secure, and he pursued the life of a roving scholar, applying his mind to whatever problem tickled his fancy. His inventions include the speedometer and the cowcatcher, a device that could be fixed to the front of steam locomotives to clear cattle from railway tracks. In terms of scientific breakthroughs, he was the first to realise that the width of a tree ring depended on that year's weather and therefore it was possible to determine past climates by studying ancient trees. He was also intrigued by statistics, and as a diversion he drew up mortality tables, a basic tool for today's insurance industry.

Babbage did not restrict himself to tackling scientific and engineering problems. The cost of sending a letter used to depend on the distance the letter had to travel, but Babbage pointed out that the cost of the labour required to calculate the price for each letter was more than the cost of the postage. Instead, he proposed the system we still use today — standard prices for all letters, regardless of where in the country the addressee lives. He was also interested in politics and social issues, and towards the end of his life he began a campaign to get rid of the organ-grinders and street musicians who roamed London. He complained that the music

> not infrequently gives rise to a dance by little ragged urchins, and sometimes half-
> intoxicated men, who occasionally accompany the noise with their own discordant voices.
> Another class who are great supporters of street music consists of ladies of elastic virtue
> and cosmopolitan tendencies, to whom it affords a decent excuse for displaying their
> fascinations at their open windows.

Unfortunately for Babbage, the musicians fought back by gathering in large groups outside his house and playing as loud as possible.

A turning point in Babbage's scientific career came in 1821, when he and the astronomer John Herschel were examining a set of mathematical tables, the sort used as the basis for astronomical, engineering and navigational calculations. The two men were disgusted by the number of errors in the tables, which would lead to flaws in important calculations. One set of tables, the *Nautical Ephemeris for Finding Latitude and*

Longitude at Sea, contained over a thousand errors. Indeed, many shipwrecks and engineering disasters were blamed on faulty tables. These mathematical tables were calculated by hand, and the mistakes were simply the result of human error. This caused Babbage to exclaim, 'I wish to God these calculations had been executed by steam!' This marked the beginning of an extraordinary endeavour to build a machine capable of faultlessly calculating tables to a high degree of accuracy (see box). Although he failed to complete such a machine, his designs embody the basic elements of the modern computer. In many ways, Babbage was the father of computing.

CHARLES BABBAGE'S COMPUTING ENGINES

In 1823 Charles Babbage designed 'Difference Engine No. 1', a magnificent calculator consisting of 25,000 precision parts, to be built with government funding. Although Babbage was a brilliant innovator, he was not a great implementer. After ten years of toil he abandoned 'Difference Engine No. 1', cooked up an entirely new design, and set to work building 'Difference Engine No. 2'.

When Babbage abandoned his first machine, the government lost confidence in him and decided to cut its losses by withdrawing from the project – it had already spent £17,470, enough to build a pair of battleships. Consequently, Babbage had insufficient funds to build Difference Engine No. 2. It was only in 1991 that the Science Museum in London completed construction

Less well known is that Babbage made an equally important contribution to codebreaking: he succeeded in breaking the Vigenère cipher, and in so doing he made the greatest breakthrough in cryptanalysis since the Arab scholars of the ninth century broke the monoalphabetic cipher by inventing frequency analysis. Babbage's work required no mechanical calculations or complex computations. Instead, he used nothing more than sheer cunning.

Babbage had become interested in ciphers at a very young age. In later life, he recalled how his childhood hobby occasionally got him into trouble: 'The bigger boys made ciphers, but if I got hold of a few words, I usually found out the key.

of the machine, shown here, according to Babbage's original designs. It worked perfectly, exactly as Babbage had planned.

The government's rejection of Babbage's project was a devastating blow to his scientific ambitions. It was probably this withdrawal of support that later prompted Babbage to make the following complaint:

> Propose to an Englishman any principle, or any instrument, however admirable, and you will observe that the whole effort of the English mind is directed to find a difficulty, a defect, or an impossibility in it. If you speak to him of a machine for peeling a potato, he will pronounce it impossible: if you peel a potato with it before his eyes, he will declare it useless, because it will not slice a pineapple.

The scientific tragedy was that Babbage's machine would have been a stepping stone to the even more ambitious Analytical Engine. Rather than merely calculating a specific set of tables, the Analytical Engine would have been able to solve a variety of mathematical problems depending on the instructions it was given. In fact, the Analytical Engine provided the template for modern computers. The design included a 'store' (memory) and a 'mill' (processor), which would allow it to make decisions and repeat instructions, which are equivalent to the 'IF . . . THEN . . .' and 'LOOP' commands in modern programming.

The consequence of this ingenuity was occasionally painful: the owners of the detected ciphers sometimes thrashed me, though the fault lay in their own stupidity.' These beatings did not discourage him, and he continued to be enchanted by cryptanalysis. He wrote in his autobiography that, 'deciphering is, in my opinion, one of the most fascinating of arts'.

Babbage expressed his cryptanalytic skills in a variety of ways. For example, young lovers in Victorian England were often forbidden from publicly expressing their affection, and could not even communicate by letter in case their parents intercepted and read the contents. This resulted in lovers sending encrypted messages to each other via the personal columns of newspapers. These 'agony columns', as they became known, provoked the curiosity of cryptanalysts, who would scan the notes and try to decipher their titillating contents. Charles Babbage is known to have indulged in this activity, along with his friends Sir Charles Wheatstone and Baron Lyon Playfair, who together were responsible for developing the deft *Playfair cipher* (see box overleaf). On one occasion, Wheatstone deciphered a note in *The Times* from an Oxford student, suggesting to his true love that they elope. A few days later, Wheatstone inserted his own message, encrypted in the same cipher, advising the couple against this rebellious and rash action. Shortly afterwards there appeared a third message, this time unencrypted and from the lady in question: 'Dear Charlie, Write no more. Our cipher is discovered.'

Babbage soon gained a reputation within London society as a cryptanalyst prepared to tackle any encrypted message, and strangers would approach him with all sorts of problems. For example, he helped a desperate biographer attempting to decipher the shorthand notes of John Flamsteed, England's first Astronomer Royal. He also came to the rescue of a historian by solving a cipher of Henrietta Maria, wife of Charles I. In 1854 he collaborated with a barrister and used cryptanalysis to reveal crucial evidence in a legal case. Over the years, he accumulated a thick file of encrypted messages which he planned to use as the basis for an authoritative book on cryptanalysis, entitled *The Philosophy of Decyphering*. The book would contain two examples of every kind of cipher, one that would be broken as a demonstration and one that would be left as an exercise for the reader. Unfortunately, as with many other of his grand plans, the book was never completed.

While most cryptanalysts had given up all hope of ever breaking the Vigenère cipher, Babbage was inspired to attempt a decipherment by an exchange of letters with John Hall Brock Thwaites, a dentist from Bristol with a rather innocent view of ciphers. In 1854 Thwaites claimed to have invented a new cipher, which in fact was equivalent to the Vigenère cipher. He wrote to the *Journal of the Society of Arts* with the intention of patenting his idea, apparently unaware that he was several centuries too late. Although the Vigenère cipher was well known to military and other professional cryptographers, it is not too surprising that an amateur like Thwaites had never seen it before. Babbage decided to set the record straight by writing to the Society, pointing out that 'the cypher . . . is a very old one, and to be found in most books'. Thwaites was unapologetic and challenged Babbage to break his cipher. Whether or not it was breakable was irrelevant to whether or not it was new, but Babbage's curiosity was sufficiently aroused for him to embark on a search for a weakness in the Vigenère cipher.

Cracking a difficult cipher is akin to climbing a sheer cliff face. The cryptanalyst is seeking any nook or cranny which will provide the slightest purchase. In a monoalphabetic cipher the cryptanalyst will latch on to the frequency of the letters, because the commonest letters, such as **e**, **t** and **a**, will stand out no matter how they have been disguised. In the polyalphabetic Vigenère cipher the frequencies are much more balanced, because the keyword is used to switch between cipher alphabets. Hence, at first sight, the rock face seems perfectly smooth.

Remember, the great strength of the Vigenère cipher is that the same letter is enciphered in different ways. For example, if the keyword is **KING**, then every letter in the plaintext can potentially be enciphered in four different ways, because the keyword contains four letters. Each letter of the keyword defines a different cipher alphabet in the Vigenère square, as shown in Table 6 (see p.66). The **e** column of the square has been highlighted to show how it is enciphered differently, depending on which letter of the keyword is defining the encipherment:

If the **K** of **KING** is used to encipher **e**, then the resulting ciphertext letter is **O**.
If the **I** of **KING** is used to encipher **e**, then the resulting ciphertext letter is **M**.
If the **N** of **KING** is used to encipher **e**, then the resulting ciphertext letter is **R**.
If the **G** of **KING** is used to encipher **e**, then the resulting ciphertext letter is **K**.

Similarly, whole words will be enciphered in different ways: the word **the**, for example, could be enciphered as **DPR**, **BUK**, **GNO** or **ZRM**, depending on its position relative to the keyword. Although this makes cryptanalysis difficult, it is not impossible. The important point is that if there are only four ways to encipher the

THE PLAYFAIR CIPHER

The Playfair cipher was popularised by Lyon Playfair, first Baron Playfair of St Andrews and Deputy Speaker of the House of Commons, but it was invented by Sir Charles Wheatstone, one of the pioneers of the electric telegraph. The two men lived close to each other, either side of Hammersmith Bridge, and they often met to discuss their ideas on cryptography.

The cipher replaces each pair of letters in the plaintext with another pair of letters. In order to encrypt and transmit a message, the sender and receiver must first agree on a keyword. For example, we can use Wheatstone's own name, CHARLES, as a keyword. Next, before encryption, the letters of the alphabet are written in a 5 by 5 square, beginning with the keyword, and combining the letters I and J into a single element:

```
C    H    A    R    L
E    S    B    D    F
G   I/J   K    M    N
O    P    Q    T    U
V    W    X    Y    Z
```

Next, the message is broken up into pairs of letters, or digraphs. The two letters in any digraph should be different, achieved in the following example by inserting an extra x between the double m in hammersmith. An extra x is added at the end to make a digraph from the single final letter:

Plaintext   meet me at hammersmith bridge tonight

Plaintext in digraphs   me-et-me-at-ha-mx-me-rs-mi-th-br-id-ge-to-ni-gh-tx

Encryption can now begin. All the digraphs fall into one of three categories – both letters are in the same row, or the same column, or neither. If both letters are in the same row, then they are replaced by the letter to the immediate right of each one; thus mi becomes NK. If one of the letters is at the end of the row, it is replaced by the letter at the beginning; thus ni becomes GK. If both letters are in the same column, they are replaced by the letter immediately beneath each one; thus ge becomes OG. If one of the letters is at the bottom of the column, then it is replaced by the letter at the top; thus ve becomes CG.

If the letters of the digraph are neither in the same row nor the same column, the encipherer follows a different rule. To encipher the first letter, look along its row until you reach the column containing the second letter; the letter at this intersection then replaces the first letter. To encipher the second letter, look along its row until you reach the column containing the first letter; the letter at this intersection replaces the second letter. Hence, me becomes GD, and et becomes DO. The complete encryption is:

Plaintext
in digraphs   me et me at ha mx me rs mi th br id ge to ni gh tx

Ciphertext   GD DO GD RQ AR KY GD HD NK PR DA MS OG UP GK IC QY

The recipient, who also knows the keyword, can easily decipher the ciphertext by simply reversing the process: for example, enciphered letters in the same row are deciphered by replacing them by the letters to their left.

Playfair was determined to promote Wheatstone's idea among the most senior politicians. He introduced Wheatstone to the Under Secretary of the Foreign Office who complained that the system was too complicated for use in battle conditions. Wheatstone replied that he could teach the method to boys from the nearest elementary school in fifteen minutes. 'That is very possible,' said the Under Secretary, 'but you could never teach it to attachés.' Eventually the British War Office secretly adopted the technique, probably using it first in the Boer War. Although it proved effective for a while, the Playfair cipher was far from impregnable. It can be attacked by looking for the most frequently occurring digraphs in the ciphertext, and assuming that they represent the commonest digraphs in English, namely th, he, an, in, er, re and es.

Sir Charles Wheatstone

Table 6 *A Vigenère square used in combination with the keyword* **KING**. *The keyword defines four separate cipher alphabets, so that the letter* **e** *may be encrypted as* **O, M, R** *or* **K**.

Plain	a b c d e f g h i j k l m n o p q r s t u v w x y z
1	B C D E F G H I J K L M N O P Q R S T U V W X Y Z A
2	C D E F G H I J K L M N O P Q R S T U V W X Y Z A B
3	D E F G H I J K L M N O P Q R S T U V W X Y Z A B C
4	E F G H I J K L M N O P Q R S T U V W X Y Z A B C D
5	F G H I J K L M N O P Q R S T U V W X Y Z A B C D E
6	G H I J K L M N O P Q R S T U V W X Y Z A B C D E F
7	H I J K L M N O P Q R S T U V W X Y Z A B C D E F G
8	I J K L M N O P Q R S T U V W X Y Z A B C D E F G H
9	J K L M N O P Q R S T U V W X Y Z A B C D E F G H I
10	K L M N O P Q R S T U V W X Y Z A B C D E F G H I J
11	L M N O P Q R S T U V W X Y Z A B C D E F G H I J K
12	M N O P Q R S T U V W X Y Z A B C D E F G H I J K L
13	N O P Q R S T U V W X Y Z A B C D E F G H I J K L M
14	O P Q R S T U V W X Y Z A B C D E F G H I J K L M N
15	P Q R S T U V W X Y Z A B C D E F G H I J K L M N O
16	Q R S T U V W X Y Z A B C D E F G H I J K L M N O P
17	R S T U V W X Y Z A B C D E F G H I J K L M N O P Q
18	S T U V W X Y Z A B C D E F G H I J K L M N O P Q R
19	T U V W X Y Z A B C D E F G H I J K L M N O P Q R S
20	U V W X Y Z A B C D E F G H I J K L M N O P Q R S T
21	V W X Y Z A B C D E F G H I J K L M N O P Q R S T U
22	W X Y Z A B C D E F G H I J K L M N O P Q R S T U V
23	X Y Z A B C D E F G H I J K L M N O P Q R S T U V W
24	Y Z A B C D E F G H I J K L M N O P Q R S T U V W X
25	Z A B C D E F G H I J K L M N O P Q R S T U V W X Y
26	A B C D E F G H I J K L M N O P Q R S T U V W X Y Z

word **the**, and the original message contains several instances of the word **the**, then it is highly likely that some of the four possible encipherments will be repeated in the ciphertext. This is demonstrated in the following example, in which the line **The Sun and the Man in the Moon** has been enciphered using the Vigenère cipher and the keyword **KING**.

Keyword	K I N G K I N G K I N G K I N G K I N G K I N G
Plaintext	t h e s u n a n d t h e m a n i n t h e m o o n
Ciphertext	D P R Y E V N T N B U K W I A O X B U K W W B T

The word **the** is enciphered as **DPR** in the first instance, and then as **BUK** on the second and third occasions. The reason for the repetition of **BUK** is that the second **the** is displaced by eight letters with respect to the third **the**, and eight is a multiple of the length of the keyword, which is four letters long. In other words, the second **the** was enciphered according to its relationship to the keyword (**the** is directly below **ING**), and by the time we reach the third **the**, the keyword has cycled round exactly twice, repeating the relationship and hence repeating the encipherment.

Babbage realised that this sort of repetition provided him with exactly the foothold he needed to conquer the Vigenère cipher. He was able to define a series of relatively simple steps which could be followed by any cryptanalyst to crack the hitherto *chiffre indéchiffrable*. To demonstrate his brilliant technique, let us imagine that we have intercepted the cipher-text shown in Figure 5. We know that it was enciphered using the Vigenère cipher, but we know nothing about the original message, and the keyword is a mystery.

The first stage in Babbage's cryptanalysis is to look for sequences of letters that appear more than once in the ciphertext. There are two ways in which such repetitions

```
W U B E F I Q L Z U R M V O F E H M Y M W T
I X C G T M P I F K R Z U P M V O I R Q M M
W O Z M P U L M B N Y V Q Q Q M V M V J L E
Y M H F E F N Z P S D L P P S D L P E V Q M
W C X Y M D A V Q E E F I Q C A Y T Q O W C
X Y M W M S E M E F C F W Y E Y Q E T R L I
Q Y C G M T W C W F B S M Y F P L R X T Q Y
E E X M R U L U K S G W F P T L R Q A E R L
U V P M V Y Q Y C X T W F Q L M T E L S F J
P Q E H M O Z C I W C I W F P Z S L M A E Z
I Q V L Q M Z V P P X A W C S M Z M O R V G
V V Q S Z E T R L Q Z P B J A Z V Q I Y X E
W W O I C C G D W H Q M M V O W S G N T J P
F P P A Y B I Y B J U T W R L Q K L L L M D
P Y V A C D C F Q N Z P I F P P K S D V P T
I D G X M Q Q V E B M Q A L K E Z M G C V K
U Z K I Z B Z L I U A M M V Z
```

Figure 5   The ciphertext, enciphered using the Vigenère cipher.

could arise. The most likely is that the same sequence of letters in the plaintext has been enciphered using the same part of the key. Alternatively, there is a slight possibility that two different sequences of letters in the plaintext have been enciphered using different parts of the key, coincidentally leading to the identical sequence in the ciphertext. If we restrict ourselves to long sequences, we can largely discount the second possibility, and in this case we shall consider repeated sequences only if they are of four letters or more. Table 7 (opposite) is a log of such repetitions, along with the spacing between them. For example, the sequence **E-F-I-Q** appears in the first line of the ciphertext and then in the fifth line, shifted forward by 95 letters.

As well as being used to encipher the plaintext into ciphertext, the keyword is also used by the receiver to decipher the ciphertext back into plaintext. So if we could identify the keyword, deciphering the text would be easy. At this stage we do not have enough information to work out the keyword, but Table 7 does provide some very good clues to its length. Having listed which sequences repeat themselves and the spacing between these repetitions, the rest of the table is given over to identifying the *factors* of the spacing – the numbers that will divide into the spacing. For example, the sequence **W-C-X-Y-M** repeats itself after 20 letters, and the numbers 1, 2, 4, 5, 10 and 20 are factors, because they divide perfectly into 20 without leaving a remainder. These factors suggest six possibilities:

(1) The key is 1 letter long and is recycled 20 times between encryptions.
(2) The key is 2 letters long and is recycled 10 times between encryptions.
(3) The key is 4 letters long and is recycled 5 times between encryptions.
(4) The key is 5 letters long and is recycled 4 times between encryptions.
(5) The key is 10 letters long and is recycled 2 times between encryptions.
(6) The key is 20 letters long and is recycled 1 time   between encryptions.

The first possibility can be excluded, because a key that is only 1 letter long gives rise to a monoalphabetic cipher – only one row of the Vigenère square would be used for the entire encryption, and the cipher alphabet would remain unchanged; it is unlikely that a cryptographer would do this. To indicate each of the other possibilities, a ✓ is placed in the appropriate column of Table 7. Each ✓ indicates a potential key length.

To identify whether the key is 2, 4, 5, 10 or 20 letters long, we need to look at the factors of all the other spacings. Because the keyword seems to be 20 letters or smaller, Table 7 lists those factors that are 20 or smaller for each of the other spacings. There is a clear propensity for a spacing divisible by 5. In fact, every spacing is

Table 7 *Repetitions and spacings in the ciphertext.*

Repeated sequence	Repeat spacing	Possible length of key (or factors)																		
		2	3	4	5	6	7	8	9	10	11	12	13	14	15	16	17	18	19	20
E-F-I-Q	95				✓															✓	
P-S-D-L-P	5				✓																
W-C-X-Y-M	20	✓		✓	✓					✓											✓
E-T-R-L	120	✓	✓	✓	✓	✓		✓		✓		✓			✓						✓

divisible by 5. The first repeated sequence, **E-F-I-Q**, can be explained by a keyword of length 5 recycled nineteen times between the first and second encryptions. The second repeated sequence, **P-S-D-L-P**, can be explained by a keyword of length 5 recycled just once between the first and second encryptions. The third repeated sequence, **W-C-X-Y-M**, can be explained by a keyword of length 5 recycled four times between the first and second encryptions. The fourth repeated sequence, **E-T-R-L**, can be explained by a keyword of length 5 recycled twenty-four times between the first and second encryptions. In short, everything is consistent with a five-letter keyword.

If we assume that the keyword is indeed 5 letters long, our next step is to work out the actual letters of the keyword. For the time being, let us call the keyword L_1-L_2-L_3-L_4-L_5, such that L_1 represents the first letter of the keyword, L_2 the second, and so on. The process of encipherment would have begun with enciphering the first letter of the plaintext according to the first letter of the keyword, L_1. The letter L_1 defines one row of the Vigenère square, and effectively provides a monoalphabetic substitution cipher alphabet for the first letter of the plaintext. However, when it comes to encrypting the second letter of the plaintext, the cryptographer would have used L_2 to define a different row of the Vigenère square, effectively providing a different monoalphabetic substitution cipher alphabet. The third letter of plaintext would be encrypted according to L_3, the fourth according to L_4, and the fifth according to L_5. Each letter of the keyword is providing a different cipher alphabet for encryption. However, the sixth letter of the plaintext would once again be encrypted according to L_1, the seventh letter of the plaintext would once again be encrypted according to L_2, and the cycle repeats itself thereafter. In other words, the polyalphabetic cipher consists of five monoalphabetic ciphers, each responsible for encrypting one-fifth of the entire message — and we already know how to cryptanalyse monoalphabetic ciphers.

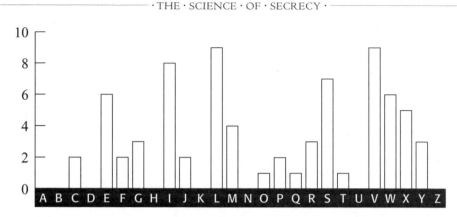

Figure 6 _Frequency distribution for letters in the ciphertext encrypted using the L_1 cipher alphabet (number of occurrences)._

We proceed as follows. We know that one of the rows of the Vigenère square, defined by L_1, provided the cipher alphabet to encrypt the 1st, 6th, 11th, 16th, . . . letters of the message. Hence, if we look at the 1st, 6th, 11th, 16th, . . . letters of the ciphertext, we should be able to use old-fashioned frequency analysis to work out the cipher alphabet in question. Figure 6 shows the frequency distribution of the letters that appear in the 1st, 6th, 11th, 16th, . . . positions of the ciphertext, which are **W, I, R, E,** . . . . Now, remember that each cipher alphabet in the Vigenère square is simply a standard alphabet shifted by a value between 1 and 26. The frequency distribution in Figure 6 should therefore have similar features to the frequency distribution of a standard alphabet, except that it will have been shifted by some distance. By comparing the L_1 distribution with the standard distribution, it should be possible to work out the shift. Figure 7 shows the standard frequency distribution for a piece of English plaintext.

Figure 7 _Standard frequency distribution (number of occurrences based on a plaintext with the same number of letters as in the ciphertext)._

The standard distribution has peaks, plateaus and valleys, and to match it with the L_1 cipher distribution we look for the most outstanding combination of features. For example, the three spikes at **R-S-T** in the standard distribution (Figure 7) and the long depression to its right that stretches across six letters from **U** to **Z** together form a very distinctive pair of features. The only similar features in the L_1 distribution (Figure 6) are the three spikes at **V-W-X**, followed by the depression stretching six letters from **Y** to **D**. This would suggest that all the letters encrypted according to L_1 have been shifted four places, or that L_1 defines a cipher alphabet which begins **E**, **F**, **G**, **H**, ... In turn, this means that the first letter of the keyword, L_1, is probably **E**. This hypothesis can be tested by shifting the L_1 distribution back four letters and comparing it with the standard distribution. Figure 8 shows both distributions for comparison. The match between the major peaks is very strong, implying that it is safe to assume that the keyword does indeed begin with **E**.

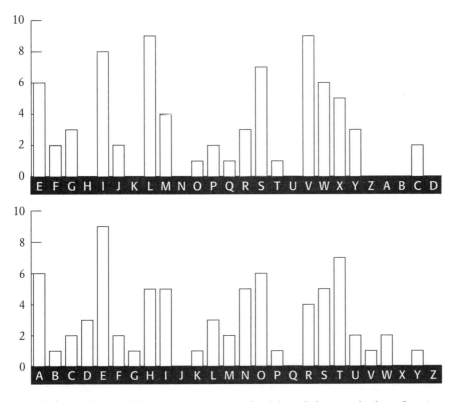

Figure 8 *The L_1 distribution shifted back four letters (top), compared with the standard frequency distribution (bottom).*

To summarise, searching for repetitions in the ciphertext has allowed us to identify the length of the keyword, which turned out to be five letters long. This allowed us to split the ciphertext into five parts, each one enciphered according to a monoalphabetic substitution as defined by one letter of the keyword. By analysing the fraction of the ciphertext that was enciphered according to the first letter of the keyword, we have been able to show that this letter, L_1, is probably **E**. This process is repeated in order to identify the second letter of the keyword. A frequency distribution is established for the 2nd, 7th, 12th, 17th, . . . letters in the ciphertext. Again, we need to compare the resulting distribution, shown in Figure 9, with the standard distribution in order to deduce the shift.

This distribution is harder to analyse. There are no obvious candidates for the three neighbouring peaks that correspond to **R-S-T**. However, the depression that stretches from **G** to **L** is very distinct, and probably corresponds to the depression we expect to see stretching from **U** to **Z** in the standard distribution. If this were the case, we would expect the three **R-S-T** peaks to appear at **D**, **E** and **F**, but the peak at **E** is missing. For the time being, we shall dismiss the missing peak as a statistical glitch, and go with our initial hunch, which is that the depression from **G** to **L** is a recognisably shifted feature. This would suggest that all the letters encrypted according to L_2 have been shifted twelve places, or that L_2 defines a cipher alphabet

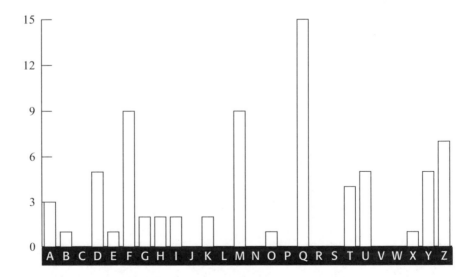

Figure 9 *Frequency distribution for letters in the ciphertext encrypted using the* L_2 *cipher alphabet (number of occurrences).*

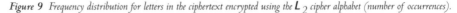

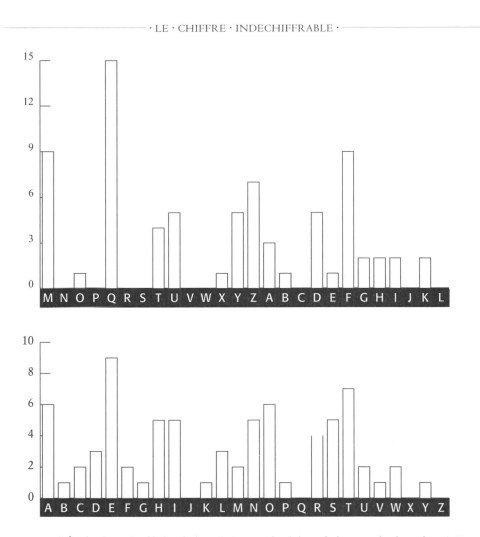

Figure 10 *The* **L**$_2$ *distribution shifted back twelve letters (top), compared with the standard frequency distribution (bottom). Most major peaks and troughs match.*

which begins **M**, **N**, **O**, **P**, . . . and that the second letter of the keyword, **L**$_2$, is **M**. Once again, this hypothesis can be tested by shifting the **L**$_2$ distribution back twelve letters and comparing it with the standard distribution. Figure 10 shows both distributions, and the match between the major peaks is again very strong, implying that it is safe to assume that the second letter of the keyword is indeed **M**.

I shall not continue the analysis; suffice it to say that analysing the 3rd, 8th, 13th, . . . letters implies that the third letter of the keyword is **I**, analysing the 4th, 9th,

14th, . . . letters implies that the fourth letter is **L**, and analysing the 5th, 10th, 15th, . . . letters implies that the fifth letter is **Y**. The keyword is **EMILY**. It is now possible to reverse the Vigenère cipher and complete the cryptanalysis. The first letter of the ciphertext is **W**, and it was encrypted according to the first letter of the keyword, **E**. Working backwards, we look at the Vigenère square, and find **W** in the row beginning with **E**, and then we find which letter is at the top of that column. The letter is **S**, which must make it the first letter of the plaintext. By repeating this process, we see that the plaintext begins **sittheedownandhavenoshamecheekbyjowl** . . . . By inserting suitable word-breaks and punctuation, we eventually get:

> Sit thee down, and have no shame,
> Cheek by jowl, and knee by knee:
> What care I for any name?
> What for order or degree?
>
> Let me screw thee up a peg:
> Let me loose thy tongue with wine:
> Callest thou that thing a leg?
> Which is thinnest? thine or mine?
>
> Thou shalt not be saved by works:
> Thou hast been a sinner too:
> Ruined trunks on withered forks,
> Empty scarecrows, I and you!
>
> Fill the cup, and fill the can:
> Have a rouse before the morn:
> Every moment dies a man,
> Every moment one is born.

These are verses from a poem by Alfred Tennyson entitled 'The Vision of Sin'. The keyword happens to be the first name of Tennyson's wife, Emily Sellwood. I chose to use a section from this particular poem as an example for cryptanalysis because it inspired some curious correspondence between Babbage and the great poet. Being a keen statistician and compiler of mortality tables, Babbage was irritated by the lines 'Every moment dies a man, Every moment one is born', which are the last lines of the plaintext above. Consequently, he offered a correction to Tennyson's 'otherwise beautiful' poem:

It must be manifest that if this were true, the population of the world would be at a standstill . . . I would suggest that in the next edition of your poem you have it read – 'Every moment dies a man, Every moment $1\frac{1}{16}$ is born.' . . . The actual figure is so long I cannot get it onto a line, but I believe the figure $1\frac{1}{16}$ will be sufficiently accurate for poetry.

I am, Sir, yours, etc.,

Charles Babbage.

Babbage's successful cryptanalysis of the Vigenère cipher was probably achieved in 1854, soon after his spat with Thwaites, but his breakthrough went completely unrecognised because he never published it. His work came to light only in the 1970s, when Ole Franksen, a Danish scholar, examined Babbage's extensive notes. In the meantime his technique was independently discovered by Friedrich Wilhelm Kasiski, a retired officer of the Prussian army. Ever since 1863, when he published his cryptanalytic breakthrough in *Die Geheimschriften und die Dechiffrir-kunst* ('Secret Writing and the Art of Deciphering'), the technique has been known as the Kasiski Test, and Babbage's contribution has been completely ignored. And why did Babbage fail to publicise his cracking of such a vital cipher? He certainly had a habit of not finishing projects and not publishing his discoveries, which might suggest that this is just one more example of his lackadaisical attitude. However, there is an alternative explanation.

Babbage was a close friend of Admiral Sir Francis Beaufort, inventor of the Beaufort scale for wind strength and for twenty-five years Hydrographer to the Royal Navy. It is well documented that they discussed cryptography and exchanged letters on the subject, so it seems likely that Babbage told Beaufort about his successful assault against the Vigenère cipher. His discovery occurred soon after the outbreak of the Crimean War (see box overleaf), and it is quite possible that Beaufort requested that Babbage keep his work secret, thus providing the British with a clear advantage over the Russian enemy and a nine-year head start over the rest of the world. If this was the case, then it would fit in with the long-standing tradition of hushing up codebreaking achievements in the interests of national security, a practice that has gone on throughout the centuries and which no doubt will continue in the twenty-first century.

Babbage's cracking of the Vigenère cipher is another stage in the evolution of cryptography, but in particular it illustrates the secretive nature of the subject.

Codebreaking, by its very nature, is a clandestine activity, and governments rarely champion the achievements of their codebreakers. Therefore the heroes of crypt-analysis rarely receive the recognition they deserve.

NEW TECHNOLOGY IN THE CRIMEAN WAR

The Crimean War of 1853–56 was the first conflict in which the electric telegraph played a significant role, and therefore one in which communication and encryption were more important than ever before. The war was fought against the background of what was known as the Eastern Question: the fear of the Western European powers, Britain especially, that the crumbling Ottoman Empire would fall under Russian domination. When Russia invaded the Balkans in 1853, British, French and Turkish troops landed on the Crimean peninsula with the objective of capturing the Russian naval base at Sebastopol.

A Russian long-distance telegraph ran from St Petersburg to Sebastopol, while the Allies laid a 550 km submarine cable – the longest ever attempted – across the Black Sea, from where it was linked to the European network at Bucharest. The War Office in London found that it could now direct military operations 'live', much to the annoyance of the British commanders in the field. In another development, news of the campaign was rapidly conveyed to Fleet Street by reporters from the press. William Howard Russell's dispatches for *The Times* did much to expose the scandalously ramshackle conduct of the war, in particular the dire medical facilities, which led to public outcry and the mission of Florence Nightingale to set up proper field hospitals.

CHAPTER THREE

Lost Languages and Ancient Messages

The discovery of the Rosetta Stone, and the decipherment of Egyptian hieroglyphs and other forgotten scripts

ALTHOUGH THE MAJORITY of codebreakers tackled military and diplomatic codes, a radical new breed of codebreaker began to emerge in the nineteenth century. This group of cryptanalysts was attempting to decipher long-forgotten languages, perhaps written in extinct scripts. If anything, the archaeological challenge is much more severe than the conventional one. For example, while military codebreakers usually have a continuous stream of words which they can attempt to identify, the information available to the archaeologist is sometimes just a small collection of clay tablets.

Deciphering ancient texts seems almost impossible, yet many men and women have devoted themselves to this arduous enterprise. The obsession is driven by the desire to understand the writing of our ancestors, thus allowing us to read their words, comprehend their culture and catch a glimpse of their thoughts. Perhaps this appetite for ancient scripts is best explained by Maurice Pope, the author of *The Story of Decipherment*: 'Decipherments are by far the most glamorous achievements of scholarship. There is a touch of magic about unknown writing, especially when it comes from the remote past, and a corresponding glory is bound to attach itself to the person who first solves its mystery.'

Deciphering forgotten scripts is not strictly cryptanalysis because there was no deliberate attempt by the scribe to hide the meaning of the text. Hence, such archae-ological work is not directly part of the continual search for secret communication systems and the parallel struggle to break into them. Nonetheless, techniques used to piece together scripts such as cuneiform and Egyptian hieroglyphs are derived largely from conventional codebreaking. Indeed, many of the twentieth century's finest military cryptanalysts were drawn towards these purer intellectual challenges, where the motivation is curiosity rather than animosity.

All attempts at archaeological decipherment may be placed in one of three classes, depending on how much is known about the language and the script. Class 1 decipherments involve languages which are well understood, but scripts which remain a mystery. They present no great difficulty to the expert as they are little more than substitution ciphers. For example, imagine that you discovered a long-lost Shakespearean play, written in a previously unseen form of shorthand in which syllables have been replaced by mysterious symbols. Frequency analysis would soon show which symbols were most common, and presumably these would relate to the most commonly used syllables. A combination of statistics and guesswork would soon lead to a translation.

Class 2 decipherments are the other way round – the script is well understood, but the language is unknown. Such decipherments are much harder than those in Class 1, and are analogous to deciphering a French newspaper without knowledge of French. Because it is written in the same Roman alphabet as English it would be possible to read aloud the words on the page, but unravelling their meaning would be virtually impossible unless there were any extra clues that could be exploited. For example, the date on the newspaper might give a lead to the events reported in the articles, or there might be pictures and captions that give some hints. The fact that French is closely related to English would also be a great help, making it possible to identify the grammatical structure and spot words derived from a common Latin root. Frequency analysis is of little use in Class 2 decipherments, so experts tend to rely on a deep knowledge of linguistics and a large amount of guesswork.

The worst case is a Class 3 decipherment – the language and the script are both a complete mystery. In many ways Class 3 decipherments provide the ultimate challenge to any cryptanalyst. If the language can be deduced, and it turns out to be a known language, or at least related in some way to a known language, then the problem moves from Class 3 to Class 1. However, if the language cannot be identified and appears to be confined to an isolated branch of the linguistic tree, then any attempt at decipherment is almost certain to end in failure. An exceptional success in Class 3 decipherment was achieved with the most ancient form of cuneiform –

an unknown script communicating an unknown tongue. This decipherment was possible only because archaeologists tackled a simpler, related Class 1 problem, namely the decipherment of a more modern form of cuneiform.

Different forms of cuneiform were used to record various languages in the Near East from the fourth millennium BC. The first breakthrough in deciphering cuneiform was in connection with a relatively recent form of the script discovered in the ruins of Persepolis, the capital of the Persian Achaemenid Dynasty between the sixth and fourth centuries BC. At the start of the nineteenth century Georg Friedrich Grotefend, a twenty-seven-year-old German schoolteacher, made a brilliant intuitive leap when he spotted a pair of repeated phrases, which he guessed were equivalent to 'X, king of kings' and 'son of king Y', phrases which often appeared in Greek texts of the same era. Working on this assumption he examined the various X's and Y's, and compared them with the names of members of the royal family. Additional clues from the histories of Herodotus suggested that the kings in question were

WEDGE WRITING ON CLAY STATIONERY

The word 'cuneiform' describes a family of scripts which all have the common feature of wedge-shaped writing – the Latin word *cuneus* means 'wedge'. Indentations were usually made by pressing a wooden or reed stylus into a damp clay tablet, which was then allowed to harden in the heat of the sun. The tablets were deliberately not baked, which meant that they could be recycled just by wetting the surface. The downside of this environmentally friendly practice was that the tablets, which were most commonly used for keeping accounts,

could easily be tampered with by moistening a thumb, smearing the original figures and writing new quantities in their place. To discourage this malpractice, clay tablets were sometimes sealed within clay envelopes, as shown here, and a copy of the original document was inscribed on the outside. Accountants could then refer to the details on the envelope, but if any party suspected that the inscription had been corrupted, the envelope could be cracked open and the master tablet consulted to settle the dispute.

Darius and Xerxes. Grotefend's next step was to insert the ancient forms of Darius and Xerxes (**d-a-r-h-e-u-sh** and **kh-sh-h-e-r-sh-e**) alongside the candidate cuneiform signs:

d	a	r	h	e	u	sh		kh	sh	h	e	r	sh	e

There was an immediate indication that he was on the right track. Four of the letters that appear in the ancient form of Darius (**r**, **h**, **e**, **sh**) also appear in the ancient form of Xerxes, and in three cases (**r**, **h**, **sh**) the respective cuneiform signs match. Grotefend was prepared to ignore the one minor problem raised by the two separate cuneiform signs for **e** on the grounds that in modern English it is quite possible for the same sound to be written differently in two different words, for example 'blue' and 'blew'.

With the sound values now tentatively established for a few cuneiform signs, Grotefend's next step was to insert these sounds into the word that he believed represented 'king':

kh	sh	e	h	?	?	h

Even though there were gaps in the word, Grotefend could easily recognise it. He was already aware of the word *khscheio*, a royal title in the Persian language, so it was clear that he was reading an ancient dialect of Persian, written in a script two thousand years old. The decipherment was now a Class 1 problem – an unknown script, but a language that could at least be partly understood by studying its modern counterpart. Once Grotefend had found a way into the script, archaeologists from around the world began to build upon his breakthrough, and bit by bit the entire script was eventually deciphered.

The decipherment of this Persian form of cuneiform was to provide the vital stepping stone to solving the much harder Class 3 problem of ancient cuneiform. In 1835 Englishman Henry Rawlinson journeyed to western Iran to examine the cuneiform inscriptions carved on the vertical face of a mountain at Behistun.

Alongside the 414 lines of Persian cuneiform, which was by now understood, were two other scripts, one of which was Akkadian, the unknown language of Babylonia and Assyria written in a much more ancient and mysterious form of cuneiform from the third millennium BC.

In an attempt to crack Akkadian cuneiform, Rawlinson spent the next ten years clinging to the sheer rock face, meticulously copying down the cuneiform texts line by line. Using information from the known Persian cuneiform, he could guess some of the sound values for visually similar signs in Akkadian. Furthermore, the meaning of the Akkadian text could be derived by reading the corresponding Persian text. This was enough to indicate that Akkadian was a member of the Semitic family of languages, thus providing linguistic clues to the decipherment.

By 1872 scholars had such a command of Akkadian cuneiform that they had deciphered the Epic of Gilgamesh, the Babylonian account of the Great Flood, which seems to have provided the basis for the Biblical tale of Noah. Thirty years later they translated the 3,600 lines of cuneiform that make up the legal code of Hammurabi, a list of crimes and prescribed punishments which bear an uncanny resemblance to the Ten Commandments that God handed to Moses. For a second time it seemed that the word of God was nothing more than a second-hand version of a Babylonian text.

Although Gilgamesh and Hammurabi's laws have had a profound effect on our understanding of the origins of the Biblical scriptures, the pinnacle of cuneiform decipherment, for me, has to be the unravelling of a cuneiform cipher. A cuneiform tablet small enough to fit into the palm of your hand and dating from 1500 BC contains a recipe for pottery glaze. As a countermeasure against Mesopotamian industrial espionage, the scribe encrypted the secret ingredients. A particular cuneiform symbol can often be used to express more than one sound, a property known as polyvalence. In his cipher, the scribe used the signs to represent their least common sound values in order to confuse the unwitting reader. Polyvalence also occurs in English, which makes learning to read and write much more difficult than it needs to be. To help young children grapple with literacy George Bernard Shaw was keen to reform the English alphabet. He demonstrated the weakness of the established English alphabet by pointing out that 'ghoti' is a perfectly logical alternative spelling for the word 'fish' — he had used the 'f' sound in 'tough', the 'i' sound in 'women', and the 'sh' sound in 'nation'. The cuneiform cipher was using a similarly baffling ploy.

Deciphering Egyptian Hieroglyphs

The most famous, and arguably the most romantic, of all decipherments was the cracking of Egyptian hieroglyphs. For centuries, hieroglyphs remained a mystery, and archaeologists could do no more than speculate about their meaning. However, thanks to a classic piece of codebreaking the hieroglyphs were eventually deciphered, and ever since archaeologists have been able to read first-hand accounts of the history, culture and beliefs of the ancient Egyptians. The decipherment of hieroglyphs has bridged the millennia between ourselves and the civilisation of the pharaohs.

The earliest hieroglyphs date back to 3000 BC, and this form of ornate writing endured for the next three and a half thousand years. Although the elaborate nature of hieroglyphs was ideal for the walls of majestic temples (the Greek word *hieroglyphica* means 'sacred carvings'), it was overly complicated for keeping track of mundane transactions. Hence, evolving in parallel with hieroglyphs was *hieratic*, an everyday script in which each hieroglyphic symbol was replaced by a stylised representation which was quicker and easier to write. In about 400 BC hieratic was replaced by an even simpler script known as *demotic*, the name being derived from the Greek *demotika* meaning 'popular', which reflects its secular function. Hieroglyphic, hieratic and demotic writing are essentially forms of the same script – one could almost regard them merely as different fonts (see box).

All three forms of writing are phonetic, which is to say that the characters largely represent distinct sounds, just like the letters in the English alphabet. As you might expect, the ancient Egyptians used these three scripts in every aspect of their lives, just as we use writing today. Then, towards the end of the fourth century AD, in the space of a few decades, the Egyptian scripts vanished. The last datable examples of ancient Egyptian writing are to be found on the island of Philae. A hieroglyphic temple inscription was carved in AD 394, and a piece of demotic graffiti has been dated to AD 450. The spread of the Christian Church was responsible for the extinction of the Egyptian scripts, outlawing their use in order to eradicate any link with Egypt's pagan past. The ancient scripts were replaced with Coptic, a script consisting of 24 letters from the Greek alphabet supplemented by 6 demotic characters used for Egyptian sounds not expressed in Greek. Coptic became so dominant that the ability to read hieroglyphic, demotic and hieratic writing rapidly vanished. The ancient Egyptian language continued to be spoken, and evolved into what became known as the Coptic language, but in due course both the Coptic language and script were displaced by the spread of Arabic in the eleventh century. The final linguistic link with Egypt's ancient kingdoms had been broken. The knowledge needed to read the tales of the pharaohs was lost.

Interest in hieroglyphs was reawakened in the seventeenth century when Pope Sixtus V reorganised the city of Rome according to a new network of avenues, erecting obelisks brought from Egypt at each intersection. Scholars attempted to decipher the meanings of the hieroglyphs on the obelisks, but were hindered by a false assumption: nobody was prepared to accept that the hieroglyphs could possibly represent phonetic characters, or *phonograms*. The idea of phonetic spelling was thought to be too advanced for such an ancient civilisation. Instead, seventeenth-century scholars were convinced that the hieroglyphs were *semagrams* — that these

THE EVOLUTION OF EGYPTIAN WRITING

Ancient Egyptian priests developed the characteristic *hieroglyphs* some time after 3000 BC. From around 1500 BC the priests evolved a less pictorial, more cursive script known as *hieratic*, which was easier to write. The final stage was the appearance of *demotic*, the everyday script, around 400 BC. The examples illustrated here show the transition from hieroglyphs that originally represented a fox-fur cape and a water-jar, via hieratic characters which are still recognisably symbolic, to demotic characters that have the appearance of what we would now call 'writing'. Hieroglyphs ceased to be used around AD 400, and demotic script soon after; the Egyptian language itself gave way to Arabic in medieval times.

Hieroglyphic	Hieratic	Demotic

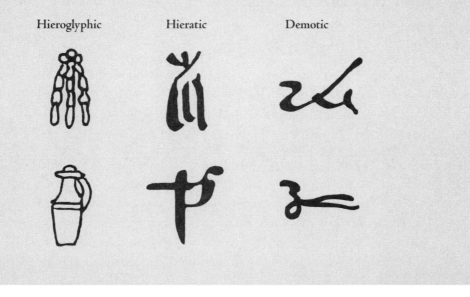

ATHANASIUS KIRCHER – 'UNIVERSAL MAN'

The extraordinary breadth of Athanasius Kircher's studies and his prolific output – over forty published books, one of them on cryptography – earned him the title of *homo universalis*. Born in Geisa, Germany, in 1601, he learned ancient languages at a Jesuit school and went on to study the sciences and humanities. In 1634, having fled the turmoil of the Thirty Years' War, he settled in Rome, where he lived until his death in 1680. Although responsible for few advances (he did not, as is often claimed, invent the magic lantern), Kircher pursued his investigations with a scientific rigour and, in an age when scholarship was equated with book-learning, he went so far as to lower himself into the crater of Vesuvius to examine it after a recent eruption. His lasting contribution lay in his hundreds of letters and reports in which he disseminated knowledge of discoveries and inventions in many different fields to other European scholars.

intricate characters represented whole ideas, and were nothing more than primitive picture-writing. The belief that hieroglyphs are merely picture-writing was even commonly held by foreigners who visited Egypt while hieroglyphic writing was still a living script. Diodorus Siculus, a Greek historian of the first century BC, wrote:

> Now it happens that the forms of the Egyptians' letters take the shape of all kinds of living creatures and of the extremities of the human body and of implements . . . For their writing does not express the intended idea by a combination of syllables, one with another, but by the outward appearance of what has been copied and by the metaphorical meaning impressed upon the memory by practice. . . . So the hawk symbolises for them everything which happens quickly because this creature is just about the fastest of winged animals. And the idea is transferred, through the appropriate metaphorical transfer, to all swift things and to those things to which speed is appropriate.

In the light of such definitive accounts, perhaps it is not so surprising that seventeenth-century scholars attempted to decipher the hieroglyphs by interpreting each one as a whole idea. For example, in 1652 the German Jesuit priest Athanasius Kircher published a dictionary of allegorical interpretations entitled *Œdipus ægyptiacus*, and used it to produce a series of weird and wonderful translations. A handful of hieroglyphs, which we now know merely represent the name of the pharaoh Apries, were translated by Kircher as 'the benefits of the divine Osiris are to be procured by means of sacred ceremonies and of the chain of the Genii, in order that the benefits of the Nile may be obtained'. Today Kircher's translations seem ludicrous, but their impact on other would-be decipherers was immense, because Kircher was widely acknowledged to be the most respected scholar of his age (see box). His ideas were to influence generations of future Egyptologists.

A century after Kircher's death, in the summer of 1798, the antiquities of ancient Egypt fell under renewed scrutiny when Napoléon Bonaparte despatched a team of historians, scientists and draftsmen to follow in the wake of his invading army (see box overleaf). These academics, or 'Pekinese dogs' as the soldiers called them, did a remarkable job of mapping, drawing, transcribing, measuring and recording everything they witnessed. In 1799 the French scholars encountered the single most famous slab of stone in the history of archaeology, found by a troop of French soldiers stationed at Fort Julien in Rosetta (the name the French gave to the town of Rashīd) in the Nile Delta. The soldiers had

The Rosetta Stone, inscribed in 196 BC and rediscovered in 1799, contains the same text written in three different scripts: hieroglyphs at the top, demotic in the middle and Greek at the bottom. This image shows the Rosetta Stone as it was before 1999. The Stone had been used as a printing block and coated in ink, but this does not explain its black appearance. The dark colour developed after its surface was coated with a wax preservative, which then absorbed dust and dirt over the decades. A major restoration returned the Stone to its original grey colour, with a pink vein running through part of it. Analysis showed that it was not made of basalt, as many had claimed, but that it was a fine- to medium-grained quartz-bearing rock.

been given the task of demolishing an ancient wall to clear the way for an extension to the fort. Built into the wall was a stone bearing a remarkable set of inscriptions: the same piece of text had been inscribed on the stone three times, in Greek, demotic and hieroglyphs. The Greek, which could easily be read, was in effect a piece of plaintext which could be compared with the demotic and hieroglyphic ciphertexts. The Rosetta Stone, as the slab became known, was potentially a means of unravelling the meaning of the ancient Egyptian symbols.

The scholars immediately recognised the stone's significance, and sent it to the National Institute in Cairo for detailed study. However, before the institute could embark on any serious research it became clear that the French army was on the verge of being defeated by advancing British forces. The French moved the Rosetta Stone from Cairo to the relative safety of Alexandria, but ironically, when the French finally surrendered, Article XVI of the Treaty of Capitulation handed all the antiquities in Alexandria to the British, whereas those in Cairo were allowed to be taken to France. In 1802 the priceless slab of rock (measuring 118 cm in height,

NAPOLÉON IN EGYPT

The France of 1798 was a land of disillusion and corruption. Within a decade the country had experienced political revolution, social upheaval, the execution of the king and queen as traitors, war with other European powers, and the reign of terror under Robespierre. Like many a failing regime, the ruling Directory had embarked upon foreign adventures to divert attention from its domestic misfortunes. In one such overseas diversion, General Napoléon Bonaparte had been dispatched on a military expedition to wrest Egypt from Turkish control. This, the Directory hoped, would frustrate British trade in the eastern Mediterranean. Napoléon, however, had his own grandiose vision of mounting a later attack on British India.

Accompanying the general's army of 25,000 men was a small army of scholars. After the defeat of the Turkish forces at the battle of the Pyramids in July 1798 – during which, it seems, one of the French cannons permanently disfigured the inscrutable gaze of the sphinx – Napoléon's academics examined the Great Pyramid with a view to unravelling its mysteries. The general himself had a guided tour. One of the leaders of the scientific expedition was the young Joseph Fourier, later to achieve fame as a physicist and mathematician. On his return to France, Fourier passed on his enthusiasm for the civilisation of ancient Egypt to a young boy in Grenoble. That boy, Jean-François Champollion, would later become known as the Father of Egyptology.

Napoléon's military ambitions were halted when his fleet was sunk by Nelson. Stranded in Africa, he resolved to march home through Syria, but was stalled there by Admiral Sir Sidney Smith. The admiral thoughtfully passed on to Napoléon news of Austria's planned attack on France. With a few companions, Napoléon eluded the British forces and escaped to the south of France. Soon after he toppled the Directory and seized power for himself.

77 cm in width and 30 cm in thickness, and weighing three-quarters of a tonne) was sent to Portsmouth on board HMS *L'Égyptienne*, and later that year it took up residence at the British Museum, where it has remained ever since.

The translation of the Greek soon revealed that the Rosetta Stone bore a decree issued in 196 BC by the general council of Egyptian priests. The text records the benefits the Pharaoh Ptolemy had bestowed upon the people of Egypt, and details the honours that the priests had, in return, piled upon the pharaoh. For example, they declared that 'a festival shall be kept for King Ptolemy, the ever-living, the beloved of Ptah, the god Epiphanes Eucharistos, yearly in the temples throughout the land from the 1st of Thoth for five days, in which they shall wear garlands and perform sacrifices and libations and the other usual honours'. The other two inscriptions contained the identical decree, so the decipherment of hieroglyphic and demotic writing would seem to be straightforward. However, three significant hurdles remained. First, the Rosetta Stone is seriously damaged, as can be seen from the photograph on page 85. The Greek text consists of 54 lines, of which the last 26 are damaged. The demotic

consists of 32 lines, of which the first 14 lines are damaged. The hieroglyphic text is in the worst condition, with half the lines missing completely and the remaining 14 lines (corresponding to the last 28 lines of the Greek text) partly missing. The second barrier to decipherment is that the two Egyptian scripts convey the ancient Egyptian language, which nobody had spoken for at least eight centuries. If it was possible to find a set of Egyptian symbols corresponding to a set of Greek words, then it would enable archaeologists to work out the meaning of the Egyptian symbols, but it would still be impossible to establish the sound of the Egyptian words. Unless archaeologists knew how the Egyptian words were spoken, they could not deduce the phonetics of the symbols. Finally, the intellectual legacy of Kircher still encouraged archaeologists to think of Egyptian writing in terms of semagrams, rather than phonograms, so few people even considered attempting a phonetic decipherment of hieroglyphs.

One of the first scholars to question the prejudice that hieroglyphs were picture-writing was the English prodigy and polymath Thomas Young. Born in 1773 in Milverton, Somerset, Young was able to read fluently at the age of two. By the age of fourteen he had studied Greek, Latin, French, Italian, Hebrew, Chaldean, Syriac,

PHENOMENON YOUNG

Thomas Young (1773–1829) performed an extraordinary series of medical experiments, many of them with the object of explaining how the human eye works. He established that colour perception is the result of three separate types of receptors, each one sensitive to one of the three primary colours. Then, by placing metal rings around a living eyeball, he showed that focusing did not require distortion of the whole eye, and postulated that the internal lens did all the work. His interest in optics led him towards physics, and another series of discoveries. He published 'The Undulatory Theory of Light' (1807), a classic paper on the nature of light; created a new and better explanation of tides; formally defined the concept of energy; and published groundbreaking papers on the subject of elasticity. He seemed to be able to tackle problems in almost any subject, but this was not entirely to his advantage. His mind was so easily fascinated that he would leap from subject to subject, embarking on a new problem before polishing off the last one.

Samaritan, Arabic, Persian, Turkish and Ethiopic, and when he became a student at Emmanuel College, Cambridge, his brilliance gained him the sobriquet 'Phenomenon Young'. At Cambridge he studied medicine, but it was said that he was interested only in the diseases, not the patients who had them. Gradually he began to concentrate less on caring for the sick and more on research, including linguistics.

When Young heard about the Rosetta Stone, it became an irresistible challenge. In the summer of 1814 he set off on his annual holiday to the south-coast resort of Worthing, taking with him a copy of the three inscriptions. Young's breakthrough came when he focused on a set of hieroglyphs surrounded by a loop, called a *cartouche*. His hunch was that these hieroglyphs were ringed because they represented something of great significance, possibly the name of the Pharaoh Ptolemy, because his Greek name, Ptolemaios, was mentioned in the Greek text. If this were the case, it would enable Young to discover the phonetics of the hieroglyphs in the cartouche, because a pharaoh's name would be pronounced roughly the same regardless of the language. The Ptolemy cartouche is repeated six times on the Rosetta Stone, sometimes in a so-called standard version, and sometimes in a longer, more elaborate version. Young assumed that the longer version was the name of Ptolemy with the addition of titles, so he concentrated on the symbols that appeared in the standard version, guessing sound values for each hieroglyph (Table 8).

Although he did not know it at the time, Young managed to correlate most of the hieroglyphs with their correct sound values. Fortunately he had placed the first two hieroglyphs (□, ◠), which appeared one above the other, in their correct phonetic order. The scribe has positioned the hieroglyphs in this way for aesthetic reasons, at

Table 8 *Young's decipherment of* (cartouche), *the cartouche of Ptolemaios (standard version) from the Rosetta Stone.*

Hieroglyph	Young's sound value	Actual sound value
□	p	p
◠	t	t
optional glyph	optional	o
lion glyph	lo or ole	l
◡	ma or m	m
double reed	i	i or y
bolt glyph	osh or os	s

the expense of phonetic clarity. Scribes tended to write in such a way as to avoid gaps and maintain visual harmony — sometimes they would even swap letters around in direct contradiction to any sensible phonetic spelling, merely to increase the beauty of an inscription. After this decipherment, Young discovered a cartouche in an inscription copied from the temple of Karnak at Thebes which he suspected was the name of a Ptolemaic queen, Berenika (or Berenice). He repeated his strategy; the results are shown in Table 9.

Of the thirteen hieroglyphs in the two cartouches, Young had identified half of them perfectly, and he got another quarter partly right. He had also correctly identified the feminine termination symbol, placed after the names of queens and goddesses. Although he could not have known the level of his success, the appearance of 𓇋𓇋 in both cartouches, representing **i** on both occasions, should have told Young that he was on the right track and given him the confidence he needed to press ahead with further decipherments. However, his work suddenly ground to a halt. It seems that he had too much reverence for Kircher's argument that hieroglyphs were semagrams, and he was not prepared to shatter that paradigm. He excused his own phonetic discoveries by noting that the Ptolemaic dynasty was descended from Lagus, a general of Alexander the Great. In other words, the Ptolemys were foreigners, and Young hypothesised that their names would have to be spelt out phonetically because there would not be a single natural semagram within the standard list of hieroglyphs. He summarised his thoughts by comparing hieroglyphs with Chinese characters, which Europeans were only just beginning to understand:

Table 9 Young's decipherment of ⟨cartouche⟩, *the cartouche of Berenika from the temple of Karnak.*

Hieroglyph	Young's sound value	Actual sound value
𓃀	bir	b
◯	e	r
〰〰	n	n
𓇋𓇋	i	i
▣	optional	k
𓄿	ke or ken	a
◯	feminine termination	feminine termination

> It is extremely interesting to trace some of the steps by which alphabetic writing seems
> to have arisen out of hieroglyphical; a process which may indeed be in some measure
> illustrated by the manner in which the modern Chinese express a foreign combination of
> sounds, the characters being rendered simply 'phonetic' by an appropriate mark, instead of
> retaining their natural signification; and this mark, in some modern printed books,
> approaching very near to the ring surrounding the hieroglyphic names.

Young called his achievements 'the amusement of a few leisure hours'. He lost
interest in hieroglyphs, and brought his work to a conclusion by summarising it in
an article for the 1819 *Supplement to the Encyclopaedia Britannica*.

The Father of Egyptology

In France, meanwhile, a promising young linguist, Jean-François Champollion,
was prepared to take Young's ideas to their natural conclusion. Although he was
still only in his late twenties, Champollion had been fascinated by hieroglyphs for
the best part of two decades. The obsession began in 1800, when the French
mathematician Joseph Fourier, who had been one of Napoléon's original
'Pekinese dogs', introduced the ten-year-old Champollion to his collection of
Egyptian antiquities, many of them decorated with bizarre inscriptions. When
Fourier explained that nobody could interpret this cryptic writing, the boy promised that one day he would solve the mystery. Just seven years later, at the age of
seventeen, he presented a paper entitled 'Egypt under the Pharaohs'. It was so innovative that he was immediately elected to the Academy in Grenoble. When he heard
that he had become a teenage professor, Champollion was so overwhelmed that he
immediately fainted.

Champollion continued to astonish his peers, mastering Latin, Greek, Hebrew,
Ethiopic, Sanskrit, Zend, Pahlevi, Arabic, Syrian, Chaldean, Persian and Chinese, all
to arm himself for an assault on hieroglyphs. His obsession is illustrated by an incident in 1808, when he bumped into an old friend in the street. The friend casually
mentioned that Alexandre Lenoir, a well-known Egyptologist, had published a
complete decipherment of hieroglyphs. Champollion was so devastated that he collapsed on the spot. (He appears to have had quite a talent for fainting.) His whole
reason for living seemed to depend on being the first to read the script of the
ancient Egyptians. Fortunately for Champollion, Lenoir's decipherments were as
fantastical as Kircher's seventeenth-century attempts, and the challenge remained.

In 1822 Champollion applied Young's approach to other cartouches. The British naturalist William Bankes had brought an obelisk with Greek and hieroglyphic inscriptions to his estate at Kingston Lacy in Dorset, and had recently published a lithograph of these bilingual texts which included cartouches of Ptolemy and Cleopatra. Champollion obtained a copy, and managed to assign sound values to individual hieroglyphs (Table 10). The letters **p**, **t**, **o**, **l** and **e** are common to both names; in four cases they are represented by the same hieroglyph in both Ptolemy and Cleopatra, and only in one case, **t**, is there a discrepancy. Champollion assumed that the **t** sound could be represented by two hieroglyphs, just as the hard **c** sound in English can be represented by **c** or **k**, as in 'cat' and 'kid'. Inspired by his success, Champollion began to address cartouches without a bilingual translation, substituting whenever possible the hieroglyph sound values that he had derived from the Ptolemy and Cleopatra cartouches. His first mystery cartouche (Table 11, opposite) contained one of the greatest names of ancient times. It was obvious to Champollion that the cartouche, which seemed to read **a-l-?-s-e-?-t-r-?**,

Jean-François Champollion

Table 10 Champollion's decipherment of ⬭ and ⬭, the cartouches of Ptolemaios and Cleopatra from the Bankes obelisk.

Hieroglyph	Sound Value	Hieroglyph	Sound Value
□	p	◿	c
◠	t	🐦	l
🦶	o	🚩	e
🐦	l	🦶	o
◡	m	🐦	p
𓏭	e	🦅	a
𓏏	s	◡	t
		◯	r
		🦅	a

represented the name **alksentrs** — Alexandros in Greek, or Alexander in English. It also became apparent to Champollion that the scribes were not fond of using vowels, and would often omit them; the scribes assumed that readers would have no problem filling in the missing vowels. With three new hieroglyphs under his belt, the young scholar studied other inscriptions and deciphered a series of cartouches. However, all this progress was merely extending Young's work. All these names, such as Alexander and Cleopatra, were still foreign, supporting the theory that phonetics was invoked only for words outside the traditional Egyptian lexicon.

The obelisk that William Bankes set up at his estate in Kingston Lacy, Dorset, as it appears today, somewhat weathered by the English climate. The obelisk stands on a foundation laid by the Duke of Wellington in 1827. Adjacent to the estate is the Iron Age hill fort of Badbury Rings, coincidentally of roughly the same antiquity.

Table 11 *Champollion's decipherment of* 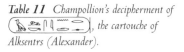 *, the cartouche of Alksentrs (Alexander).*

Hieroglyph	Sound Value
🦅	a
	l
	?
	s
	e
	?
	t
	r
	?

Then, on 14 September 1822, Champollion received reliefs from the temple of Abu Simbel, bearing cartouches that predated the period of Graeco-Roman domination. The significance of these cartouches was that they were old enough to contain traditional Egyptian names, yet they were still spelt out – evidence against the theory that spelling was used only for foreign names. Champollion concentrated on a cartouche containing four hieroglyphs: ⊙⋔⋔⋔. The first two symbols were unknown, but the repeated hieroglyphs at the end, ⋔⋔, were known from the cartouche of Alexander (**alksentrs**) to correspond to the letter **s**. This meant that the cartouche represented (?-?-**s-s**). At this point Champollion brought to bear his vast linguistic knowledge. Although Coptic, the direct descendant of the ancient Egyptian language, had ceased to be a living language in the eleventh century AD, it still existed in a fossilised form in the liturgy of the Christian Coptic Church. Champollion had learnt Coptic as a teenager, and was so fluent in it that he used it to record entries in his journal. However, until this moment he had never considered that Coptic might also be the language of the hieroglyphs.

Champollion wondered whether the first sign in the cartouche, ⊙ , might be a semagram representing the sun, i.e. a picture of the sun was the symbol for the word 'sun'. Then, in an act of intuitive genius, he assumed the sound value of the semagram to be that of the Coptic word for sun, **ra**. This gave him the sequence (**ra**-?-**s-s**). Only one pharaonic name seemed to fit. Allowing for the irritating omission of vowels, and assuming that the missing letter was **m**, then surely this had to be the name of Rameses, one of the greatest pharaohs, and one of the most ancient. The spell was broken. Even ancient traditional names were written phonetically. Champollion dashed into his brother's office and proclaimed, 'Je tiens l'affaire!' ('I've got it!'), but once again his intense passion for hieroglyphs got the better of him. He promptly collapsed and was bedridden for the next five days.

Champollion had demonstrated that the scribes sometimes used the rebus principle. In a rebus, still found in children's puzzles, long words are broken into their phonetic components which are then represented by semagrams. For example, the word 'belief' can be broken down into two syllables, *be-lief*, which can then be rewritten as *bee-leaf*. Instead of writing the word alphabetically, it can be represented by the image of a bee followed by the image of a leaf. In the example discovered by Champollion, only the first syllable (**ra**) is represented by a rebus image, a picture of the sun, while the remainder of the word is spelt more conventionally.

The significance of the sun semagram in the Rameses cartouche is enormous, because it clearly restricts the possibilities for the language spoken by the scribes.

For example, the scribes could not have spoken Greek, because this would have meant that the cartouche would be pronounced 'helios-meses'. The cartouche makes sense only if the scribes spoke a form of Coptic, because the cartouche would then be pronounced 'ra-meses'.

Although this was just one more cartouche, its decipherment clearly demonstrated the four fundamental principles of hieroglyphs. First, the language of the script is at least related to Coptic and, indeed, examination of other hieroglyphs showed that it was archaic Coptic. Second, semagrams are used to represent some words; for example, the word 'sun' is represented by a simple picture of the sun. Third, some long words are built wholly or partly according to the rebus principle. Finally, for most of their writing the ancient scribes relied on using a relatively conventional phonetic

DECIPHERING THE RAMESES CARTOUCHE

Champollion succeeded in identifying the name of Rameses. But our modern understanding of ancient Egyptian hieroglyphs reveals some subtleties that would not have been apparent to him.

The cartouche of Rameses illustrates several aspects of hieroglyphic writing. As Champollion correctly guessed, the first hieroglyph is a rebus, a picture of the sun representing the sound of the Coptic word for 'sun', **ra**. The second hieroglyph actually represents the combined letters **ms**, showing that some symbols represent double consonants. The two remaining hieroglyphs both represent the letter **s**, so the complete name could be read as **ramsss**. The first of the two **s** hieroglyphs is there merely to reinforce the final letter of the **ms** combination. Hence, we have just **ramss**. The only remaining problem is that some vowels appear to be missing. In fact, hieroglyphic writing (in common with Arabic) often omits vowels, because they can usually be inserted by the reader, who can guess them from the context of the word.

The Rameses in question was Rameses II (1304–1237 BC), known as Rameses the Great. He fought then made peace with the Hittites, and married a Hittite princess, after which the rest of his reign was a long period of stability and prosperity. He was responsible for many huge constructions, including the rock temple at Abu Simbel.

To the ancient Egyptians, personal names written in hieroglyphs embodied a person's identity. The line around the cartouche was there to give the name — and thus the person — protection.

EGYPTIAN HIEROGLYPHS

Dr Bill Manley, co-author of How to Read Egyptian Hieroglyphs, *explains how to make sense of a hieroglyphic inscription.*

The beautiful inscription shown here decorates a pillar in the White Chapel of King Senwosret I (c. 1917–1872 BC) in the temple of Karnak. On the left the king himself is shown making an offering to a god, who is identified by his crown of high plumes. In order to complement such scenes, the script was flexible enough to be written in columns (reading top to bottom) or in rows (reading either left to right, or right to left). There is a simple rule to tell which direction to read: any sign that has a face or a front will normally look towards the beginning of the text.

In this scene the texts provide captions explaining what is going on. The texts appear in three sections:

1. The top row labels the vulture as the goddess Nekhbet.
2. The four columns on the main part of the pillar form two texts. The two columns above the king face right, and so read from right to left. They identify the king, who faces in the same direction. The two columns above the god Amun-Re contain a speech by him. These hieroglyphs face left and so read left to right. Therefore, there is an elegant symmetry in the two texts, which begin on the central axis of the pillar and then read out towards the edges.
3. The hieroglyphs at the bottom between the two figures explain that the king is actually offering water.

Hieroglyphs do not usually 'picture' words, rather they spell out sounds in the Egyptian language, much as we do with our own alphabet. The main difference is that usually they are only used to spell out the consonants of a word, which seems odd bt y cn prbbly rd ths. To take an example, the name of the god Amun-Re is written in front of his plumes. In Egyptian this consisted of two words with the consonants *imn r*. The first word is spelled out as follows: ⟨ gives us the sound *i* (this is not 'i' but more like our 'y'). ⬛ spells out the sounds *m + n* together. 〰〰 reads *n* but here is only used to confirm the reading of ⬛, so ⬛ and 〰〰 together give us *mn* not *mnn*.

Copy of an inscription from P. Lacau & H Chevrier: Une chapelle se Sésostris I à Karnak *(IFAO, Cairo, 1956).*

Hence we read *i* + *mn* = *imn*. The ◎ hieroglyph is a semagram representing the Egyptian word for sun – *re* – but in this case it represents the sound of the second word in the name Amun-Re. The ⟦ below ◎ does not represent any sound. Instead it fills what would otherwise be an awkward gap. Notice that the signs are not written in a straight line but are organised into a neat group, emphasising that the appearance of hieroglyphs is every bit as important as legibility.

alphabet. This final point is the most important one. Champollion called phonetics the 'soul' of hieroglyphs.

Using his deep knowledge of Coptic, Champollion began an unhindered and prolific decipherment of hieroglyphs beyond the cartouches. Within two years he had identified phonetic values for the majority of hieroglyphs, and discovered that some of them represented combinations of two or even three consonants. This sometimes gave scribes the option of spelling a word using several simple hieroglyphs or with just a few multi-consonant hieroglyphs.

Champollion sent his initial results in a letter to Monsieur Dacier, the permanent secretary of the French Académie des Inscriptions. Then, in 1824, at the age of thirty-four, Champollion published all his achievements in a book entitled *Précis du système hiéroglyphique*. For the first time in fourteen centuries it was possible to read the history of the pharaohs, as written by their scribes. For linguists, here was an opportunity to study the evolution of a language and a script across a period of over three thousand years. Hieroglyphs could be understood and traced from the third millennium BC through to the fourth century AD. Furthermore, the evolution of hieroglyphs could be compared with the scripts of hieratic and demotic, which could now also be deciphered.

For several years, politics and envy prevented Champollion's magnificent achievement from being universally accepted. Thomas Young was a particularly bitter critic. On some occasions Young denied that hieroglyphs could be largely phonetic; at other times he accepted the argument but complained that he himself had reached this conclusion before Champollion, and that the Frenchman had merely filled in the gaps. Much of Young's hostility resulted from Champollion's failure to give him any credit, even though it is likely that Young's initial breakthrough provided the inspiration for the full decipherment.

In July 1828 Champollion set off on his first expedition to Egypt, which lasted eighteen months. It was a remarkable opportunity for him to examine at first hand the inscriptions he had previously seen only in drawings or lithographs. Thirty years earlier, Napoléon's scholars had guessed wildly at the meaning of the hieroglyphs which adorned the temples, but now Champollion could simply read them character by character and interpret them correctly. His visit came just in time. Three years later, having written up the notes, drawings and translations from his Egyptian expedition, he suffered a severe stroke. The fainting spells he had suffered throughout his life were perhaps symptomatic of a more serious illness, exacerbated by his obsessive and intense study. He died on 4 March 1832, aged forty-one.

Exercises for the Interested Reader

In the two centuries since Champollion's breakthrough, Egyptologists have continued to improve their understanding of the intricacies of hieroglyphs. Their level of comprehension is now so high that scholars are able to unravel encrypted hieroglyphs, which are among the world's most ancient ciphertexts. Some of the inscriptions to be found on the tombs of the pharaohs were encrypted using a variety of techniques, including the substitution cipher. Sometimes fabricated symbols would be used in place of the established hieroglyph, and on other occasions a phonetically different but visually similar hieroglyph would be used instead of the correct one. For example, the horned asp hieroglyph, which usually represents **f**, might be used in place of the serpent, which represents **z**. Usually these encrypted epitaphs were not intended to be unbreakable, rather they acted as cryptic puzzles to arouse the curiosity of passers-by, who would thus be tempted to linger at a tomb rather than move on.

Having conquered hieroglyphs, archaeologists went on to decipher many other ancient scripts, including the cuneiform texts of Babylon, the Kök-Turki runes of Turkey, the Brahmi alphabet of India, the Linear B script of Crete (see box), and the Mayan script of southern Mexico (see box overleaf). However, the good news for budding Champollions is that there are several outstanding scripts waiting to be solved, such as the Etruscan and Indus scripts.

Readers might be encouraged to learn that some of the greatest decipherments have been made by amateurs. For example, Georg Grotefend, who made the first breakthrough in interpreting cuneiform, was a schoolteacher and Michael Ventris, who made a key contribution towards deciphering Linear B, was an architect. Although it is almost half a century since the decipherment of Linear B, its ancestor, Linear A, has defied all attempts at decipherment, largely due to a lack of material. However, if archaeologists were to uncover a new hoard of tablets, this would shed valuable light on a so far intractable problem. With over ten thousand inscriptions there would seem to be more than enough material for an attack on the Etruscan script, but the subject matter is highly stereotypical, and this lack of variety means that progress has been inordinately painful. The signs seem to be related to the Greek alphabet, and by applying the appropriate sound values archaeologists believe that they can pronounce some Etruscan words. However, the few words that have been identified seem to bear no relation to any language on earth, past or present. Iberian, another pre-Roman script, is equally unfathomable.

THE CRACKING OF LINEAR B

On 31 March 1900 the eminent archaeologist Sir Arthur Evans began to unearth hundreds of clay tablets on the island of Crete. Some tablets, subsequently dated to 2000–1650 BC, consisted merely of drawings, while more recent tablets contained two forms of writing, apparently related to each other, but never previously seen. One script (1750–1450 BC) was dubbed Linear A, while the other one (1450–1375 BC) became known as Linear B. Attempts to decipher the scripts began immediately, most effort being directed at the more recent form of writing, Linear B. It would be fifty years before there was a breakthrough. Michael Ventris and John Chadwick, building on the work of Alice Kober, showed that Linear B represented an archaic form of Greek. Their discovery revolutionised our view of the period that preceded the Classical Greek age.

This drawing of a tablet (*c.* 1400 BC) shows the sort of characters used in Linear B. The script is phonetic, each symbol representing a syllable. On 24 June 1953 Michael Ventris gave a public lecture explaining the

Alice Kober

Michael Ventris   John Chadwick

rules of Linear B. The following day it was reported in *The Times*, next to a comment on the recent conquest of Mount Everest, which led to the achievement being known as the 'Everest of Greek Archaeology'. In 1954 Ventris and Chadwick decided to write an authoritative three-volume account of their work, to include a description of the decipherment, a detailed analysis of three hundred tablets, and a dictionary of 630 words. The account was completed in the summer of 1955 and was ready for publication in the autumn of 1956. However, a few weeks before printing, on 6 September 1956, Michael Ventris was killed while driving home late at night on the Great North Road near Hatfield, when his car collided with a lorry. John Chadwick paid tribute to his colleague, a man who matched the genius of Champollion, and who also died at a tragically young age: 'The work he did lives, and his name will be remembered so long as the ancient Greek language and civilisation are studied.'

MAYAN NUMBER GLYPHS

The Mayan civilisation of southern Mexico and northern Central America thrived between the third and ninth centuries AD. In common with the other great historical empires of the region, Mayan culture featured great cities with ziggurats, monumental carvings, pottery, agriculture and blood sacrifice. The civilisation had long been in decline when the conquistadors arrived in the fifteenth century and virtually obliterated what was left of it.

Later explorers who chanced upon the remains of Mayan cities early in the nineteenth century found written records in the form of carvings in stone that had survived destruction by the Spanish. These elaborate and stylised carvings, known as *glyphs* – often of human faces – were not recognised for what they were. It was assumed that the people who had carved them were too primitive to have developed a written language.

It was not until the late twentieth century that the glyphic writing became well understood. An extensive system of glyphs representing words and syllables were combined according to complex rules to represent the syntax, grammar and sounds of speech.

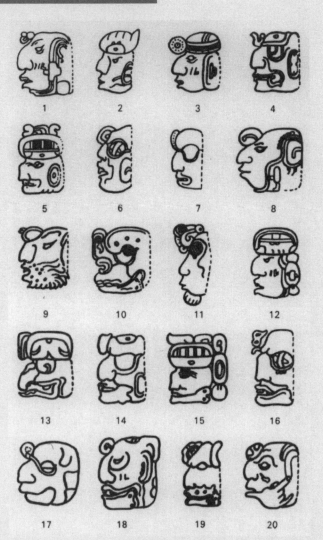

Other glyphs represent numbers, and in fact it was these that were the first to be deciphered. The Maya had several number systems and possessed sophisticated mathematics and astronomy which they used to construct a number of interlocking calendars. The simplest and commonest set of numerals consisted of bars representing 5 and dots representing 1. But there was also an elaborate 'head variant' system (shown here), based on the number 20, in which numerals were represented by portrait-like glyphs.

The most intriguing ancient European script appears on the unique Phaistos Disk, discovered in southern Crete in 1908. It is a circular tablet dating from 1700 BC bearing writing arranged in two spirals, one on each side. The signs are not handmade impressions; instead, they were made using a variety of stamps, making this the world's oldest example of type-writing. Remarkably, no other similar document has ever been found, so decipherment relies on very limited information – there are 242 characters divided by lines into 61 groups (possibly words), and the number of different characters is 45. It is probable that the total number of available characters in the script is between 50 and 60, suggesting that it is a syllabic form of writing, but beyond this there is little agreement. Solutions have been announced but have not been convincing, and with such a paucity of material there is no immediate expectation of decipherment. On the other hand, a type-written document implies mass production, so the hope is that eventually archaeologists will discover a hoard of disks.

In Asia the outstanding problem is the Bronze Age script of the Indus civilisation which can be found on thousands of seals dating from the third millennium BC. Each seal depicts an animal accompanied by a short inscription, but the meaning of these inscriptions has so far eluded all the experts. In one exceptional example, the script has been found on a large wooden board with giant letters 37 cm in height. This could be the world's oldest billboard. It implies that literacy was not restricted to the elite, and begs the question as to what was being advertised. The most likely answer is that it was part of a promotional campaign for the king, and if the identity of the king can be established then the billboard could provide a way into the rest of the script.

In conclusion, there are plenty of existing ancient scripts waiting for those who wish to follow in the footsteps of Champollion. However, the greatest challenge of all may be yet to come – a message from outer space. The attempt to communicate with extra-terrestrial life dates back to at least the nineteenth century when the German mathematician Carl Friedrich Gauss suggested planting avenues of trees in the barren plains of Siberia to form a giant right-angled triangle. He was attempting to signify to any watching Martians that there was life on Earth intelligent enough to appreciate the wonders of geometry. The Viennese astronomer Josef Johann von Littrow proposed a more brilliant version of the plan, to be implemented in the Sahara Desert. He suggested digging canals to form a geometrical shape 15 km in length, and at night he wanted to fill them with kerosene and set them alight.

Towards the end of the nineteenth century in Colorado the maverick physicist Nikola Tesla constructed a transmitter tower capped with a copper sphere, in which he generated intense electric surges. He intended to alter the Earth's magnetic field, which would act as a beacon to passing aliens, but he merely succeeded in illuminating light bulbs in towns up to 40 km away. In 1899 he picked up a mysterious signal which he could not explain, leading him to write, 'The feeling is constantly growing in me that I had been the first to hear the greeting of one planet to another.' In 1920 Guglielmo Marconi also reported tentative signals from outer space. It is now believed that these messages were nothing more than 'whistlers', electromagnetic radiation caused by lightning.

Serious research began in 1960 when the 30-metre radio telescope at Green Bank, Virginia, began a brief but concerted effort to scan the skies. Project Ozma (named after the Queen of Oz – 'a place very far away, difficult to reach, and populated by exotic beings') picked up one or two false alarms before it was brought to a halt in the summer when the telescope was needed for more conventional uses. The following year interest increased when the respected journal *Nature* published an article entitled 'Searching for Interstellar Communications' by Philip Morrison and Giuseppe Cocconi. They began by summarising the arguments in favour of extra-terrestrial civilisations, adding that:

> To the beings of such a society, our Sun must appear as a likely site for the evolution of a new society. We shall assume that long ago they established a channel of communication that would one day become known to us as ... What sort of channel would it be?

Morrison and Cocconi believed that any interstellar communication would have to be via radio waves, which can travel vast distances and are easy to transmit and receive. The radio waveband ranges from 1 to 10,000 Megahertz, which is an enormous region to scan, but the article pointed out some likely radio frequencies based on the radio waves emitted by hydrogen atoms, because this is the most abundant element in the Universe. When a hydrogen atom is heated, or excited in some other way, it emits radiation at a frequency of 1,420 Megahertz. This frequency would be known by all civilisations, and one which could be used as a standard for communication. However, the article did not recommend searching at this exact frequency, as any signal would be swamped by natural emissions from cosmic hydrogen. It recommended instead searching at frequencies either side of the hydrogen frequency, or at twice or half the value.

When Morrison and Cocconi published their article nobody was even aware if planets existed outside our solar system, but in 1995 scientists searching for intelligent life received a huge fillip when Michel Mayor and Didier Queloz discovered a planet orbiting the star 51 Pegasi. Since then several other so-called extrasolar planets have been discovered, but the majority of them are hostile and would not provide an environment conducive to life. Just like Goldilocks, astronomers would prefer to find planets with a sun-to-planet distance which results in a climate that is not too hot and not too cold, but just right. The SETI (Search for Extra-Terrestrial Intelligence) Project, the descendant of Project Ozma, would then have a clear clue as to where to aim its radio receivers and look for an alien signal.

An alien message might be relatively easy to decipher if it was written in the language of mathematics. To signify an intelligent presence, the sender might transmit a series of blips and bleeps to represent a pattern of numbers, such as prime numbers (2, 3, 5, 7, 11, …): 2 blips, bleep, 3 blips, bleep, 5 blips, …. Subsequently, images could be sent via a kind of faxing principle, a blip representing a black pixel, a bleep representing a white one.

However, what would happen if they started sending a form of natural alien language? And what if the signal we received was not a deliberate message to Earth, but merely a personal communication between two gossiping aliens or an alien television broadcast? It is worth bearing in mind that our own transmissions to the rest of the cosmos are dominated by television broadcasts. Soap operas are our emissaries to the universe.

The challenge of such a decipherment would be truly enormous, an extreme example of a Class 3 decipherment. Furthermore, deciphering an alien message, according to some academics, would be potentially dangerous. Once we had heard and understood a message from another life form, it would be tempting to reply and establish a dialogue. However, imagine that the alien civilisation had a habit of spraying messages throughout the universe, in order to destroy those civilisations that replied. This would allow them to find comfortable planets to colonise. When the physicist Chen Ning Yang was asked what we should do if we ever received a message from outer space, he categorically replied, 'Don't answer!'

CHAPTER FOUR

The Zimmermann Telegram

Codes versus ciphers, and how to break a code
without arousing the enemy's suspicion

A T THE END of the nineteenth century, cryptography was in disarray. Ever since Babbage and Kasiski had destroyed the security of the Vigenère cipher, cryptographers had been searching for a new cipher, something that would re-establish secret communication, thereby allowing business and the military to exploit the immediacy of the telegraph without fearing that their communications might be intercepted and deciphered. Furthermore, at the turn of the century the Italian physicist Guglielmo Marconi invented an even more powerful form of telecommunication, which made the need for secure encryption even more pressing.

In 1894 Marconi began to experiment with a curious property of electrical circuits. Under certain conditions, if one circuit was carrying an electric current, this could induce a current in another isolated circuit some distance away. By enhancing the design of the two circuits, increasing the power and adding aerials, Marconi soon found that he could transmit and receive pulses of information over distances of up to 2.5 km. He had invented radio. The telegraph had already been established for half a century, but it required a wire to transport a message between sender and receiver. Marconi's system had the great advantage of being wireless — the signal travelled, as if by magic, through the air.

In 1896, in search of financial backing for his idea, Marconi emigrated to Britain, where he filed his first patent. In just five years he succeeded in extending the range of his radio transmissions by enough to span the Atlantic (see box overleaf).

MARCONI AND WIRELESS TELEGRAPHY

Having moved to Britain in 1896, Marconi continued his experiments in wireless telegraphy. He gradually increased the range of his radio communications, first transmitting a message 15 km across the Bristol Channel, and then 53 km across the English Channel to France. At the same time he began to look for commercial applications for his invention, pointing out to potential backers the two main advantages of radio: it did not require the construction of expensive telegraph lines, and it had the potential to send messages between otherwise isolated locations. He pulled off a magnificent publicity stunt in 1899 when he equipped two ships with radios so that journalists covering the America's Cup, the world's most important yacht race, could send reports back to New York for the following day's newspapers.

Interest increased still further when Marconi shattered the myth that radio communication was limited by the horizon. Critics had argued that because radio waves could not bend and follow the curvature of the Earth, radio communication would be limited

Guglielmo Marconi

to a hundred kilometres or so. Marconi attempted to prove them wrong by sending a message from Poldhu in Cornwall to St John's in Newfoundland, a distance of 3,500 km. In December 1901, for three hours each day, the Poldhu transmitter sent the letter S (dot-dot-dot) over and over again while Marconi stood on the windy cliffs of Newfoundland trying to detect the radio waves. Day after day he wrestled to raise aloft a giant kite, which in turn hoisted his antenna high into the air. A little after midday on 12 December, Marconi detected three faint dots – the first transatlantic radio message. The explanation of Marconi's achievement remained a mystery until 1924, when physicists discovered the ionosphere, a layer of the atmosphere whose lower boundary is about 60 km above the Earth. The ionosphere acts as a mirror, allowing radio waves to bounce off it. Radio waves also bounce off the Earth's surface, so radio messages could effectively reach anywhere in the world after a series of reflections between the ionosphere and the Earth.

His invention tantalised the military, who viewed it with a mixture of desire and trepidation. The tactical advantages of radio are obvious: it allows direct communication between any two points without the need for a wire between the locations. Laying such a wire is often impractical, sometimes impossible. Previously, a naval commander based in port had no way of communicating with his ships, which might disappear for months on end, but radio would enable him to coordinate the manoeuvres of a fleet wherever the ships might be. Similarly, radio would allow generals to direct their campaigns, keeping them in continual contact with battalions, regardless of their movements. All this is made possible by the nature of radio waves, which emanate in all directions and reach receivers wherever they may be. However, this all-pervasive property of radio is also its greatest military weakness, because messages will inevitably reach the enemy as well as the intended recipient. Consequently, reliable encryption became a necessity. If the enemy were going to be able to intercept every radio message, then cryptographers had to find a way of preventing them from deciphering these messages.

The mixed blessings of radio – ease of communication and ease of interception – were brought into sharp focus at the outbreak of the First World War. All sides were keen to exploit the power of radio, but were also unsure of how to guarantee security. Together, the advent of radio and the Great War intensified the need for effective encryption. The hope was that there would be a breakthrough, some new cipher that would re-establish secrecy for military commanders. Indeed, several new ciphers were invented between 1914 and 1918, such as the German *ADFGVX cipher* (see box overleaf), but none of them provided the necessary security, and the cracking of them resulted in a catalogue of cryptographic failures.

In addition to ciphers there was a widespread use of codes, but these were also often inadequate. The weakness of codes is best illustrated by the decipherment of a German telegram that was intercepted by the British on 17 January 1917. The story of this decipherment shows how cryptanalysis can affect the course of war at the very highest level, and demonstrates the potentially devastating repercussions of employing inadequate encryption. Within a matter of weeks, the deciphered telegram would force America to rethink its policy of neutrality, thereby shifting the balance of the war.

Despite calls from politicians in Britain and America, President Woodrow Wilson had spent the first two years of the war steadfastly refusing to send American troops to support the Allies. Besides not wanting to sacrifice his nation's youth on the bloody battlefields of Europe, he was convinced that the war could be ended only by a negotiated settlement, and he believed that he could best serve the world if he

THE ADFGVX CIPHER

The ADFGVX cipher, used by Germany in the First World War, features both substitution and transposition. Encryption begins by drawing up a 6 by 6 grid, and filling the 36 squares with a random arrangement of the 26 letters and the 10 digits. Each row and column of the grid is identified by one of the six letters A, D, F, G, V or X. The arrangement of the elements in the grid acts as part of the key, so the receiver needs to know the details of the grid in order to decipher messages. The first stage of encryption is to take each letter of the message, locate its position in the grid, and substitute it with the letters that label its row and column. For example, 8 would be substituted by AA, and p would be replaced by AD.

	A	D	F	G	V	X
A	8	p	3	d	1	n
D	l	t	4	o	a	h
F	7	k	b	c	5	z
G	j	u	6	w	g	m
V	x	s	v	i	r	2
X	9	e	y	0	f	q

Here is a short message encrypted according to this system:

Message	attack at 10 pm
Plaintext	a t t a c k a t 1 0 p m
Stage 1 Ciphertext	DV DD DD DV FG FD DV DD AV XG AD GX

So far this is a simple monoalphabetic substitution cipher, and frequency analysis would be enough to crack it. However, the second stage of the ADFGVX is a transposition, which makes cryptanalysis much harder. The transposition depends on a keyword, which in this case happens to be the word MARK. Transposition is carried out according to the following recipe. First, the letters of the keyword are written in the top row of a fresh grid. Next, the stage 1 ciphertext is written underneath it in a series of rows, as shown opposite. The columns of the grid are then rearranged so that the letters of the keyword are in alphabetical order. The final ciphertext is achieved by going down each column and then writing out the letters in this new order.

M	A	R	K
D	V	D	D
D	D	D	V
F	G	F	D
D	V	D	D
A	V	X	G
A	D	G	X

Rearrange columns so that the letters of the keyword are in alphabetical order

→

A	K	M	R
V	D	D	D
D	V	D	D
G	D	F	F
V	D	D	D
V	G	A	X
D	X	A	G

Final Ciphertext **V D G V V D D V D D G X D D F D A A D D F D X G**

The final ciphertext would then be transmitted in Morse code, and the receiver would reverse the encryption process in order to retrieve the original text. The entire ciphertext is made up of just six letters (i.e. A, D, F, G, V, X), because these are the labels of the rows and columns of the initial 6 by 6 grid. People often wonder why these letters were chosen as labels, as opposed to, say, A, B, C, D, E and F. The answer is that A, D, F, G, V and X are highly dissimilar from one another when translated into Morse dots and dashes, so this choice of letters minimises the risk of errors during transmission. The cipher was eventually cracked in June 1918 by the great French codebreaker Georges Painvin. It required such enormous effort that he lost 15 kg in weight.

Georges Painvin

remained neutral and acted as a mediator. Indeed, on 7 November 1916 the president was re-elected by campaigning with the slogan 'He kept us out of the war'.

Wilson soon saw hope for a settlement when Germany appointed a new Foreign Minister, Arthur Zimmermann, a jovial giant of a man who appeared to herald a new era of enlightened German diplomacy. American newspapers ran headlines such as OUR FRIEND ZIMMERMANN and LIBERALIZATION OF GERMANY, and one article proclaimed him to be 'one of the most auspicious omens for the future of German–American relations'. However, unknown to the Americans, Zimmermann had no intention of pursuing peace. Instead, he was plotting to extend Germany's military aggression.

By the end of 1916, Germany and the Allies were in deadlock. During the five-month Battle of the Somme the two sides had between them suffered over a million casualties and made no progress. The Allies were drained and desperate, and in Germany the situation was no better. The Kaiser had resorted to conscripting fifteen-year-olds, while the civilian population survived on a diet of potatoes. It was now time, Zimmermann believed, for Germany to grab victory by unleashing all its naval power, reversing a policy of restraint that had been enforced by America.

Back in 1915, a submerged German U-boat had been responsible for sinking the ocean liner *Lusitania*, drowning 1,198 passengers, including 128 US civilians (see box overleaf). The loss of the *Lusitania* would have drawn America into the war were it not for Germany's reassurances that henceforth U-boats would surface before attacking, a restriction that was intended to avoid accidental attacks on civilian ships. However, on 9 January 1917, Zimmermann attended a momentous meeting at the German castle of Pless, where the Supreme High Command was trying to persuade the Kaiser that it was time to renege on the promise and embark on a course of unrestricted submarine warfare. The German U-boat commanders knew that they were almost invulnerable if they launched their torpedoes while remaining submerged, and they believed that this would prove to be the decisive factor in determining the outcome of the war. Germany had been constructing a fleet of two hundred U-boats, and the Supreme High Command argued that unrestricted U-boat aggression would cut off Britain's supply lines and starve it into submission within six months.

A swift victory was essential. Unrestricted submarine warfare and the inevitable sinking of US civilian ships would almost certainly provoke America into declaring war on Germany. Bearing this in mind, Germany needed to force an Allied surrender before America could mobilise its troops and make an impact in the European

WOODROW WILSON AND AMERICA'S NEUTRALITY

Germany's invasion of Belgium in 1914 came as a shock to the population of America, safe and sound in their booming land of plenty. They felt enormous sympathy for all those who became swept up in the tide of war – indeed, many had relatives on one or other side of the conflict – but they also felt relief that they were not involved themselves. As the war dragged on, American public opinion swung one way and the other. The sinking of the *Lusitania* in 1915 stirred anti-German feeling; British searches of US vessels and confiscation of goods, and the suppression of the Dublin Easter Rising of 1916, had the opposite effect.

President Woodrow Wilson was an Anglophile who modelled himself on Gladstone, but he was also an avowed pacifist, having witnessed as a boy the devastation of the American Civil War, and he urged neutrality. However, US manufacturers, denied a market in Germany by the British naval blockade, were only too pleased to supply Britain with essential war supplies, and the British sought to borrow money on Wall Street. Wilson acquiesced, but tried to retain the illusion of neutrality by pretending that Germany was free to trade with America if it could evade the blockade.

In 1916 Wilson was re-elected to the White House, and set about peacemaking. German diplomats were keen to respond to Wilson's overtures, but the generals had their way and announced the resumption of unrestricted submarine warfare. British politicians hoped that this would precipitate America's entry into the war, but Wilson continued to declare neutrality.

Woodrow Wilson

THE SINKING OF THE *LUSITANIA*

On 1 May 1915 the RMS *Lusitania*, under the command of Captain Turner, set out on her 202nd voyage across the Atlantic. She was carrying 1,257 passengers, a crew of 702, cargoes of meat, medical supplies, copper, cheese, oil and machinery, as well as a secret consignment of approximately 173 tonnes of weapons, including rifles and shells. By 5 May, the submarine U-20 commanded by Kapitänleutnant Walter Schwieger was lurking in the Irish Channel, already having torpedoed and destroyed three ships in the area. On 7 May, the *Lusitania* entered the fog-bound Irish Channel, slowing to a few knots in the appalling conditions. At 1.20 Schwieger wrote in his log, 'Starboard ahead, four funnels and two masts of a steamer.' By 1.40 the two ships were about 750 metres apart. Schwieger fired the first torpedo. As he noted in his war diary:

> An unusually heavy explosion takes place with a huge cloud of smoke. The explosion of the torpedo must have been followed by a second one. The superstructure right above the point of impact and the bridge are torn asunder, fire breaks out, and smoke envelops the high bridge. The ship stops immediately and keels over to starboard very quickly, the bow section sinking at the same time … great confusion ensues on board. On the bow the name *Lusitania* becomes visible in golden letters.

arena. By the end of the meeting at Pless, the Kaiser was convinced that a swift victory could be achieved, and he signed an order to proceed with unrestricted U-boat warfare, which would take effect on 1 February.

In the three weeks that remained, Zimmermann devised an insurance policy. If unrestricted U-boat warfare increased the likelihood of America entering the war, then Zimmermann had a plan that would delay and weaken American involvement in Europe, and which might even discourage it completely. Zimmermann's idea was to propose an alliance with Mexico, and persuade the President of Mexico to invade America and reclaim territories such as Texas, New Mexico and Arizona that had been lost to their neighbour in the nineteenth century. Germany would support Mexico in its battle with their common enemy, aiding it financially and militarily.

Mexico had long posed a threat to the United States, partly because of Mexico's own military ambitions and partly because it offered overseas powers a gateway into North and South America, a region in which the United States had so far been the sole dominant influence. America's relationship with Mexico had not been helped by a series of unstable and despotic leaders, who could potentially increase their popularity by regaining territory. At the beginning of 1918 the president was General Venustiano Carranza, a particularly weak leader, whose failures had created anarchy in Mexico, allowing local leaders to seize control of several provinces.

In addition to inciting Mexican aggression, Zimmermann wanted the Mexican president to act as a mediator and persuade Japan that it too should attack America. Japan was officially one of the Allied powers, but Zimmermann was optimistic that they would switch sides if there was an opportunity to steal a piece of America. This way, Germany would pose a threat to America's east coast, Japan would attack from the west, while Mexico invaded from the south. Zimmermann's main motive was to create such problems for America at home that it could not afford to send troops to Europe. Thus Germany could win the battle at sea, win the war in Europe and then withdraw from the American campaign. On 16 January, Zimmermann encapsulated his proposal in a telegram to the German ambassador in Washington, who would then retransmit it to the German ambassador in Mexico, who would finally deliver it to the Mexican president. The message was as follows:

> We intend to begin unrestricted submarine warfare on the first of February. We shall endeavour in spite of this to keep the United States neutral. In the event of this not succeeding, we make Mexico a proposal of alliance on the following basis: make war together, make peace together,

generous financial support, and an understanding on our part that Mexico is to reconquer the lost territory in Texas, New Mexico and Arizona. The settlement in detail is left to you.

You will inform the President [of Mexico] of the above most secretly, as soon as the outbreak of war with the United States is certain, and add the suggestion that he should, on his own initiative, invite Japan to immediate adherence and at the same time mediate between Japan and ourselves.

Please call the President's attention to the fact that the unrestricted employment of our submarines now offers the prospect of compelling England to make peace within a few months. Acknowledge receipt.

Zimmermann

Obviously, it was essential to protect such a vital telegram. Zimmermann's communication office protected the message with one of their many codes rather than a cipher. The Germans used several distinct codes, each one reserved for a particular circle of communication. For example, code 0086 was used by German missions in South America, while code 0064 was used between Berlin and Madrid. Each code would require a separate codebook, and each member of the communication circle would possess a copy. The codebook consisted of thousands of words and phrases, each one associated with a different random number. A message would be encoded by substituting each word with the corresponding number listed in the codebook.

The Zimmermann telegram, as it would eventually become known, was encoded according to code 0075, a two-part codebook used for diplomatic communications. 'Two-part' refers to the fact that there were, in fact, two codebooks: one for encoding and one for decoding. The encoding book lists all the words alphabetically, along with the corresponding number. Encoding is quick because finding words alphabetically is easy. However, decoding with such a codebook is painfully slow, because if the numbers are random the receiver looks at a number in the encoded message and then has to search through every number in the codebook. The encoding book is like a telephone book — if given a name, it is easy to find a number, but if given a number it

Arthur Zimmermann

WESTERN UNION TELEGRAM									

via Galveston

JAN 19 1917

GERMAN LEGATION

MEXICO CITY

130	13042	13401	8501	115	3528	416	17214	6491	11310
18147	18222	21560	10247	11518	23677	13605	3494	14936	
98092	5905	11311	10392	10371	0302	21290	5161	39695	
23571	17504	11269	18276	18101	0317	0228	17694	4473	
22284	22200	19452	21589	67893	5569	13918	8958	12137	
1333	4725	4458	5905	17166	13851	4458	17149	14471	6706
13850	12224	6929	14991	7382	15857	67893	14218	36477	
5870	17553	67893	5870	5454	16102	15217	22801	17138	
21001	17388	7446	23638	18222	6719	14331	15021	23845	
3156	23552	22096	21604	4797	9497	22464	20855	4377	
23610	18140	22260	5905	13347	20420	39689	13732	20667	
6929	5275	18507	52262	1340	22049	13339	11265	22295	
10439	14814	4178	6992	8784	7632	7357	6926	52262	11267
21100	21272	9346	9559	22464	15874	18502	18500	15857	
2188	5376	7381	98092	16127	13486	9350	9220	76036	14219
5144	2831	17920	11347	17142	11264	7667	7762	15099	9110
10482	97556	3569	3670						

BERNSTORFF.

The Zimmermann telegram, as forwarded by von Bernstorff, the German ambassador in Washington, to von Eckhardt, the German ambassador in Mexico City. Numbers in lines 7 and 8 of the message correspond to the territories that Germany was expecting Mexico to recover from America: 36477 is Texas (part of Mexico until 1836), 17553 67893 is New Mexico and 5454 16102 15217 22801 is Arizona (states ceded to America in 1848 after the Mexican War). The word 'Arizona' was not in the codebook and so had to be spelt out syllable by syllable, with the four number groups representing 'ar', 'iz', 'on' and 'a'.

is difficult to find the name. To make decoding easier, it is necessary to have a decoding book which lists the numbers in ascending order, along with the associated word. Code 0075 consisted of 10,000 words and phrases.

Encryption was essential because Germany was aware that the Allies were intercepting all its transatlantic communications, a consequence of Britain's first offensive action of the war. Before dawn on the first day of the First World War, the British ship *Telconia* approached the German coast under cover of darkness, dropped anchor, and hauled up a clutch of undersea cables. These were Germany's transatlantic cables — its communication links to the rest of the world. By the time the sun had risen, they had been severed. This act of sabotage was aimed at destroying Germany's most secure means of communication, thereby forcing German messages to be sent via insecure radio links or via cables owned by other countries. The exact details are unclear, but it is likely that Zimmermann sent his encrypted telegram via Sweden and, as a back-up, via the more direct American-owned cable. Both routes touched England, which meant that the text of the telegram soon fell into British hands.

The intercepted telegram was immediately sent to Room 40, the Admiralty's decoding office, named after the room in which it was initially housed. Room 40 was a strange mixture of linguists, classical scholars and puzzle addicts, capable of the most ingenious feats of cryptanalysis. For example, the Reverend Montgomery, a tall grey-haired figure, was a gifted translator of German theological works. He had demonstrated his talents by deciphering a secret message hidden in a postcard addressed to Sir Henry Jones, 184 King's Road, Tighnabruaich, Scotland. The postcard had been sent from Turkey, so Sir Henry had assumed that it was from his son, a prisoner of the Turks. However, he was puzzled because the postcard was blank, and the address was peculiar — the village of Tighnabruaich was so tiny that none of the houses had numbers and there was no King's Road. Eventually, the Reverend Montgomery spotted the postcard's cryptic message. The address alluded to the Bible, First Book of Kings, Chapter 18, Verse 4: 'Obadiah took a hundred prophets, and hid them fifty in a cave, and fed them with bread and water.' Sir Henry's son was simply reassuring his family that he was being well looked after by his captors.

When the Zimmermann telegram arrived in Room 40, Montgomery was one of the people responsible for deciphering it, along with Nigel de Grey, a thirty-year-old Eton graduate with movie-star good looks and an incisive mind. De Grey was a publisher by profession, seconded from the firm of William Heinemann, but in Room 40 he had found his true calling. Together, de Grey and Montgomery recognised immediately that they were dealing with a form of encryption used only for high-level diplomatic communications, and tackled the telegram with a sense of urgency.

To a limited extent, an encoded message can be cracked by frequency analysis, but applied to words and phrases rather than letters. The analysis is much harder than with a cipher because the codebreaker has to identify thousands of words, not just twenty-six letters. On the other hand, the task is made much easier by the large amount of material that is available for analysis. A code relies on a codebook, a vast tome that may take weeks to compile and then more weeks to distribute. Therefore, a codebook is generally used for several years before being discarded, which in turn means that the codebreaker may have access to several years' worth of correspondence encoded in the same manner.

Given enough material, it is possible to establish several of the most common words. Furthermore, the most frequently occurring number probably represents a full stop, which then allows the codebreaker to split the message into sentences for closer analysis. At this point, a cryptanalyst would use syntax to identify the type of words that numbers represent. For example, in German the verb is usually the second element in a sentence, unless the past tense is being used, in which case the verb moves to the end of the sentence.

Unfortunately, even after applying frequency analysis and syntax analysis to lots of material, a codebreaker can probably identify only a few words with confidence. To really crack the code, something else is needed – military intelligence. Imagine that a coded message has just been intercepted. At first the codebreaker may have little or no idea of the contents of the encoded message. A few hours later, there may arrive an intelligence report of the sinking of some enemy ships. If the sinkings occurred just before the message was transmitted, then perhaps the message is about the sinkings, in which case the codebreaker may be able to deduce some of the words of the message. Over the course of several months, by extensive cross-checking between intelligence reports and encoded messages, the codebreaker can begin to identify the meanings of certain number groups.

Sometimes there will be a chance to mount a less analytic but still very effective form of attack. If a codebreaker can somehow steal a decoded message and compare it with a coded version, he can immediately identify with certainty the meanings of dozens of numbers. He might even get his hands on a complete codebook, perhaps confiscated from an enemy soldier. Remember, because of the immense effort required to make and distribute a new codebook, the same book might be in use for many years, so there will inevitably be lapses in security. In comparison, a cipher is much less vulnerable because a key is generally simple and short so it can be changed much more frequently, perhaps daily. The capture of a cipher key jeopardises security for only a day.

By using a combination of frequency analysis, military intelligence and captured plaintext messages, de Grey and Montgomery had over the course of several months compiled a partially complete copy of the 0075 codebook. With this resource it was only a matter of hours before they were able to decipher a few chunks of text from the Zimmermann telegram, enough to see that they were uncovering a message of the utmost importance. Montgomery and de Grey persevered with their task, and by the end of the day they could discern the outline of Zimmermann's terrible plans. They realised the dreadful implications of unrestricted U-boat warfare, but at the same time they could see that the German Foreign Minister was discussing the possibility of an attack on America – if this information were to be passed to the Americans then it was likely to provoke President Wilson into abandoning his policy of American neutrality. The telegram contained the deadliest of threats, but carried with it the possibility of America joining the Allies.

Eventually de Grey took the partially deciphered telegram to Admiral Sir William Hall, Director of Naval Intelligence, expecting him to pass the information to the Americans, thereby drawing them into the war. However, Admiral Hall merely placed the partial decipherment in his safe, encouraging de Grey to continue filling in the gaps. He was reluctant to hand the Americans an incomplete decipherment, in case there was a vital caveat that had not yet been deciphered. He also had another concern at the back of his mind. If the British gave the Americans the deciphered Zimmermann telegram, and the Americans reacted by publicly condemning Germany's proposed aggression, then the Germans would conclude that their method of encryption had been broken. This would goad them into developing a new and stronger encryption system, thus cutting off a vital channel of intelligence. In any case, Hall was aware that the all-out U-boat onslaught would begin in just two weeks, which in itself might be enough to incite President Wilson to declare war on Germany. There was no point in jeopardising a valuable source of intelligence when the desired outcome might happen anyway.

On 1 February, as ordered by the Kaiser, Germany re-instigated unrestricted naval warfare. On 2 February President Wilson held a cabinet meeting to decide the

American response. On 3 February he addressed Congress and announced that America would continue to remain neutral, acting as a peacemaker, not a combatant. This was contrary to Allied and German expectations. American reluctance to join the Allies left Admiral Hall with no choice but to exploit the Zimmermann telegram.

Fortunately, in the fortnight since de Grey had first dashed into Hall's office, Room 40's clandestine skills had removed the two obstacles that had prevented Hall from handing the telegram to the Americans: namely, incomplete decipherment, and betraying to the Germans the fact that their code had been breached. Hall had realised that von Bernstorff, the German ambassador in Washington, would have decoded the telegram from Berlin, read the contents, and then encoded it once again before forwarding the message to von Eckhardt, the German ambassador in Mexico.

Crucially, the German ambassador in Mexico did not have a copy of code 0075, only the 13040 codebook, so that was what the ambassador in Washington would have used to protect the telegram during its onward journey. This code, however, had been in use since 1907, and Room 40 had had almost a decade in which to build up a virtually complete copy of the 13040 codebook.

Cracking 13040 had been helped by the fact that it was, to some extent, a one-part code, which means that the same codebook is used to encode and decode messages. This is only possible because the words are ordered alphabetically and then numbered more or less in ascending order. It contained, for example, the following encodings (taken from the Zimmermann telegram):

Februar	**13605**
Fest	**13732**
Finalzielle	**13850**
Folgender	**13918**

Hence if we know these four words and numbers, and we encounter a new number, say **13621**, we know that it represents a word beginning with 'fe'. This makes code-breaking much quicker.

If Hall could somehow obtain this Mexican version of the Zimmermann telegram, then completing the decipherment would be straightforward. But this was not the only benefit. Before re-encoding and resending the telegram, von Eckhardt would have removed the instructions aimed at himself and would have changed the address. If a decipherment of this version of the telegram were to be published in the newspapers, then the Germans would assume that it had been stolen from the Mexicans after they had decoded it, not intercepted and cracked by the British on its way to America. Room 40 would be able to continue with its activities.

Fortunately for Hall, there was a British secret agent in Mexico City who was ideally placed to obtain a copy of the Mexican telegram. The agent, known only as Mr H, had a friend in the Mexico City telegraph office who was deeply indebted to him because of a previous incident. The friend had sought help for an old chum, an English printer who had been falsely accused of forging Mexican currency. Forgery was so rife that it was undermining the whole economy and punishable by death. Mr H intervened and asked the British ambassador to request a stay of execution, during which time the real forger was apprehended and the honest printer was released. Later, when Mr H requested a copy of the 13040 encoded Zimmermann telegram, the mutual friend was only too happy to help.

It was the decipherment of this version of the telegram that Hall handed to Arthur Balfour, the British Secretary of State for Foreign Affairs. On 23 February, Balfour summoned the American ambassador, Walter Page, and presented him with the Zimmermann telegram, later calling this 'the most dramatic moment in all my life'. Four days later, President Wilson saw for himself the 'eloquent evidence', as he called it, proof that Germany was encouraging direct aggression against America.

It is difficult to underestimate the scale of Zimmermann's threat. Although Germany was already fighting a war, its massive U-boat fleet could still inflict terrible losses against the U.S. Navy. Furthermore, Mexico's troops could have stormed north, capturing American territory and endangering American lives. And on top of all this, Japan would attack America's west coast. For many years there had been scare stories about the 'Yellow Peril' invading America, and now Germany was attempting to precipitate just such an invasion.

The telegram was released to the press and, at last, on 1 March 1917 the American nation was confronted with the reality of Germany's intentions. Although the initial reaction was that America should retaliate, there was some concern within the administration that the telegram might be a hoax by the British to engineer American involvement in the war. However, doubts over the telegram's authenticity soon vanished when Zimmermann publicly admitted his authorship. At a press conference in Berlin, without being pressured, he simply stated, 'I cannot deny it. It is true.'

'Exploding in his Hands', a cartoon by Rollin Kirby published on 3 March 1917 in The World.

The press began to speculate about how the telegram had been intercepted. One story claimed that four American soldiers had discovered it while arresting a German agent crossing the border into Mexico. Another theory claimed that it had been found while examining the belongings of Ambassador von Bernstorff, who was expelled from Washington when Germany began its unrestricted naval aggression.

In Germany, the Foreign Office began an investigation into how the Americans had obtained the Zimmermann telegram. They fell for Admiral Hall's ploy, and came to the conclusion that 'various indications suggest that the treachery was committed in Mexico'. Meanwhile, Hall continued to distract attention from the work of British cryptanalysts. He planted a story in the British press criticising his own organisation for not intercepting the Zimmermann telegram, which in turn led to a spate of articles attacking the British secret service and praising the Americans.

At the beginning of the year, Wilson had said that it would be a 'crime against civilisation' to lead his nation to war, but by 2 April 1917 he had changed his mind: 'I advise that the Congress declare the recent course of the Imperial Government to be in fact nothing less than war against the government and people of the United States, and that it formally accept the status of belligerent which has thus been thrust upon it.' A single breakthrough by Room 40 cryptanalysts had succeeded where three years of intensive diplomacy had failed. Barbara Tuchman, American historian and author of *The Zimmermann Telegram*, offered the following analysis:

> Had the telegram never been intercepted or never been published, inevitably the Germans would have done something else that would have brought us in eventually. But the time was already late and, had we delayed much longer, the Allies might have been forced to negotiate. To that extent the Zimmermann telegram altered the course of history . . . In itself the Zimmermann telegram was only a pebble on the long road of history. But a pebble can kill a Goliath, and this one killed the American illusion that we could go about our business happily separate from other nations. In world affairs it was a German Minister's minor plot. In the lives of the American people it was the end of innocence.

Lessons for the Second World War

The First World War saw a series of victories for cryptanalysts, culminating in the decipherment of the Zimmermann telegram. Room 40's codebreakers had demonstrated the fundamental weakness of all codes. Once a sender has compiled a codebook and agreed it with the receiver, the first message to be encoded and sent between them is highly secure. But a message encoded several years later is much less secure because the codebreaker will have had time to build up a duplicate codebook. Another lesson that emerged from Room 40 was that information gained via cryptanalysis had to be exploited cautiously, otherwise the enemy would suspect that its code had been broken and upgrade its encryption to re-establish security. At the outbreak of the Second World War, the issues of better encryption and how to exploit information gained from cracking codes were still of paramount importance, as illustrated by the story of Enigma.

In 1918 the German inventor Arthur Scherbius and his close friend Richard Ritter founded the company of Scherbius & Ritter, an innovative engineering firm that dabbled in everything from turbines to heated pillows. One of Scherbius's pet projects was to replace the inadequate systems of cryptography used in the First World War by swapping pencil-and-paper ciphers with a form of encryption that exploited twentieth-century technology. Having studied electrical engineering in Hanover and Munich, he developed a piece of cryptographic machinery that he called the Enigma cipher (see box overleaf). Scherbius's invention would become the most notorious system of encryption in history.

Scherbius's Enigma consisted of a number of ingenious components, which he combined into a formidable and intricate cipher machine. The basic form of Scherbius's invention consists of three elements connected by wires: a keyboard for inputting each plaintext letter, a scrambling unit that encrypts each plaintext letter into a corresponding ciphertext letter, and a display board consisting of various lamps for indicating the ciphertext letter. To encrypt a plaintext letter, the operator presses the appropriate letter on the keyboard, which sends an electric pulse via the central scrambling unit through to a lampboard, where it illuminates and indicates the corresponding ciphertext letter.

The scrambling unit is what makes the Enigma machine so powerful. The scrambler changes after each letter is typed, which means that it is regularly altering its overall mode of encryption. Initially typing **a** might illuminate **J** (i.e. **a** is encrypted as **J**), but then the internal structure of the scrambler changes, so that typing **a** again might illuminate **T** (i.e. **a** is encrypted as **T**). The constantly changing encryption mode and its apparent randomness are what make the Enigma cipher extraordinarily difficult to crack.

The initial encryption mode of the scrambler and all subsequent modes are dictated by how the machine is set up before encryption. The number of possible settings depends on the type of Enigma machine, but typically there are 159,000,000,000,000,000,000.

If we think of the Enigma machine in terms of a general cipher system, then the initial setting is what determines the exact details of the encryption. In other words, the initial setting provides the key. The initial setting is usually dictated by a book of keys which lists the key for each day and which is available to everybody within the communications network. Distributing the book of keys requires time and effort, but because only one key per day is needed it could be arranged for a book containing twenty-eight keys to be sent out just once every four weeks.

Once the scrambler has been set according to the key agreed for that day, the sender can begin encrypting. After a brief protocol, he types in the first letter of

ARTHUR SCHERBIUS AND THE ENIGMA CIPHER MACHINE

The Enigma cipher machine was housed in a compact box measuring only 34 × 28 × 15 cm, but it weighed a hefty 12 kg. The particular machine shown here has its cover removed to reveal more of its features, in particular the scrambler unit, which consists of three so-called rotors. Each letter of the message is typed into the keyboard which sets off an electrical signal. Encryption is implemented by altering the pathway of the electrical signal. First, the signal is turned into another letter by the plugboard, which consists of a series of cables designed to swap pairs of letters. Next, the signal enters the scrambler unit via the entry wheel. The scrambler unit consists of three rotors. Each rotor contains a series of wires that take the incoming signal and change its path. The change in the path depends on the orientation of the rotor. (Crucially, the orientation of at least one rotor changes after each letter is typed in.) The signal then reaches the reflector, which sends the signal back through the scrambler and plugboard to light up a lamp, signalling how the original letter has been encrypted.

Arthur Scherbius took out his first patent in 1918, but at roughly the same time inventors in other parts of the world were developing a very similar concept. In the Netherlands in 1919, Alexander Koch took out Dutch Patent No. 10,700, but he failed to turn his encryption

Arthur Scherbius

machine into a commercial success and eventually sold the patent rights in 1927. In Sweden, Arvid Damm also took out a patent, but by the time he died in 1927 he also had failed to find a market. In America, the inventor Edward Hebern had complete faith in his invention, the so-called 'Sphinx of the wireless', but his failure was the greatest of all. Hebern built a $380,000 factory but sold only twelve machines at a total price of roughly $1,200, and in 1926 he was brought to trial by dissatisfied shareholders and found guilty under California's Corporate Securities Act.

Fortunately for Scherbius, security failures in the First World War made the German military sympathetic to his invention. Part of the reason for Germany's awareness of its own security weaknesses in the First World War was a report published in 1923 by the British Royal Navy, which stated that cryptanalysis of German communications had provided the Allies with a clear advantage. The Germans acknowledged in their own report that, 'the German fleet command, whose radio messages were intercepted and deciphered by the English, played, so to speak, with open cards against the British command.' By 1925 Scherbius was mass-producing Enigma machines, which went into military service the following year. Over the next two decades over 30,000 Enigma machines were manufactured.

Scrambler unit
containing three
scramblers

Reflector

Entry wheel

Lamps (visible
after removal of
lampboard)

Keyboard

Plugboard

the message, sees which letter is illuminated on the lampboard, and notes it down as the first letter of the ciphertext. Then, the first scrambler having automatically stepped on by one place, the sender inputs the second letter of the message, and so on. Once he has generated the complete ciphertext, he hands it to a radio operator who transmits it to the intended receiver. In order to decipher the message, the receiver needs to have another Enigma machine and a copy of the book of keys that contains the initial scrambler settings for that day. He sets up his machine according to the book, types in the ciphertext letter by letter, and the lampboard indicates the plaintext. In other words, the sender types in the plaintext to generate the ciphertext, and then the receiver types in the ciphertext to generate the plaintext – as long as sender and receiver have the same initial set-up for their respective Enigma scramblers, then everything runs smoothly.

At the outbreak of the Second World War, the Enigma machine seemed to give Germany an enormous advantage in terms of secure communication. To crack the Enigma cipher a codebreaker would have to identify which of the vast number of possible keys had been used to encrypt a particular message. It is impossible to accomplish this by checking every single key because there are simply too many possibilities. One way to find the key is to somehow steal the information. However, even if a key is found, the consequences would not be catastrophic for Germany because a single key jeopardises security for only one day. Even if a codebreaker captures a book of keys, then the security breach lasts for, at most, twenty-eight days. In comparison, a codebook falling into the wrong hands would have led to a long-term security failure, perhaps lasting for years. Germany had clearly learnt a lesson from the First World War.

Unfortunately for the German military, the Enigma machine was not all it was cracked up to be. In theory Scherbius had developed a highly secure cipher system, but in practice the Enigma machine contained subtle flaws that would eventually undermine its apparent invulnerability. Like many pioneers, Scherbius was the first to make a brilliant invention and the first to make serious mistakes. Similarly, the German army was the first to use such a cipher machine and the first to use it improperly, thereby helping potential cryptanalysts. Allied cipher machines, which were developed and employed later, did not suffer the problems encountered by the pioneering Germans.

The British cryptanalysts responsible for cracking Enigma worked at Bletchley Park, Britain's codebreaking centre during the Second World War. They used a variety of techniques to crack the Enigma cipher and exploited all of its subtle flaws.

For example, one design flaw meant that it was impossible for Enigma to encrypt a letter as itself. For example, **a** could never be encrypted as **A**, nor **b** as **B**, and so on.

A flaw in the way the machine was used stemmed from the formulaic composition of many German messages. This allowed British codebreakers to guess the first few words of a message, which gave them an enormous advantage in deciphering the rest of it (see box overleaf).

The military intelligence derived from cracking the German Enigma was part of an intelligence-gathering operation codenamed Ultra. The Ultra files, which also contained decipherment of Italian and Japanese messages, gave the Allies a clear advantage in all the major arenas of the war. In North Africa, Ultra helped to destroy German supply lines and informed the Allies of the status of General Rommel's forces, enabling the Eighth Army to fight back against the German advances. Ultra also warned of the German invasion of Greece, allowing British troops to retreat without suffering heavy losses. In fact, Ultra provided accurate reports on the enemy's situation

In 1938 the Government Code and Cypher School, Britain's primary codebreaking organisation, decided that it required larger premises outside London. The Buckinghamshire estate of Bletchley Park, which included a large Victorian Tudor-Gothic mansion built by the nineteenth-century financier Sir Herbert Leon, was bought for the purpose, and the first codebreakers moved into the building in August 1939. This photograph shows a preliminary visit made by senior cryptanalysts in order to assess the suitability of the site. To avoid arousing the suspicion of local people, they claimed to be part of 'Captain Ridley's shooting party'.

ALAN TURING AND THE BOMBES

Among the many great codebreakers at Bletchley Park, one mathematician in particular is often singled out as the greatest cryptanalyst of all. Alan Turing arrived at Bletchley from his post at Cambridge University and set to work to expose the flaws of the Enigma cipher and search for weaknesses in the way that it was used.

He eventually realised that *cribs* offered a way of cracking the German code. A crib is a piece of encrypted text whose true meaning is known or can be guessed. For example, Bletchley might intercept some encrypted material from a German weather ship and would be able to guess that the first line of encrypted text was about weather conditions or might contain a time of transmission. By knowing a few of the original words and the corresponding letters after encryption, the codebreakers could place severe

Alan Turing

constraints on the set-up of the Enigma machine – in other words, it was possible to home in on the key. It was still necessary to check thousands of Enigma scrambler settings in order to see which one satisfied the constraints. Turing designed a codebreaking machine known as a *bombe* (shown opposite) to check all these settings within a few hours. The name was taken from a Polish term used to describe a codebreaking machine that they had built before the outbreak of war (named, perhaps, after its persistent ticking, or because the inventors got the idea while eating an ice cream known as a bombe). The Polish cryptanalysts had passed their work on to the British just a few days before the invasion of Poland, providing Bletchley Park with a vital head start in its battle against the Enigma cipher.

throughout the entire Mediterranean region. This information was particularly valuable when the Allies landed in Italy and Sicily in 1943.

In 1944 Ultra played a major role in the Allied invasion of Europe. For example, in the months before D-Day the Bletchley decipherments provided a detailed picture of German troop concentrations along the French coast. Sir Harry Hinsley, official historian of British Intelligence during the war, wrote:

> As Ultra accumulated, it administered some unpleasant shocks. In particular, it revealed in the second half of May – following earlier disturbing indications that the Germans were concluding that the area between Le Havre and Cherbourg was a likely, and perhaps even the main, invasion area – that they were sending reinforcements to Normandy and the Cherbourg peninsula. But this evidence arrived in time to enable the Allies to modify the

BOMBE

plans for the landings on and behind the Utah beach; and it is a singular fact that before the expedition sailed the Allied estimate of the number, identification, and location of the enemy's divisions in the west, fifty-eight in all, was accurate in all but two items that were to be of operational importance.

Throughout the war the Bletchley codebreakers knew that their decipherments were vital, but they were rarely given any operational details or told how their decipherments were being used. For example, the codebreakers were given no information about the date for D-Day, and they arranged a dance for the evening before the landings. This worried Commander Travis, the Director of Bletchley and one of the few people on site who was privy to the plans for D-Day. He could not inform the Hut 6 dance committee that they should cancel the event because this would have been a clear hint that a major offensive was in the offing, and as such a breach of security. The dance was allowed to go ahead. As it happened, bad weather postponed the landings for twenty-four hours, so the codebreakers had time to recover from the frivolities.

At the other end of the information chain, commanders in the battlefield or at sea had no idea that they were benefiting from intelligence gained by cracking Enigma. Only a few of Churchill's most trusted colleagues were given Ultra intelligence, and it was they who decided how it would be used without making it obvious to Germany that Enigma was no longer secure.

As with the Zimmermann telegram, the information had to be used in such a way as not to arouse the suspicion of the German military. In order to maintain the Ultra secret, Churchill's commanders took a variety of precautions. For example, the Enigma decipherments gave the locations of numerous U-boats, but it would have been unwise to have attacked every single one of them because a sudden unexplained increase in successful British attacks would suggest to Germany that its communications were being deciphered. Consequently, some U-boat coordinates were not passed on to the commanders at sea, allowing some U-boats to escape. Other U-boats were attacked only after a spotter plane had been sent out first, thus justifying the approach of a destroyer some hours later. Alternatively, the Allies might send fake messages describing sightings of U-boats which likewise provided sufficient explanation for the ensuing attack.

Despite this policy of minimising telltale signs that Enigma had been broken, British actions did sometimes raise concerns among Germany's security experts. On one occasion Bletchley deciphered an Enigma message giving the exact location of a group of German tankers and supply ships, nine in total. Those responsible for exploiting the Ultra intelligence decided not to sink all the ships in case this aroused German suspicions. Instead, they informed destroyers of the exact location of just seven of the ships, which should have allowed the *Gedania* and the *Gonzenheim* to escape unharmed. The seven targeted ships were indeed sunk, but Royal Navy destroyers accidentally encountered the two ships that were supposed to be spared, and sank them too. The destroyers did not know about Enigma or the policy of not arousing suspicion — they merely believed they were doing their duty. Back in Berlin, Admiral Kurt Fricke instigated an investigation into this and other similar attacks, exploring the possibility that the British had broken the Enigma cipher. The report concluded that the numerous losses were either the result of natural misfortune, or caused by a British spy who had infiltrated the Kriegsmarine. The breaking of Enigma was considered impossible and inconceivable.

Stuart Milner-Barry, one of the Hut 6 cryptanalysts, wrote: 'I do not imagine that any war since classical times, if ever, has been fought in which one side read consistently the main military and naval intelligence of the other.' An American report came to a similar conclusion:

Ultra created in senior staffs and at the political summit a state of mind which transformed the taking of decisions. To feel that you know your enemy is a vastly comforting feeling. It grows imperceptibly over time if you regularly and intimately observe his thoughts and ways and habits and actions. Knowledge of this kind makes your own planning less tentative and more assured, less harrowing and more buoyant.

It has been argued, albeit controversially, that Bletchley Park's achievements were the decisive factor in the Allied victory. What is certain is that the Bletchley codebreakers significantly shortened the war. This becomes evident by re-running the Battle of the Atlantic and speculating what might have happened without the benefit of Ultra intelligence. To begin with, more ships and supplies would certainly have been lost to the dominant U-boat fleet, and that would have compromised the vital link to America and forced the Allies to divert manpower and resources into the building of new ships. Historians have estimated that this would have delayed Allied plans by several months, which would have meant postponing the D-Day invasion until at least the following year. According to Sir Harry Hinsley, 'the war, instead of finishing in 1945, would have ended in 1948 had the Government Code and Cypher School [at Bletchley Park] not been able to read the Enigma cyphers and produce the Ultra intelligence'. During this period of delay, additional lives would have been lost in Europe, and Hitler would have been able to make greater use of his V-weapons, inflicting damage throughout southern England. The historian David Kahn summarises the impact of breaking Enigma:

It saved lives. Not only Allied and Russian lives but, by shortening the war, German, Italian, and Japanese lives as well. Some people alive after World War II might not have been but for these solutions. That is the debt that the world owes to the codebreakers; that is the crowning human value of their triumphs.

However, cryptanalysis is a clandestine activity, so Bletchley's accomplishments remained a closely guarded secret even after 1945. Having successfully deciphered messages during the war, Britain wanted to continue its intelligence operations and was reluctant to divulge its capabilities. In fact, Britain had captured thousands of

Enigma machines and distributed them among its former colonies, who believed that the cipher was as secure as it had seemed to the Germans. The British did nothing to disabuse them of this belief, and routinely deciphered their secret communications in the years that followed.

Consequently, the thousands of men and women who had contributed to the creation of Ultra received no recognition for their achievements. Most of the code-breakers returned to their civilian lives, sworn to secrecy, unable to reveal their pivotal role in the Allied war effort. While those who had fought conventional battles could talk of their heroic achievements, those who had fought intellectual battles of no less significance had to endure the embarrassment of having to evade questions about their wartime activities. According to Gordon Welchman, one of the young cryptanalysts working with him in Hut 6 received a scathing letter from his old headmaster, accusing him of being a disgrace to his school for not being at the front. Derek Taunt, who also worked in Hut 6, summed up the true contribution of his colleagues: 'Our happy band may not have been with King Harry on St Crispin's Day, but we had certainly not been abed and have no reason to think ourselves accurs't for having been where we were.'

After three decades of silence, the cloud of secrecy over Bletchley Park was dispersed in the early 1970s. Captain F.W. Winterbotham, who had been responsible for distributing the Ultra intelligence, badgered the British Government, arguing that the Commonwealth countries had stopped using the Enigma cipher and that there was now nothing to be gained by concealing the fact that Britain had broken it. The intelligence services reluctantly agreed, and permitted him to write a book about Bletchley Park. Published in the summer of 1974, Winterbotham's book *The Ultra Secret* was the signal that Bletchley personnel were at last free to discuss their wartime activities. Gordon Welchman felt enormous relief: 'After the war I still avoided discussions of wartime events for fear that I might reveal information obtained from Ultra rather than from some published account . . . I felt that this turn of events released me from my wartime pledge of secrecy.' At last, those who had contributed so much to the war effort would receive the recognition they deserved.

For some, the publication of Winterbotham's book came too late. Many years after the death of Alastair Denniston, Bletchley's first director, his daughter received a letter from one of his colleagues: 'Your father was a great man in whose debt all English-speaking people will remain for a very long time, if not for ever. That so few should know exactly what he did is the sad part.'

Alan Turing was another cryptanalyst who did not live long enough to receive any public recognition. Before the war Turing had shown himself to be a mathematical genius, publishing work that laid down the ground rules for computers and computing. At Bletchley Park he turned his mind to cracking Enigma, arguably making the single most important contribution to finding the flaws in the German cipher machine. After the war, instead of being acclaimed a hero, he was persecuted for his homosexuality. In 1952, while reporting a burglary to the police, he naively revealed that he was having a homosexual relationship. The police felt they had no option but to arrest and charge him with 'Gross Indecency contrary to Section 11 of the Criminal Law Amendment Act 1885'. The newspapers reported the subsequent trial and conviction, and Turing was publicly humiliated.

Turing's secret had been exposed, and his sexuality was now public knowledge. The British Government withdrew his security clearance. He was forbidden to work on research projects relating to the development of the computer. He was forced to consult a psychiatrist and to undergo hormone treatment, which made him impotent and obese. Over the next two years he became severely depressed, and on 7 June 1954 he went to his bedroom, carrying with him a jar of cyanide solution and an apple. He dipped the apple in the cyanide and took several bites. At the age of just forty-two, one of the true geniuses of cryptanalysis committed suicide.

CHAPTER FIVE

Alice and Bob Go Public

The solution to the so-called key-distribution problem, and the secret history of non-secret encryption

THE STORY OF cryptography since the First and Second World Wars has been dominated by a single technology — the computer. This seems only appropriate, as it was cryptography that spurred the development of computing. During the course of the Second World War, the Germans began to use the Lorenz cipher to encrypt communications between Hitler and his generals. The encryption was performed by the Lorenz SZ40 machine, which operated in a similar way to the Enigma machine, but the Lorenz was far more complicated, and it provided the Bletchley codebreakers with an even greater challenge. However, two of Bletchley's codebreakers, John Tiltman and Bill Tutte, discovered a weakness in the way that the Lorenz cipher was used, a flaw that Bletchley could potentially exploit and thereby read Hitler's messages.

Breaking the Lorenz cipher required a mixture of searching, matching, statistical analysis and careful judgement, all of which was beyond the capability of any available technology. Therefore Lorenz-encrypted messages had to be broken by hand, which took weeks of painstaking effort, by which time the messages were largely out of date. Eventually, Max Newman, a Bletchley mathematician, came up with a way to mechanise the cryptanalysis of the Lorenz cipher. Drawing heavily on some theoretical work about the nature of computing, Newman designed a machine that was capable of adapting itself to different problems, what we today would call a computer.

COLOSSUS AND THE BIRTH OF THE MODERN COMPUTER

Where does the Colossus machine fit into the early history of modern electronic computing? There is no doubt that it deserves the name 'computer'. Its specific purpose was to decrypt messages encrypted by the German Lorenz SZ40 machine, so it was not designed as a general-purpose computer. Nevertheless, it was programmable, some programs being implemented through permanent wiring, and others via a plugboard. And it had the ability to jump between programs, which would be triggered if its internal counters reached certain values. Colossus can certainly claim to be the world's first large programmable electronic computer (and it was large – the size of a room and a tonne in weight). Tommy Flowers, who built Colossus, had made the crucial realisation that the pattern of the encrypted message could be replicated as electronic signals in valves – 2,400 of them in the Colossus Mk II – as opposed to the motions of rotors in the bombes used to crack the Enigma ciphers. In America, John V. Atansoff and Clifford Berry had constructed a prototype computer with valves in 1942, but the Colossus was a much more impressive machine.

The Colossus machines and their blueprints were destroyed at the end of the war, except for one. It is now known that a Colossus survived, at least until 1958, within the walls of GCHQ in Cheltenham, where it was kept a closely guarded secret. So, although Colossus embodied many of the principles of the modern computer, it had no direct influence on the subsequent evolution of computers.

Implementing Newman's design was deemed technically impossible, so Bletchley's senior officials shelved the project. Fortunately, Tommy Flowers, an engineer who had taken part in discussions about Newman's design, decided to ignore Bletchley's scepticism and went ahead with building the machine. At the Post Office's research centre at Dollis Hill, North London, Flowers took Newman's blueprint and spent ten months turning it into the Colossus machine, which he delivered to Bletchley Park on 8 December 1943. It contained 1,500 electronic valves, which made it considerably faster than the bombes, with their sluggish electromechanical relay switches. But more important than Colossus's speed was the fact that it was programmable. It was this that made Colossus a precursor of the modern digital computer (see box).

Colossus, as with everything else at Bletchley Park, remained a secret after the war, and those who worked on it were forbidden to talk about it. When Tommy Flowers was ordered to dispose of the Colossus blueprints, he obediently took them down to the boiler room and burnt them. The plans for the world's first computer were lost for ever. This secrecy meant that other scientists gained the credit for the invention of the computer. In 1945 J. Presper Eckert and John W. Mauchly of the University of Pennsylvania completed ENIAC (Electronic Numerical Integrator And Calculator), consisting of 18,000 electronic valves and capable of performing 5,000 calculations per second. For decades, ENIAC, not Colossus, was considered to be the world's first computer.

Having contributed to the birth of the modern computer, cryptanalysts continued after the war to develop and employ computer technology in order to break all sorts of ciphers. They could now exploit the speed and flexibility of programmable computers to search through all possible keys until the correct one was found. In due course the cryptographers began to fight back, exploiting the power of computers to create increasingly complex ciphers. In short, the computer played a crucial role on both sides in the post-war battle between codemakers and codebreakers.

Using a computer to encipher a message is, to a large extent, very similar to traditional forms of encryption. Indeed, there are only two significant differences between computer encryption and the sort of mechanical encryption that was the basis for ciphers like Enigma.

The first difference is simply a matter of speed. Electronics can operate far more quickly than mechanical scramblers: a computer programmed to mimic the Enigma cipher could encipher a lengthy message in an instant. Alternatively, a computer programmed to perform a vastly more complex form of encryption could still accomplish the task within a reasonable time.

The second and perhaps more significant difference is that a computer scrambles numbers rather than letters. Computers deal only in binary numbers — sequences of ones and zeros known as *binary digits*, or *bits* for short. Before encryption, any message must therefore be converted into binary digits. This conversion can be performed according to various protocols, such as the American Standard Code for Information Interchange, known familiarly by the acronym ASCII, pronounced 'ass-key'. ASCII assigns a 7-digit binary number to each letter of the alphabet. For the time being it is sufficient to think of a binary number as merely a pattern of ones and zeros that uniquely identifies each letter (Table 12), just as Morse code identifies each letter with a unique series of dots and dashes. There are 128 (2^7) ways of arranging a combination of 7 binary digits, so ASCII can identify up to 128 distinct characters. This allows plenty of room to define all the lower-case letters (e.g. **a = 1100001**) and all necessary punctuation (e.g. **! = 0100001**), as well as other symbols (e.g. **& = 0100110**). Once the message has been converted into binary, encryption can begin.

Even though we are dealing with computers and numbers, and not machines and letters, the encryption still proceeds by the age-old principles of substitution and transposition, in which elements of the message are substituted for other elements, or their positions are switched, or both. Every encipherment, no matter how complex, can be broken down into combinations of these simple operations. The following two examples demonstrate the essential simplicity of computer encipherment by showing how a computer might perform an elementary substitution cipher and an elementary transposition cipher.

First, imagine that we wish to encrypt the message **HELLO**, employing a simple computer version of a transposition cipher. Before encryption can begin, we must translate the message into ASCII according to Table 12:

Plaintext = **HELLO** = **1001000 1000101 1001100 1001100 1001111**

One of the simplest forms of transposition cipher would be to swap the first and second digits, the third and fourth digits, and so on. In this case the final digit would remain unchanged because there are an odd number of digits. In order to see the operation more clearly, I have removed the spaces between the ASCII blocks in the original plaintext to generate a single string, and then lined it up against the resulting ciphertext for comparison:

Plaintext   = **10010001000101100110010011001001111**
Ciphertext = **01100010001010011001100011000110111**

An interesting aspect of transposition at the level of binary digits is that it can happen within a single letter. Furthermore, bits of one letter can swap places with bits of the neighbouring letter. For example, by swapping the seventh and eighth numbers, the final 0 of H is swapped with the initial 1 of E. The encrypted message is a single string of 35 binary digits, which can be transmitted to the receiver, who then reverses the transposition to recreate the original string of binary digits. Finally, the receiver reinterprets the binary digits via ASCII to regenerate the message **HELLO**.

Next, imagine that we wish to encrypt the same message, **HELLO**, this time employing a simple computer version of a substitution cipher. Once again we begin by converting the message into ASCII before encryption. As usual, substitution relies on a key that has been agreed between sender and receiver. In this case the key is the word **DAVID** translated into ASCII, and it is used in the following way. Each element of the plaintext is 'added' to the corresponding element of the key. Adding binary digits can be thought of in terms of two simple rules. If the elements in the plaintext and the key are the same, the element in the plaintext is substituted for **0** in the ciphertext. But if the elements in the message and key are different, the element in the plaintext is substituted for **1** in the ciphertext:

Message	**HELLO**
Message in ASCII	1001000100010110011001001 1001001111
Key = DAVID	1000100100000110101101001 0011000100
Ciphertext	0001100000010000110100000 1010001011

Table 12 *ASCII binary numbers for the capital letters.*

A	1 0 0 0 0 0 1		N	1 0 0 1 1 1 0
B	1 0 0 0 0 1 0		O	1 0 0 1 1 1 1
C	1 0 0 0 0 1 1		P	1 0 1 0 0 0 0
D	1 0 0 0 1 0 0		Q	1 0 1 0 0 0 1
E	1 0 0 0 1 0 1		R	1 0 1 0 0 1 0
F	1 0 0 0 1 1 0		S	1 0 1 0 0 1 1
G	1 0 0 0 1 1 1		T	1 0 1 0 1 0 0
H	1 0 0 1 0 0 0		U	1 0 1 0 1 0 1
I	1 0 0 1 0 0 1		V	1 0 1 0 1 1 0
J	1 0 0 1 0 1 0		W	1 0 1 0 1 1 1
K	1 0 0 1 0 1 1		X	1 0 1 1 0 0 0
L	1 0 0 1 1 0 0		Y	1 0 1 1 0 0 1
M	1 0 0 1 1 0 1		Z	1 0 1 1 0 1 0

The resulting encrypted message is a single string of 35 binary digits which can be transmitted to the receiver, who uses the same key to reverse the substitution, thus recreating the original string of binary digits. Finally, the receiver reinterprets the binary digits via ASCII to regenerate the message **HELLO**.

Computer encryption was restricted to those who had computers, which in the early days meant governments and the military. However, a series of scientific, technological and engineering breakthroughs made computers, and computer encryption, far more widely available. In 1947 AT&T Bell Laboratories invented the transistor, a cheap alternative to the electronic valve. Commercial computing became a reality in 1951 when companies such as Ferranti began to make computers to order. In 1953 IBM launched its first computer, and four years later it introduced Fortran, a programming language that allowed 'ordinary' people to write computer programs. Then, in 1959, the invention of the integrated circuit heralded a new era of computing.

During the 1960s computers became increasingly powerful, and at the same time they became cheaper. Businesses were more easily able to afford computers, and could use them to encrypt important communications such as money transfers or delicate trade negotiations. However, as more and more businesses bought computers, and as encryption between businesses spread, cryptographers were confronted with a major problem known as *key distribution*.

Imagine that a bank wants to send some confidential data to a client over a telephone line, but is worried that there might be somebody tapping the wire. The bank picks a key (remember, the key defines the exact recipe for scrambling the message) and uses some encryption software to scramble the data message. In order to decrypt the message the client needs not only to have a copy of the encryption software on his computer, but also to know which key was used to encrypt the message. How does the bank inform the client of the key? It cannot send the key via the telephone line, because it suspects that there is an eavesdropper on the line. The only truly secure way to send the key is to hand it over in person, which is clearly a time-consuming task. A less secure but more practical solution is to send the key via a courier. In the 1970s, banks attempted to distribute keys by employing special dispatch riders who had been vetted and who were among the company's most trusted employees. These dispatch riders would race across the world with padlocked briefcases, personally distributing keys to everyone who would receive messages from the bank over the next week. As business networks grew in size, as more messages were sent, and as more keys had to be delivered, the banks found that this distribution process became a horrendous logistical nightmare, and the overhead costs became prohibitive.

The problem of key distribution has plagued cryptographers throughout history. For example, during the Second World War the German High Command had to distribute the monthly book of keys to all its Enigma operators, which was a major burden. Also, U-boats, which tended to spend extended periods away from base, had somehow to obtain a regular supply of keys. In earlier times, users of the Vigenère cipher had to find a way of getting the keyword from the sender to the receiver. No matter how secure a cipher is in theory, in practice it can be undermined by the problem of key distribution.

To some extent, governments and the military have been able to deal with the problem of key distribution by throwing money and resources at it. Their messages are so important that they will go to any lengths to ensure secure key distribution. The U.S. Government keys are managed and distributed by COMSEC, short for Communications Security. In the 1970s COMSEC was responsible for transporting tonnes of keys every day. When ships carrying COMSEC material came into dock, cryptocustodians would march on board, collect stacks of cards, paper tapes, floppy disks, or whatever other medium the keys might be stored on, and deliver them to the intended recipients.

Key distribution might seem a mundane issue, but it became the overriding problem for post-war cryptographers. If two parties wanted to communicate securely, they had to rely on a third party to deliver the key, and this became the weakest link in the chain of security. The problem for businesses was straightforward: if governments with all their money were struggling to guarantee the secure distribution of keys, then how could civilian companies ever hope to achieve reliable key distribution without bankrupting themselves?

Despite claims that the problem of key distribution was unsolvable, in the mid-1970s a team of mavericks triumphed against the odds and came up with a brilliant solution. They devised an encryption system that appeared to defy all logic. Although computers transformed the implementation of ciphers, the greatest revolution in twentieth-century cryptography was the development of techniques to overcome the problem of key distribution. Indeed, this breakthrough is generally considered to be the greatest cryptographic achievement since the invention of the monoalphabetic cipher over two thousand years ago.

The Californian Mavericks

Whitfield Diffie is one of the most ebullient cryptographers of his generation. The mere sight of him is a striking and somewhat contradictory image. His impeccable suit reflects the fact that for most of the 1990s he has been employed by one of America's giant computer companies — currently his official job title is Distinguished Engineer at Sun Microsystems. However, his shoulder-length hair and long white beard betray the fact that his heart is still in the 1960s. He spends much of his time in front of a computer workstation, but he looks as if he would be equally comfortable in a Bombay ashram. Diffie is aware that his dress and personality can have quite an impact on others, and comments that, 'People always think that I am taller than I really am, and I'm told it's the Tigger effect — "No matter his weight in pounds, shillings and ounces, he always seems bigger because of the bounces."'

Diffie was born in 1944, and spent most of his early years in Queens, New York. As a child he became fascinated by mathematics, reading books ranging from *The Chemical Rubber Company Handbook of Mathematical Tables* to G.H. Hardy's *Course of Pure Mathematics*. He went on to study mathematics at the Massachusetts Institute of Technology, graduating in 1965. He then took a series of jobs related to computer security, and by the early 1970s he had matured into one of the few truly independent security experts, a freethinking cryptographer, not employed by the government or by any of the big corporations. In hindsight, he was the first cypherpunk.

Diffie was particularly interested in the key-distribution problem, and he realised that whoever found a solution would go down in history as one of the all-time great cryptographers. Diffie was so captivated by the problem of key distribution that it became the most important entry in his special notebook, entitled 'Problems for an Ambitious Theory of Cryptography'.

Part of Diffie's motivation came from his vision of a wired world. Back in the 1960s, the U.S. Department of Defense began funding a cutting-edge research organisation called the Advanced Research Projects Agency (ARPA),

Whitfield Diffie

and one of ARPA's front-line projects was to find a way of connecting military computers across vast distances. This would allow a computer that had been damaged to transfer its responsibilities to another one in the network. The main aim was to make the Pentagon's computer infrastructure more robust in the face of nuclear attack, but the network would also allow scientists to send messages to each other, and perform gigantic calculations by exploiting the spare capacity of remote computers. The ARPAnet was born in 1969, and by the end of the year there were four connected sites (see box overleaf).

Although the ARPAnet was still in its infancy, Diffie was farsighted enough to see that it would expand and develop into what we now call the Internet. He predicted the arrival of the information superhighway and the digital revolution, and looked forward to the day when ordinary people would own computers interconnected via phone lines. Diffie could see the great potential of the ARPAnet, but at the same time he was concerned because people who used their computers to exchange e-mails would not have privacy. In order to have privacy people would have to encrypt their messages, but encryption required the secure exchange of keys. It was already known that large corporations were having trouble coping with key distribution; surely the public would find the task impossible, and would effectively be deprived of the right to privacy.

Diffie imagined two strangers meeting via the Internet, and wondered how they could send each other an encrypted message. He also thought about someone using the Internet to buy a commodity. How could that person send an e-mail containing encrypted credit-card details so that only the Internet retailer could decipher them? In both cases it seemed that the two parties needed to share a key, but how could they exchange keys securely? The number of casual contacts and the amount of spontaneous e-mails among the public would be enormous, and this would mean that key distribution would be impractical. Diffie feared that the necessity of key distribution would prevent the public from having access to digital privacy, and he became obsessed with the idea of finding a solution to the problem.

In 1974 Diffie, still an itinerant cryptographer, paid a visit to IBM's Thomas J. Watson Laboratory, where he had been invited to give a talk. He spoke about various strategies for attacking the key-distribution problem, but all his ideas were very tentative, and his audience was sceptical about the prospects for a solution. The only positive response to Diffie's presentation was from Alan Konheim, one of IBM's senior cryptographic experts, who mentioned that someone else had recently

FROM THE ARPANET TO THE INTERNET

Today's Internet is the vision of J. C. R. Licklider, who in the early 1960s worked at the U.S. Department of Defense's Advanced Research Projects Agency (ARPA). He conceived of a 'Galactic Network' of many linked computers to which everyone would have access. The 1960s saw the development of time-sharing between computers, packet switching (a technique for transmitting data over networks) and protocols (communication settings), which led to the establishment in 1969 of ARPAnet, a network linking several American defence and academic institutions. ARPAnet was a closed network, but other networks began to appear. For example, American libraries developed their own network in the 1970s, and in the 1980s the first Usenet Newsgroups were set up, and were soon linked to ARPAnet.

The military withdrew from ARPAnet in 1983, a year after the establishment of the dedicated Defense Data Network. The Department of Defense had seen ARPAnet as providing a communications system that could survive nuclear attack. There was no central command, and all the computers in the network were on an equal footing. Packet switching would ensure that, whichever computers and links might be destroyed, devices called rerouters would divert traffic between the surviving computers over the surviving links. This design ethos is largely responsible for the qualities of the modern Internet, particularly its anarchic (or, if you prefer, democratic) nature.

In 1986 the National Science Foundation (NSF) set up NSFnet, a high-speed data link – the 'backbone' – connecting several supercomputer centres, to which other networks could be linked. Decentralisation was now complete, and the Internet can be said to have come into existence: potentially anyone could access the system. The late 1980s also saw the first commercial e-mail services (e-mail had been developed by Ray Tomlinson in 1972), and the first Internet Service Provider. In 1989 ARPAnet was decommissioned, and in 1995 the NSF withdrew, leaving the maintenance and expansion of the backbone to private enterprise. The Internet explosion of the 1990s was sparked by the arrival of cheap personal computers and the appearance of the World Wide Web (WWW). The WWW, proposed by Tim Berners-Lee at CERN (the European centre for nuclear research based in Switzerland), was a user interface based on http, the hypertext transfer protocol, allowing users to navigate using hypertext links. In 1992 there appeared the first browser, named Mosaic; Netscape Navigator, released in 1994, became the first widely used browser.

visited the laboratory and given a lecture on the issue of key distribution. That speaker had been Martin Hellman (see box overleaf), a professor from Stanford University in California. That evening Diffie got in his car and began the 5,000 km journey to the West Coast to meet the only person who seemed to share his obsession. The alliance of Diffie and Hellman would become one of the most dynamic partnerships in cryptography.

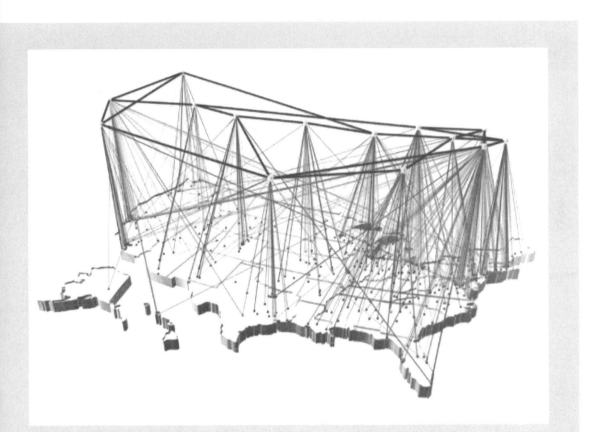

*This map illustrates the decentralised structure of the Internet within America. There are many possible routes between any two computers. Home computers are linked to Internet Service Providers (ISPs) via telephone lines, while computers within universities and businesses are connected to ISPs via a Local Area Network (LAN). ISPs are connected to each other via 'backbones' of fibre-optics. Backbones in America are connected to overseas backbones via undersea cables or satellite links. A normal phone line can can handle data at a rate of roughly **50,000** bits per second, whereas major connections within the Internet can handle up to **10,000,000,000** bits per second.*

Martin Hellman had been conducting research into cryptography entirely alone, until September 1974 when he received an unexpected phone call from Whitfield Diffie. Hellman had never heard of Diffie, but grudgingly agreed to a half-hour appointment later that afternoon. By the end of the meeting Hellman realised that Diffie was the best-informed person he had ever met. The feeling was mutual. As Hellman recalls:

I'd promised my wife I'd be home to watch the kids, so he came home with me and we had dinner together. He left at around midnight. Our personalities are very different – he is much more counter-culture than I am – but eventually the personality clash was very symbiotic. It was just such a breath of fresh air for me. Working in a vacuum had been really hard.

Since Hellman did not have a great deal of funding, he could not afford to employ his new soulmate as a researcher. Instead, Diffie was enrolled as a graduate student. Together, Hellman and Diffie began to study the key-distribution problem, desperately trying to find an alternative to the tiresome task of physically transporting keys over vast distances. In due course they were joined by Ralph Merkle. Merkle was an intellectual refugee, having emigrated from another research group where the professor had no sympathy for the impossible dream of solving the key-distribution problem.

The whole problem of key distribution is a classic catch-22. If two people want to exchange a secret message over the phone, the sender must encrypt it. To encrypt

MARTIN HELLMAN – THE MAKING OF A CRYPTOGRAPHER

Martin Hellman was born in 1945 in a Jewish neighbourhood in the Bronx, but at the age of four his family moved to a predominantly Irish Catholic neighbourhood. According to Hellman, this permanently changed his attitude to life: 'The other kids went to church and they learned that the Jews killed Christ, so I got called "Christ killer". I also got beat up. To start with, I wanted to be like the other kids, I wanted a Christmas tree and I wanted Christmas presents. But then I

realised that I couldn't be like all the other kids, and in self-defence I adopted an attitude of "Who would want to be like everybody else?"' Hellman traces his interest in ciphers to this enduring desire to be different. His colleagues had told him he was crazy to do research in cryptography, because he would be competing with the NSA and their multibillion-dollar budget. How could he hope to discover something that they did not know already? And if he did discover anything, the NSA would classify it.

the secret message the sender must use a key, which is itself a secret, so then there is the problem of transmitting the secret key to the receiver in order to transmit the secret message. In short, before two people can exchange a secret (an encrypted message) they must already share a secret (the key).

When thinking about the problem of key distribution, it is helpful to consider Alice, Bob and Eve, three fictional characters who have become the industry standard for discussions about cryptography. In a typical situation, Alice wants to send a message to Bob, or vice versa, and Eve is trying to eavesdrop. If Alice is sending private messages to Bob she will encrypt each one before sending it, using a separate key each time. Alice is continually faced with the problem of key distribution because she has to convey the keys to Bob securely, otherwise he cannot decrypt the messages. One way to solve the problem is for Alice and Bob to meet up once a week and exchange enough keys to cover the messages that might be sent during the next seven days. Exchanging keys in person is certainly secure, but it is inconvenient, and if either Alice or Bob is taken ill the system breaks down. Alternatively, Alice and Bob could hire couriers, which would be less secure and more expensive, but at least they will have delegated some of the work. Either way, it seems that the distribution of keys is unavoidable. For two thousand years this was considered to be an axiom of cryptography – an indisputable truth. However, there is a thought-experiment that seems to defy the axiom.

Imagine that Alice and Bob live in a country where the postal system is completely corrupt, and postal employees will read any unprotected correspondence. Alice wants to send an intensely personal message to Bob. She puts it inside a strongbox, closes it, and secures it with a padlock and key. She puts the padlocked box in the post and keeps the key. However, when the box reaches Bob he is unable to open it because he does not have the key. Alice might consider putting the key inside another strongbox, padlocking it and sending it to Bob, but without the key to the second padlock he is unable to open the second box, so he cannot obtain the key that opens the first box. The only way around the problem seems to be for Alice to make a copy of her key and give it to Bob in advance when they meet for coffee. So far, I have just restated the same old problem in a new scenario. Avoiding key distribution seems logically impossible: surely, if Alice wants to lock something in a box so that only Bob can open it, she must give him a copy of the key. Or, in terms of cryptography, if Alice wants to encipher a message so that only Bob can decipher it, she must give him a copy of the key. Key exchange is an inevitable part of encipherment – or is it?

Now picture the following scenario. As before, Alice wants to send an intensely personal message to Bob. Again, she puts her secret message in a strongbox, padlocks it and sends it to Bob. When the box arrives, Bob adds his own padlock and sends the box back to Alice. When Alice receives the box, it is now secured by two padlocks. She removes her own padlock, leaving just Bob's padlock to secure the box. Finally she sends the box back to Bob. And here is the crucial difference: Bob can now open the box because it is secured only with his own padlock – to which he alone has the key.

The implications of this little story are enormous. It demonstrates that a secret message can be securely exchanged between two people without them first exchanging a key. For the first time we have a suggestion that key exchange might not be an inevitable part of cryptography. We can reinterpret the story in terms of encryption. Alice uses her own key to encrypt a message to Bob, who encrypts it again with his own key and returns it. When Alice receives the doubly encrypted message, she removes her own encryption and returns it to Bob, who can then remove his own encryption and read the message.

It seems that the problem of key distribution might have been solved, because the doubly encrypted scheme requires no exchange of keys. However, there is a fundamental obstacle to implementing a system in which Alice encrypts, Bob encrypts, Alice decrypts and Bob decrypts. The problem is the order in which the encryptions and decryptions are performed. In general, the order of encryption and decryption is crucial, and should obey the maxim 'last on, first off'. In other words, the last stage of encryption should be the first to be decrypted. In the above scenario Bob performed the last stage of encryption, so this should have been the first to be decrypted, but it was Alice who removed her encryption first, before Bob removed his. The importance of order is most easily grasped by examining something we do every day. In the morning we put on our socks, and then we put on our shoes, and in the evening we remove our shoes before removing our socks – it is impossible to remove the socks before the shoes. We must obey the maxim 'last on, first off'.

Some very elementary ciphers, such as the Caesar cipher, are so simple that order does not matter. However, in the 1970s it seemed that any form of strong encryption must always obey the 'last on, first off' rule. If a message is encrypted with Alice's key and then with Bob's key, then it must be decrypted with Bob's key before it can be decrypted with Alice's key. Order is crucial even with a monoalphabetic substitution cipher. Imagine that Alice and Bob have their own keys, and look at what happens

GOD REWARDS FOOLS

The trio of Martin Hellman, Whitfield Diffie and Ralph Merkle were determined to solve the key-distribution problem, which was generally considered to be an impossible task. According to Hellman, they adopted a radical attitude to their work:

> The way to get to the top of the heap in terms of developing original research is to be a fool, because only fools keep trying. You have idea number 1, you get excited, and it flops. Then you have idea number 2, you get excited, and it flops. Then you have idea number 99, you get excited, and it flops. Only a fool would be excited by the 100th idea, but it might take 100 ideas before one really pays off. Unless you're foolish enough to be continually excited, you won't have the motivation, you won't have the energy to carry it through. God rewards fools.

Ralph Merkle, Martin Hellman and Whitfield Diffie

when the order is incorrect. Alice uses her key to encrypt a message to Bob, then Bob re-encrypts the result using his own key; Alice uses her key to perform a partial decryption, and finally Bob attempts to use his key to perform the full decryption.

Alice's key

a b c d e f g h i j k l m n o p q r s t u v w x y z
H F S U G T A K V D E O Y J B P N X W C Q R I M Z L

Bob's key

a b c d e f g h i j k l m n o p q r s t u v w x y z
C P M G A T N O J E F W I Q B U R Y H X S D Z K L V

Message	m e e t	m e	a t	n o o n
Encrypted with Alice's key	Y G G C	Y G	H C	J B B J
Encrypted with Bob's key	L N N M	L N	O M	E P P E
Decrypted with Alice's key	Z Q Q X	Z Q	L X	K P P K
Decrypted with Bob's key	w n n t	w n	y t	x b b x

The result is nonsense. However, you can check for yourself that if the decryption order were reversed, and Bob decrypts before Alice, thus obeying the 'last on, first off' rule, then the result will be the original message. But if order is so important, why did the padlock system seem to work in the anecdote about padlocked strongboxes? The answer is that order is not important for padlocks. I can apply twenty padlocks to a box and undo them in any order, and at the end the box will open. Unfortunately, encryption systems are far more sensitive than padlocks when it comes to order.

Although the doubly padlocked box approach would not work for real-world cryptography, it inspired Diffie and Hellman to search for a practical method of circumventing the key-distribution problem. They spent month after month attempting to find a solution. Although every idea ended in failure, they supported each other and persevered. Diffie often went through long periods of barren contemplation, and on one occasion in 1975 he became so frustrated that he told his wife Mary that he was just a failed scientist who would never amount to anything. He even told her that she ought to find someone else. Mary told him that she had absolute faith in him, and just two weeks later Diffie came up with his truly brilliant idea.

He can still recall how the idea flashed into his mind, and then almost vanished: 'I walked downstairs to get a Coke, and almost forgot about the idea. I remembered that I'd been thinking about something interesting, but couldn't quite recall what it was. Then it came back in a real adrenaline rush of excitement. I was actually aware for the first time in my work on cryptography of having discovered something really valuable. Everything that I had discovered in the subject up to this point seemed to me to be mere technicalities.' It was mid-afternoon, and he had to wait a couple of hours before Mary returned. 'Whit was waiting at the door,' she recalls. 'He said he had something to tell me and he had a funny look on his face. I walked in and he said, "Sit down, please, I want to talk to you. I believe that I have made a great discovery — I know I am the first person to have done this." The world stood still for me at that moment. I felt like I was living in a Hollywood film.'

Diffie had concocted a new type of cipher, one that incorporates a so-called *asymmetric key*. So far, all the encryption techniques described in this book have been *symmetric*, which means that the unscrambling process is simply the opposite of scrambling. For example, the Enigma machine uses a certain key setting to encipher a message, and the receiver uses an identical machine in the same key setting to decipher it. Both sender and receiver effectively have equivalent knowledge, and they both use the same key to encrypt and decrypt — their relationship is symmetric. In an asymmetric key system, as the name suggests, the encryption key and the decryption key are not identical. In an asymmetric cipher, if Alice knows the encryption key she can encrypt a message, but she cannot decrypt a message. In order to decrypt, Alice must have access to the decryption key. This distinction between the encryption and decryption keys is what makes an asymmetric cipher special.

Although Diffie had come up with the general concept of an asymmetric cipher, he did not actually have a specific example of one. However, the mere concept of an asymmetric cipher was revolutionary. If cryptographers could find a genuine working asymmetric cipher, a system that fulfilled Diffie's requirements, then the implications for Alice and Bob would be enormous. Alice could create her own pair of keys: an encryption key and a decryption key. If we assume that the asymmetric cipher is a form of computer encryption, then Alice's encryption key is a number, and her decryption key is a different number. Alice keeps the decryption key secret, so it is commonly referred to as Alice's *private-key*. However, she publishes the encryption key so that everybody has access to it, which is why it is commonly referred to as Alice's *public-key*. If Bob wants to send Alice a message, he simply looks up her public-key, which would be listed in something akin to a telephone directory. Bob then uses Alice's public-key to encrypt the message. He sends the encrypted message to Alice, and when it arrives Alice can decrypt it using her private decryption key. Similarly, if Charlie or Dawn want to send Alice an encrypted message, they too can look up Alice's public encryption key, and in each case only Alice has access to the private decryption key required to decrypt the messages.

The great advantage of this system is that it overcomes the problem of key distribution. Alice does not have to transport the public encryption key securely to Bob: in complete contrast, she wants to publicise her public encryption key as widely as possible. She wants everybody to know her public encryption key so that anybody can use it to send her encrypted messages. At the same time, even if the whole world knows Alice's public-key, nobody, including Eve, can decrypt any messages encrypted with it, because knowledge of the public-key is no help in decryption. In fact, once Bob has encrypted a message using Alice's public-key, even he cannot decrypt it. Only Alice, who alone possesses her private-key, can decrypt the message.

This is the exact opposite of a traditional symmetric cipher, in which Alice has to go to great lengths to transport the encryption key securely to Bob. In a symmetric cipher the encryption key is the same as the decryption key, so Alice and Bob must take the utmost precautions to ensure that the key does not fall into Eve's hands. This is the root of the key-distribution problem.

Returning to padlock analogies, asymmetric cryptography can be thought of in the following way. Anybody can close a padlock simply by clicking it shut, but only the person who has the key can open it. Locking (encryption) is easy, something everybody can do, but unlocking (decryption) can be done only by the owner of the key. The trivial knowledge of knowing how to click the padlock shut does not equip you to unlock it. Taking the analogy further, imagine that Alice designs a padlock and key. She guards the key, but she manufactures thousands of replica padlocks and distributes them to post offices all over the world. If Bob wants to send a message, he puts it in a box, goes to the local post office, asks for an 'Alice padlock' and padlocks the box. Now he is unable to unlock the box, but when Alice receives it she can open it with her unique key. The padlock and the process of clicking it shut is equivalent to the public encryption key, because everyone has access to the padlocks, and everyone can use a padlock to seal a message in a box. The padlock's key is equivalent to the private decryption key, because only Alice has it, only she can open the padlock, and only she can gain access to the message in the box.

The system seems simple when it is explained in terms of padlocks, but it is far from trivial to find a mathematical function that does the same job, something that can be incorporated into a workable cryptographic system. To turn asymmetric ciphers from a great idea into a practical invention, somebody had to discover an appropriate mathematical function to act as a mathematical padlock. A function is any mathematical operation that turns one number into another number. For example, 'doubling' is a type of function because it turns the number 3 into 6, or the number 9 into 18. Furthermore, we can think of all forms of computer encryption as functions because they turn one number (the plaintext) into another number (the ciphertext).

Most mathematical functions are classified as two-way functions because they are easy to do, and easy to undo. For example, 'doubling' is a two-way function because it is easy to double a number to generate a new number, and just as easy to undo the function and get from the doubled number back to the original number. If we know that the result of doubling is 26, then it is trivial to reverse the function and deduce that the original number was 13. The easiest way to understand the concept of a two-way function is in terms of an everyday activity. We can think of the act of turning on a light switch as a function, because it turns an ordinary light bulb into an illuminated one. This function is two-way because if a switch is turned on, it is easy enough to turn it off and return the light bulb to its original state.

However, Diffie and Hellman were not interested in two-way functions. They focused their attention on one-way functions. As the name suggests, a one-way function is easy to do but very difficult to undo. In other words, two-way functions are reversible, but one-way functions are not reversible. Once again, the best way to illustrate a one-way function is in terms of an everyday activity. Mixing yellow and blue paint to make green paint is a one-way function because it is easy to mix the paint, but impossible to unmix it. Another one-way function is the cracking of an egg, because it is easy to crack an egg but impossible then to return the egg to its original condition. For this reason, one-way functions are sometimes called Humpty Dumpty functions.

Padlocks are also real-world examples of a one-way function, because they are easy to lock but very difficult to unlock. Diffie's idea relied on a mathematical padlock, and this is why the Stanford team of Diffie, Hellman and Merkle focused their attention on studying one-way functions.

Modular arithmetic, sometimes called *clock arithmetic* in schools, is an area of mathematics that is rich in one-way functions. It deals with a finite group of numbers arranged in a loop, rather like the numbers on a clock. For example, Figure 11 shows a clock for modular 7 (or mod 7), which has only the 7 numbers from 0 to 6. To work out 2 + 3, we start at 2 and move around 3 places to reach 5, which is the same answer as in normal arithmetic. To work out 2 + 6 we start at 2 and move around 6 places, but this time we go around the loop and arrive at 1, which is not the result we would get in normal arithmetic. These results can be expressed as:

$$2 + 3 = 5 \,(\text{mod } 7) \quad \text{and} \quad 2 + 6 = 1 \,(\text{mod } 7)$$

Modular arithmetic is relatively simple, and in fact we do it every day when we talk about time. If it is 9 o'clock now, and we have a meeting 8 hours from now, we would say that the meeting is at 5 o'clock, not 17 o'clock. We have mentally calculated 9 + 8 in (mod 12). Imagine a clockface, look at 9, and then move around 8 spaces, and we end up at 5:

$$9 + 8 = 5 \,(\text{mod } 12)$$

Rather than visualising clocks, mathematicians often take the short cut of performing modular calculations according to the following recipe. First, perform the calculation in normal arithmetic. Second, if we want to know the answer in (mod x), we divide the normal answer by x and note the remainder. This remainder is the answer in (mod x). To find the answer to $11 \times 9 \,(\text{mod } 13)$, we do the following:

$$11 \times 9 = 99$$
$$99 \div 13 = 7, \ \text{remainder } 8$$
$$11 \times 9 = 8 \,(\text{mod } 13)$$

Functions performed in the modular arithmetic environment tend to behave erratically, which in turn sometimes makes them one-way functions. This becomes evident when a simple function in normal arithmetic is compared with the same simple function in modular arithmetic. In the former environment the function will be two-way

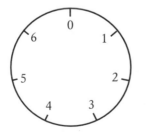

Figure 11 *Modular arithmetic is performed on a finite set of numbers, which can be thought of as numbers on a clock face. In this case, we can work out 6 + 5 in modular 7 by starting at 6 and moving around five spaces, which brings us to 4.*

and easy to reverse; in the latter environment it will be one-way and hard to reverse. As an example, let us take the function 3^x. This means take a number x, then multiply 3 by itself x times in order to get the new number. For example, if $x = 2$, and we perform the function, then:

$$3^x = 3^2 = 3 \times 3 = 9$$

In other words, the function turns 2 into 9. In normal arithmetic, as the value of x increases so does the result of the function. So if we were given the result of the function it would be relatively easy to work backwards and deduce the original number. For example, if the result is 81, we can deduce that x is 4 because $3^4 = 81$. If we made a mistake and guessed that x is 5, we could work out that $3^5 = 243$, which tells us that our choice of x is too big. We would then reduce our choice of x to 4, and we would have the right answer. In short, even when we guess wrongly we can home in on the correct value of x, and thereby reverse the function.

However, in modular arithmetic this same function does not behave so sensibly. Imagine we are told that 3^x in $(\mathrm{mod}\ 7)$ is 1, and we are asked to find the value of x. No value springs to mind, because we are generally unfamiliar with modular arithmetic. We could take a guess that $x = 5$, and we could work out the result of 3^5 $(\mathrm{mod}\ 7)$. The answer turns out to be 5, which is too big, because we are looking for an answer of just 1. We might be tempted to reduce the value of x and try again. But we would be heading in the wrong direction, because the actual answer is $x = 6$.

In normal arithmetic we can test out numbers and sense whether we are getting warmer or colder. The environment of modular arithmetic gives no such helpful clues, and reversing functions is much harder. Often, the only way to reverse a function in modular arithmetic is to compile a table by calculating the function for many values of x until the right answer is found. Table 13 shows the result of calculating several values of the function in both normal arithmetic and modular arithmetic. It clearly demonstrates the erratic behaviour of the function when calculated in modular arithmetic.

Although drawing up such a table is only a little tedious when we are dealing with relatively small numbers, it would be excruciatingly painful to build a table to deal

x	1	2	3	4	5	6
3^x	3	9	27	81	243	729
$3^x (\mathrm{mod}\ 7)$	3	2	6	4	5	1

Table 13 *Values of the function 3^x calculated in normal arithmetic (row 2) and modular arithmetic (row 3). The function increases continuously in normal arithmetic, but is highly erratic in modular arithmetic.*

with a function such as $453^x \pmod{21{,}997}$. This is a classic example of a one-way function, because I could pick a value for x and calculate the result of the function, but if I was given a result, say 5,787, I would have enormous difficulty in reversing the function and deducing the value of x. It would take me hours to draw up the table and thereby work out the correct value of x.

However, this particular one-way function is not adequate to act as a mathematical padlock, because padlocks exhibit a special type of one-way functionality. It is easy to click a padlock and lock it, but it is very difficult to unlock the padlock . . . unless, of course, you have the key! The key is what makes a padlock a special type of one-way function. The true mathematical equivalent of a padlock is a function that is always easy to perform in one direction, but generally hard to perform in the opposite direction, unless you have some special piece of information (the key).

If such a function existed, then Alice would personalise it, which would give her the special piece of information for reversing the function. She would keep this information secret, but distribute the personalised function so that Bob and everyone else can use it to encrypt messages to her. She can decrypt these messages by using the special piece of information. She unlocks the encrypted messages sent to her by using her secret key. Similarly, Bob would personalise the function so that he has his own piece of special secret information. He too distributes his mathematical padlock so that Alice and anybody else can encrypt and send messages to him. Only Bob has the special piece of information required to decrypt the messages sent to him, which have been encrypted using his personalised padlock.

So it was clear what the one-way function had to do, but finding one that could be reversed with a secret key proved to be fiendishly difficult and beyond the reach of Diffie, Hellman and Merkle. Diffie published an outline of his idea in the summer of 1975, whereupon other scientists joined the search for an appropriate one-way function, one that fulfilled the criteria for an asymmetric cipher. The team of Diffie, Hellman and Merkle had invigorated the world of cryptography. They had persuaded the rest of the world that a solution to the key-distribution problem lay just over the horizon. They had proposed the concept of an asymmetric cipher – a perfect but as yet unworkable system. They continued their research at Stanford University, attempting to find a special one-way function that would make asymmetric ciphers a reality. However, they failed to make the discovery. They were overtaken in the race to find an asymmetric cipher by another trio of researchers, based 5,000 km away on the east coast of America.

Prime Suspects

'I walked into Ron Rivest's office', recalls Leonard Adleman, 'and Ron had this paper in his hands. He started saying, "These Stanford guys have this really blah, blah, blah." And I remember thinking, "That's nice, Ron, but I have something else I want to talk about." I was entirely unaware of the history of cryptography and I was distinctly uninterested in what he was saying.' The paper that had made Ron Rivest so excited was by Whitfield Diffie and it described the concept of asymmetric ciphers. Eventually Rivest persuaded Adleman that there might be some interesting mathematics in the problem, and together they resolved to try to find a one-way function that fitted the requirements of an asymmetric cipher. They were joined in the hunt by Adi Shamir. All three men were researchers on the eighth floor of the MIT Laboratory for Computer Science.

Rivest, Shamir and Adleman formed a perfect team. Rivest is a computer scientist with a tremendous ability to absorb new ideas and apply them in unlikely places. He always kept up with the latest scientific papers, which inspired him to come up with a whole series of weird and wonderful candidates for the one-way function at the heart of an asymmetric cipher. However, each candidate was flawed in some way. Shamir, another computer scientist, has a lightning intellect and an ability to cut through the debris and focus on the core of a problem. He too regularly generated ideas for formulating an asymmetric cipher, but his ideas were also inevitably flawed. Adleman, a mathematician with enormous stamina, rigour and patience, was largely responsible for spotting the flaws in the ideas of Rivest and Shamir, ensuring that they did not waste time following false leads. Rivest and Shamir spent a year coming up with new ideas, and Adleman spent a year shooting them down. The threesome began to lose hope, but they were unaware that this process of continual failure was a necessary part of their research, gently steering them away from sterile mathematical territory and towards more fertile ground. In due course, their efforts were rewarded.

In April 1977, Rivest, Shamir and Adleman spent Passover at the house of a student, and had consumed significant amounts of Manischewitz wine before returning to their respective homes some time around midnight. Rivest, unable to sleep, lay on his couch reading a mathematics textbook. He began mulling over the question that had been puzzling him for weeks — is it possible to build an asymmetric cipher? Is it possible to find a one-way function that can be reversed only if the

ARS OR RSA?

The great breakthrough on asymmetric ciphers was made by Ron Rivest, but it would not have been possible without the year-long collaboration with his two colleagues. So when Rivest wrote up the discovery, he ended by listing the three names alphabetically: Adleman, Rivest, Shamir. Although Leonard Adleman found no fault with the paper, he was not happy with being included as one of its authors.

'I told Ron to take my name off the paper,' he recalls. 'I told him that it was his invention, not mine. But Ron refused and we got into a discussion about it. We agreed that I would go home and contemplate it for one night, and consider what I wanted to do. I went back the next day and suggested to Ron that I be the third author. I recall thinking that this paper would be the least interesting paper that I will ever be on.' Adleman could not have been more wrong. The system, dubbed RSA (Rivest, Shamir and Adleman, from left to right in the picture) as opposed to ARS, went on to become the most influential cipher in modern cryptography.

receiver has some special information? Suddenly, the mists began to clear and he had a revelation. He spent the rest of that night formalising his idea, effectively writing a complete scientific paper before daybreak. The next morning, Rivest handed the paper to Adleman, who went through his usual process of trying to tear it apart, but this time he could find no faults.

Before exploring Rivest's idea, here is a quick reminder of what scientists were looking for in order to build an asymmetric cipher:

(1) Alice must create a public-key, which she would then publish so that Bob (and everybody else) can use it to encrypt messages to her. Because the public-key is a one-way function, it must be virtually impossible for anybody to reverse it and decrypt Alice's messages.

(2) However, Alice needs to decrypt the messages being sent to her. She must therefore have a private-key, some special piece of information, which allows her to reverse the effect of the public-key. Therefore, Alice (and Alice alone) has the power to decrypt any messages sent to her.

At the heart of Rivest's asymmetric cipher is a one-way function based on the sort of modular functions described earlier in the chapter. Rivest's one-way function can be used to encrypt a message — the message, which is effectively a number, is put into the function, and the result is the ciphertext, another number. Rivest's one-way function is described in detail in the box overleaf, but here I shall explain only one particular aspect of it, a number known simply as N, because it is N that makes this one-way function reversible under certain circumstances, and therefore ideal for use as a mathematical padlock.

N is important because it is a flexible component of the one-way function, which means that each person can choose a different value of N, and personalise the one-way function. In order to choose her personal value of N, Alice picks two prime numbers, p and q, and multiplies them together. A prime number is one that has no divisors except itself and 1. For example, 7 is a prime number because no numbers except 1 and 7 will divide into it without leaving a remainder. Likewise, 13 is a prime number because no numbers except 1 and 13 will divide into it without leaving a remainder. However, 8 is not a prime number, because it can be divided by 2 and 4.

So, Alice could choose her numbers to be $p = 17,159$ and $q = 10,247$. Multiplying these two prime numbers together gives $N = 17,159 \times 10,247 = 175,828,273$. Alice's choice of N effectively becomes her public encryption key, and she could print it on her business card, post it on the Internet, or publish it in a public-key directory along with everybody else's value of N. If Bob wants to encrypt a message to Alice, he looks up Alice's value of N (175,828,273) and then inserts it into the general form of the one-way function, which would also be public knowledge. Bob now has a one-way function tailored according to Alice's public-key, so it could be called Alice's one-way function. To encrypt a message to Alice, he takes her one-way function, inserts the message, notes down the result and sends it to her.

THE MATHEMATICS OF RSA

This is a straightforward mathematical description of the mechanics of RSA encryption and decryption.

(1) Alice picks two prime numbers, p and q. The primes should be enormous, but for simplicity we assume that Alice chooses $p = 17$, $q = 11$. She must keep these numbers secret.

(2) Alice multiplies them together to get another number, N. In this case $N = 187$. She now picks another number e, and in this case she chooses $e = 7$.

[e and $(p-1) \times (q-1)$ should be what is known as relatively prime, but this is a technicality.]

(3) Alice can now publish e and N in something like a telephone directory. Since these two numbers are necessary for encryption, they must be available to anybody who might want to encrypt a message to Alice. Together these two numbers are called the public-key. (As well as being part of Alice's public-key, e could also be part of everybody else's public-key. However, everybody must have a different value of N, which depends on their choice of p and q.)

(4) To encrypt a message, it must first be converted into a number, M. For example, a word is changed into ASCII binary digits, and the binary digits can be considered as a decimal number. M is then encrypted to give the ciphertext, C, according to the formula

$$C = M^e \pmod{N}$$

(5) Imagine that Bob wants to send Alice a simple kiss: just the letter X. In ASCII this is represented by 1011000, which is equivalent to 88 in decimal. So, $M = 88$.

(6) To encrypt this message, Bob begins by looking up Alice's public-key, and discovers that $N = 187$ and $e = 7$. This provides him with the encryption formula required to encrypt messages to Alice. With $M = 88$, the formula gives

$$C = 88^7 \pmod{187}$$

(7) Working this out directly on a calculator is not straightforward, because the display cannot cope with such large numbers. However, there is a neat trick for calculating exponentials in modular arithmetic. We know that, since $7 = 4 + 2 + 1$,

$88^7 \pmod{187} = [88^4 \pmod{187} \times 88^2 \pmod{187} \times 88^1 \pmod{187}] \pmod{187}$

$88^1 = 88 = 88 \pmod{187}$

$88^2 = 7,744 = 77 \pmod{187}$

$88^4 = 59,969,536 = 132 \pmod{187}$

$88^7 = 88^1 \times 88^2 \times 88^4 = 88 \times 77 \times 132 = 894,432 = 11 \pmod{187}$

Bob now sends the ciphertext, $C = 11$, to Alice.

(8) We know that exponentials in modular arithmetic are one-way functions, so it is very difficult to work backwards from $C = 11$ and recover the original message, M. Hence, Eve cannot decipher the message.

(9) However, Alice can decipher the message because she has access to some special information: she knows the values of p and q. She can use this secret information to calculate a special number, d, the decryption key, otherwise known as her private-key. The number d is calculated according to the formula

$$[e \times d = 1] \ (\mathrm{mod}\ (p - 1) \times (q - 1))$$

$$[7 \times d = 1] \ (\mathrm{mod}\ 16 \times 10)$$

$$[7 \times d = 1] \ (\mathrm{mod}\ 160)$$

$$d = 23$$

(Deducing the value of d is not straightforward, but a technique known as Euclid's algorithm allows Alice to find d quickly and easily.)

(10) To decrypt the message, Alice simply uses the formula

$$M = C^d \ (\mathrm{mod}\ 187)$$

$$M = 11^{23} \ (\mathrm{mod}\ 187)$$

$$M = [11^1 \ (\mathrm{mod}\ 187) \times 11^2 \ (\mathrm{mod}\ 187) \times 11^4 \ (\mathrm{mod}\ 187) \times 11^{16} \ (\mathrm{mod}\ 187)] \ (\mathrm{mod}\ 187)$$

$$M = 11 \times 121 \times 55 \times 154 \ (\mathrm{mod}\ 187)$$

$$M = 88 = \mathrm{X\ in\ ASCII}$$

Rivest, Shamir and Adleman had created a special one-way function, one that could be reversed only by somebody with access to privileged information, namely the values of p and q. Each function can be personalised by choosing p and q, which multiply together to give N. The function allows everybody to encrypt messages to a particular person by using that person's choice of N, but only the intended recipient can decrypt the message because the recipient is the only person who knows p and q, and hence the only person who knows the decryption key, d.

Using the analogy of the padlock, the one-way function is the padlock. Choosing p and q means that anybody can insert their value of N into the padlock and can thereby personalise the padlock. The padlock can then be freely distributed, The values of p and q provide the mechanism for undoing the padlock and therefore are equivalent to the key.

At this point the encrypted message is secure because nobody can decipher it. The message has been encrypted with a one-way function, so reversing the one-way function and decrypting the message is, by definition, very difficult. However, the question remains — how can Alice decrypt the message? In order to read messages sent to her, Alice must have a way of reversing the one-way function: she needs to have access to some special piece of information that allows her to decrypt the message. Fortunately for Alice, Rivest designed the one-way function so that it is reversible to someone who knows the values of p and q, the two prime numbers that are multiplied together to give N. Although Alice has told the world that her value for N is 175,828,273, she has not revealed her values for p and q, so only she has the special information required to decrypt her own messages.

We can think of N as the public-key, the information that is available to everybody, the information required to encrypt messages to Alice; whereas p and q are the private-key, available only to Alice, the information required to decrypt these messages. The exact details of how p and q can be used to reverse the one-way function are outlined in the box on pages 160-1. However, there is one question that must be addressed immediately. If everybody knows N, the public-key, then surely people can deduce p and q, the private-key, and read Alice's messages? After all, N was created from p and q. In fact, it turns out that if N is large enough, it is virtually impossible to deduce p and q from N, and this is perhaps the most beautiful and elegant aspect of Rivest's asymmetric cipher.

Alice created N by choosing p and q, and then multiplying them together. The fundamental point is that this is in itself a one-way function. To demonstrate the one-way nature of multiplying primes, we can take two prime numbers, such as 9,419 and 1,933, and multiply them together. With a calculator it takes just a few seconds to get the answer, 18,206,927. However, if instead we were given 18,206,927 and asked to find the prime factors (the two numbers that were multiplied to give 18,206,927) it would take us much longer. If you doubt the difficulty of finding prime factors, then consider the following. It took me just ten seconds to generate the number 1,709,023, but it will take you and a calculator the best part of an afternoon to work out the prime factors.

This system of asymmetric cryptography, known as RSA after the initials of its inventors, is said to be a form of *public-key cryptography*. To find out how secure RSA is, we can examine it from Eve's point of view, and try to break a message from Alice to Bob. To encrypt a message to Bob, Alice must look up Bob's public-key. To create his public-key, Bob picked his own prime numbers, p_B and q_B, and multiplied them together to get N_B. He has kept p_B and q_B secret, because these make up his private decryption key, but he has published N_B, which is equal to 408,508,091. So Alice inserts Bob's public-key N_B into the general one-way encryption function, and then encrypts her message to him. When the encrypted message arrives, Bob can reverse the function and decrypt it using his values for p_B and q_B, which make up his private-key. Meanwhile, Eve has intercepted the message en route. Her only hope of decrypting the message is to reverse the one-way function, and this is possible only if she knows p_B and q_B. Bob has kept p_B and q_B secret, but Eve, like everybody else, knows that N_B is 408,508,091. Eve then attempts to deduce the values for p_B and q_B by working out which numbers when multiplied together give 408,508,091, a process known as *factoring*.

Factoring is very time-consuming, but exactly how long would it take Eve to find the factors of 408,508,091? There are various recipes for trying to factor N_B. Although some recipes are faster than others, they all consist essentially of checking each prime number to see if it divides into N_B without a remainder. For example, 3 is a prime number, but it is not a factor of 408,508,091 because 3 will not perfectly divide into 408,508,091. So Eve moves on to the next prime number, 5. Similarly, 5 is not a factor, so Eve moves on to the next prime number, and so on. Eventually, Eve arrives at 18,313, the 2,000th prime number, which is indeed a factor of 408,508,091. Having found one factor, it is easy to find the other one, which turns out to be 22,307. If Eve had a calculator and was able to check four primes a minute, then it would have taken her 500 minutes, or more than 8 hours, to find p_B and q_B. In other words, Eve would be able to work out Bob's private-key in less than a day, and could therefore decipher the intercepted message in less than a day.

This is not a very high level of security, but Bob could have chosen much larger prime numbers and increased the security of his private-key. For example, he could have chosen primes that are as big as 10^{65} (this means 1 followed by 65 zeros, or one hundred thousand million million million million million million million million million million). This would have given him a value for N of roughly $10^{65} \times 10^{65}$, which is 10^{130}. A computer could multiply the two primes and generate N in just a second, but if Eve wanted to reverse the process and work out p and q, it would take inordinately longer. Exactly how long depends on the speed of Eve's computer. In 1995 security expert Simson Garfinkel estimated that a 100 MHz Intel Pentium computer with 8 MB of RAM would take roughly fifty years to factor a number as big as 10^{130}. Cryptographers tend to have a paranoid streak and consider worst-case scenarios, such as a worldwide conspiracy to crack their ciphers. So, Garfinkel considered what would happen if a hundred million personal computers (the number sold in 1995) ganged up together. The result is that a number as big as 10^{130} could be factored in about 15 seconds. Consequently, it is now generally accepted that for genuine security it is necessary to use even larger primes. For important banking transactions, N tends to be at least 10^{308}, which is ten million billion times bigger than 10^{130}. Even with the combined efforts of a hundred million personal computers, it would take more than one thousand years to crack such a cipher. With sufficiently large values of p and q, RSA is impregnable.

The only caveat for the security of RSA public-key cryptography is that at some time in the future somebody might find a quick way to factor N. It is conceivable that a decade from now, or even tomorrow, somebody will discover a method for rapid factoring, and thereafter RSA will become useless. However, for over two thousand years mathematicians have tried and failed to find a short cut, and at the moment factoring remains an enormously time-consuming calculation. Most mathematicians believe that factoring is an inherently difficult task, and that there is some mathematical law that forbids any short cut. If we assume they are right, then RSA seems secure for the foreseeable future.

The great advantage of RSA public-key cryptography is that it does away with all the problems associated with traditional ciphers and key exchange. Alice no longer has to worry about securely transporting the key to Bob, or that Eve might intercept the key. In fact, Alice does not care who sees the public-key — the more the merrier, because the public-key helps only with encryption, not decryption. The only thing that needs to remain secret is the private-key used for decryption, and Alice can keep this with her at all times.

RSA was first announced in August 1977, when Martin Gardner wrote an article entitled 'A New Kind of Cipher that Would Take Millions of Years to Break' for his 'Mathematical Games' column in *Scientific American*. After explaining how public-key cryptography works, Gardner issued a challenge to his readers. He printed a ciphertext and also provided the public-key that had been used to encrypt it:

$N = 114,381,625,757,888,867,669,235,779,976,146,612,010,218,296,$
$721,242,362,562,561,842,935,706,935,245,733,897,830,597,123,563,$
$958,705,058,989,075,147,599,290,026,879,543,541$

The challenge was to factor N into p and q, and then use these numbers to decrypt the message. The prize was $100. Gardner did not have space to explain the nitty-gritty of RSA, and instead he asked readers to write to MIT's Laboratory for Computer Science, which would send back a technical memorandum that had just been prepared. Rivest, Shamir and Adleman were astonished by the three thousand requests they received. However, they did not respond immediately because they were concerned that public distribution of their idea might jeopardise their chances of getting a patent. When the patent problem was eventually resolved, the trio held a celebratory party at which professors and students consumed pizzas and beer while stuffing envelopes with technical memoranda for the readers of *Scientific American*.

As for Gardner's challenge, it would be seventeen years before the cipher was broken. On 26 April 1994, a team of six hundred volunteers announced the factors of N:

$q = 3,490,529,510,847,650,949,147,849,619,903,898,133,417,764,638,$
   $493,387,843,990,820,577$

$p = 32,769,132,993,266,709,549,961,988,190,834,461,413,177,642,967,$
   $992,942,539,798,288,533$

Using these values as the private-key, they were able to decipher the message. The message was a series of numbers, but when converted into letters it read 'the magic words are squeamish ossifrage'. The factoring problem had been split among the volunteers, who came from countries as far apart as Australia, Britain, America and Venezuela. The volunteers used spare time on their workstations, mainframes and supercomputers, each of them tackling a fraction of the problem. In effect, a network of computers around the world had united and worked simultaneously in order to meet Gardner's challenge. Even bearing in mind the mammoth parallel effort, some readers may still be surprised that RSA was broken in such a short time, but it should be noted that Gardner's challenge used a relatively small value of N — it was only of the order of 10^{129}. Today, users of RSA would pick a much larger value to secure important information. It is now routine to encrypt a message with a sufficiently large value of N so that all the computers on the planet would need longer than the age of the universe to break the cipher.

The Alternative History of Public-Key Cryptography

Over the past twenty years, Diffie, Hellman and Merkle have become world-famous as the cryptographers who invented the concept of public-key cryptography, while Rivest, Shamir and Adleman have been credited with developing RSA, an elegant implementation of public-key cryptography. However, a recent announcement means that the history books are having to be rewritten. According to a report first released on the Internet, public-key cryptography was originally invented at the Government Communications Headquarters (GCHQ) in Cheltenham, the top-secret establishment that was formed from the remnants of Bletchley Park after the Second World War. This is a story of remarkable ingenuity, anonymous heroes and a government cover-up that endured for decades.

The story begins in the late 1960s, when the British military started to worry about the problem of key distribution. Looking ahead to the 1970s, senior military officials imagined a scenario in which miniaturisation of radios and a reduction in cost meant that every soldier could be in continual radio contact with his officer. The advantages of widespread communication would be enormous, but communications would have to be encrypted, and the problem of distributing keys would be insurmountable. This was an era when the only form of cryptography was

FROM GC&GS TO GCHQ

The organisation known as GCHQ – the Government Communications Headquarters – can trace its origins back to the end of the First World War, when the Government Code and Cypher School (GC&CS) was established to study the methods of cipher communication used by other nations and to advise on British ciphers and codes. The Foreign Office took control of GC&CS in 1922. During the Second World War, the School was greatly expanded at its new country home of Bletchley Park, where it performed a vital role in cracking the German Enigma cipher.

After the war the organisation was transformed into GCHQ. Most of the wartime staff departed, and a new generation of signals intelligence officers was recruited. After a sojourn in London, GCHQ moved into its permanent home in Cheltenham in 1952. Despite having a staff of several thousand, this was still a covert operation and remained so until 1983, when its function was officially recognised in the British Parliament. It was not until 1994 that its role was made explicit by the Intelligence Services Act.

In 1983 GCHQ attracted wide media attention when the right to membership of a trade union was removed from its staff by the Conservative Government; the right was restored in 1997.

symmetric, so an individual key would have to be securely transported to every member of the communications network. Any expansion in communications would eventually be choked by the burden of key distribution. At the beginning of 1969, the military asked James Ellis, one of Britain's foremost government cryptographers, to look into ways of coping with the key-distribution problem.

Ellis was a curious and slightly eccentric character. He proudly boasted of travelling halfway round the world before he was even born — he was conceived in Australia, but was born in Britain. Growing up in London's East End in the 1920s, he became interested in science and he went on to study physics at Imperial College before joining the Post Office Research Station at Dollis Hill, where Tommy Flowers had built Colossus, the first codebreaking computer. The cryptographic division at Dollis Hill was eventually absorbed into GCHQ, so on 1 April 1965 Ellis moved

James Ellis

to Cheltenham to join the newly formed Communications–Electronics Security Group (CESG), a special section of GCHQ devoted to ensuring the security of British communications. Because his work involved issues of national security, Ellis was sworn to secrecy throughout his career. Although his wife and family knew that he worked at GCHQ, they were unaware of his discoveries and had no idea that he was one of the nation's most distinguished codemakers.

Despite his skills as a codemaker, Ellis was never put in charge of any of the important GCHQ research groups. He was brilliant, but he was also unpredictable, introverted and not a natural teamworker. His colleague Richard Walton recalled:

> He was a rather quirky worker, and he didn't really fit into the day-to-day business of GCHQ. But in terms of coming up with new ideas he was quite exceptional. You had to sort through some rubbish sometimes, but he was very innovative and always willing to challenge the orthodoxy. We would be in real trouble if everybody in GCHQ was like him, but we can tolerate a higher proportion of such people than most organisations. We put up with a number of people like him.

One of Ellis's greatest qualities was his breadth of knowledge. He read any scientific journal he could get his hands on, and never threw anything away. For security reasons, GCHQ employees must clear their desks each evening and place everything in locked cabinets, and Ellis's cabinets became stuffed full with the most obscure publications imaginable. He gained a reputation as a cryptoguru, and if other researchers found themselves with impossible problems they would knock on his door in the hope that his vast knowledge and originality would provide a solution. It was probably because of this reputation that he was asked to examine the key-distribution problem.

The cost of key distribution was already enormous, and would become the limiting factor to any expansion in encryption. Even a reduction of 10 per cent in the cost of key distribution would significantly cut the military's security budget. However, instead of merely nibbling away at the problem, Ellis immediately looked for a radical and complete solution or, as Richard Walton puts it, 'James being James, one of the first things he did was to challenge the requirement that it was necessary to share secret data, by which I mean the key. There was no theorem that said you had to have a shared secret. This was something that was challengeable.'

Ellis began his attack on the problem by searching through his treasure trove of scientific journals. Many years later, he recorded the moment when he discovered that key distribution was not an inevitable part of cryptography:

> The event which changed this view was the discovery of a wartime Bell Telephone report by an unknown author describing an ingenious idea for secure telephone speech. It proposed that the recipient should mask the sender's speech by adding noise to the line. He could subtract the noise afterwards since he had added it and therefore knew what it was. The obvious practical disadvantages of this system prevented it being actually used, but it has some interesting characteristics. The difference between this and conventional encryption is that in this case the recipient takes part in the encryption process . . . So the idea was born.

'Noise' is the technical term for any signal that impinges on a communication. Normally it is generated by natural phenomena, and its most irritating feature is that it is entirely random, which means that removing noise from a message is very difficult. If a radio communications system is well designed, then the level of noise is low and the message is clearly audible, but if the noise level is high and it swamps the message, there is no way to recover the message. Ellis was suggesting that the receiver, Alice, deliberately create noise, which she could measure before adding it to the communication channel that connects her with Bob. Bob could then send a message to Alice, and if Eve tapped the communications channel she would be unable to read the message because it would be swamped by the noise. The only person who can remove the noise and read the message is Alice, because she is in the unique position of knowing the exact nature of the noise, having put it there in the first place. Ellis realised that security had been achieved without exchanging any key. The key was the noise, and only Alice needed to know the details of the noise. In a memorandum, Ellis detailed his thought processes:

> The next question was the obvious one. Can this be done with ordinary encipherment? Can we produce a secure encrypted message, readable by the authorised recipient without any prior secret exchange of the key? This question actually occurred to me in bed one night, and the proof of the theoretical possibility took only a few minutes. We had an existence theorem. The unthinkable was actually possible.

An existence theorem shows that a particular concept is possible, but is not concerned with the details of the concept. In other words, until this moment, searching for a solution to the key-distribution problem was like looking for a needle in a haystack, with the possibility that the needle might not even be there. However, thanks to the existence theorem, Ellis now knew that the needle was in there somewhere.

Ellis's idea was very similar to that of Diffie, Hellman and Merkle, except that he was several years ahead of them. However, nobody knew of Ellis's work because he was an employee of the British Government and therefore sworn to secrecy. By the end of 1969, Ellis appears to have reached the same impasse that the Stanford trio would reach in 1975. He had proved to himself that public-key cryptography (or non-secret encryption, as he called it) was possible, and he had developed the concept of separate public-keys and private-keys. He also knew that he needed to find a special one-way function, one that could be reversed if the receiver had access to a piece of special information. Unfortunately, Ellis was not a mathematician. He experimented with a few mathematical functions, but he soon realised that he would be unable to progress any further on his own.

At this point Ellis revealed his breakthrough to his bosses. Their reactions are still classified material, but in an interview with Richard Walton he was prepared to paraphrase for me the various memoranda that were exchanged. Sitting with his briefcase on his lap, the lid shielding the papers from my view, Walton flicked through the documents:

> I can't show you the papers that I have in here because they still have naughty words like TOP SECRET stamped all over them. Essentially, James's idea goes to the top man, who farms it out, in the way that top men do, so that the experts can have a look at it. They state that what James is saying is perfectly true. In other words, they can't write this man off as a crank. At the same time they can't think of a way of implementing his idea in practice. And so they're impressed by James's ingenuity, but uncertain as to how to take advantage of it.

For the next three years, GCHQ's brightest minds struggled to find a one-way function that satisfied Ellis's requirements, but nothing emerged. Then, in September 1973, a new mathematician joined the team. Clifford Cocks had recently graduated from Cambridge University, where he had specialised in number theory, one of the purest forms of mathematics. When he joined GCHQ he knew very little about encryption and the shadowy world of military and diplomatic communication, so he was assigned a mentor, Nick Patterson, who guided him through his first few weeks at GCHQ.

After about six weeks Patterson told Cocks about 'a really whacky idea'. He outlined Ellis's theory for public-key cryptography, and explained that nobody had yet been able to find a mathematical function that fitted the bill. Patterson was telling Cocks because this was the most titillating cryptographic idea around, not because he expected him to try to solve it. However, as Cocks explains, later that day he set

Clifford Cocks

to work: 'There was nothing particular happening, and so I thought I would think about the idea. Because I had been working in number theory, it was natural to think about one-way functions, something you could do but not undo. Prime numbers and factoring was a natural candidate, and that became my starting point.' Cocks was beginning to formulate what would later be known as the RSA asymmetric cipher. Rivest, Shamir and Adleman discovered their formula for public-key cryptography in 1977, but four years earlier the young Cambridge graduate was going through exactly the same thought processes. Cocks recalls: 'From start to finish, it took me no more than half an hour. I was quite pleased with myself. I thought, "Ooh, that's nice. I've been given a problem, and I've solved it."'

Cocks did not fully appreciate the significance of his discovery. He was unaware that GCHQ's brightest minds had been struggling with the problem for three years, and had no idea that he had made one of the most important cryptographic breakthroughs of the century. Cocks's naivety may have been part of the reason for his success, allowing him to attack the problem with confidence rather than timidly prodding at it. Cocks told his mentor about his discovery, and it was Patterson who then reported it to the management. Cocks was quite diffident and very much still a rookie, whereas Patterson fully appreciated the context of the problem and was more capable of addressing the technical questions that would inevitably arise. Soon complete strangers started approaching Cocks, the wonderkid, and began to congratulate him. One of the strangers was James Ellis, keen to meet the man who had turned his dream into a reality. Because Cocks still did not understand the enormity of his achievement, the details of this meeting did not make a great impact on him, so that now, over two decades later, he has no memory of Ellis's reaction.

When Cocks did eventually realise what he had done, it struck him that his discovery might have disappointed G.H. Hardy, one of the great English mathematicians of the early part of the century. In his *The Mathematician's Apology*, written in 1940, Hardy had proudly stated: 'Real mathematics has no effects on war. No one has yet discovered any warlike purpose to be served by the theory of numbers.' Real mathematics means pure mathematics, such as the number theory that was at the heart of Cocks's work. Cocks had proved Hardy wrong. The intricacies of number theory could now be used to help generals plan their battles in complete secrecy. Because his work had implications for military communications, Cocks, like Ellis, was forbidden from telling anybody outside GCHQ about what he had done. Working at a top-secret government establishment meant that he could tell neither his parents nor his former colleagues at Cambridge University. The only person he could tell was his wife, Gill, since she was also employed at GCHQ.

In due course, the two Britons had to sit and watch as their discoveries were rediscovered by Diffie, Hellman, Merkle, Rivest, Shamir and Adleman over the next three years. The scientific press reported the breakthroughs at Stanford and MIT, and the researchers who had been allowed to publish their work in the scientific journals became famous within the community of cryptographers. A quick look on the Internet with a search engine turns up 15 Web pages mentioning Clifford Cocks, compared to 1,382 pages that mention Whitfield Diffie. Cocks's attitude is admirably restrained: 'You don't get involved in this business for public recognition.'

When the teams at MIT and Stanford filed for patents, one might have expected GCHQ's bosses to go public and block the American application, but instead they remained silent. They were not far-sighted enough to foresee the digital revolution and the potential of public-key cryptography. By the early 1980s they were beginning to regret their decision, as developments in computers and the embryonic Internet made it clear that RSA would be an enormously successful commercial product. In 1996, RSA Data Security, Inc., the company responsible for RSA products, was sold for $200 million. It is currently valued at $2.5 billion.

Although the work at GCHQ was still classified, there was one other organisation that was aware of the breakthroughs that had been achieved in Britain. By the early 1980s the National Security Agency (NSA), the American equivalent of GCHQ, knew about the work of Ellis and Cocks, and it was via the NSA that Whitfield Diffie heard a rumour about the British discoveries. In September 1982, Diffie decided to see if there was any truth in the rumour, and he and his wife went to Cheltenham to talk to James Ellis face to face. They met at a local pub, and very quickly Mary Diffie was struck by Ellis's remarkable character:

> We sat around talking, and I suddenly became aware that this was the most wonderful person you could possibly imagine. The breadth of his mathematical knowledge is not something I could confidently discuss, but he was a true gentleman, immensely modest, a person with great generosity of spirit and gentility. When I say gentility, I don't mean old-fashioned and musty. This man was a *chevalier*. He was a good man, a truly good man. He was a gentle spirit.

Diffie and Ellis discussed various topics, from archaeology to how rats in the barrel improve the taste of cider, but whenever the conversation drifted towards cryptography, Ellis changed the subject. At the end of Diffie's visit, as he was ready to drive away, he could no longer resist directly asking Ellis the question that was really on his mind: 'Tell me about how you invented public-key cryptography?' There was a long pause. Ellis eventually whispered, 'Well, I don't know how much I should say. Let me just say that you people did much more with it than we did.'

GCHQ were the first to discover public-key cryptography, but this should not diminish the achievements of the academics who rediscovered it. It was the academics who were the first to realise the potential of public-key encryption, and it was they who drove its implementation. Furthermore, were it not for the Americans, it is quite possible that GCHQ would never have revealed their work, thus blocking a form of encryption that has enabled the digital revolution to reach its full potential. Finally, the discovery by the academics was wholly independent of GCHQ's discovery, and on an intellectual par with it. The academic environment is completely isolated from the top-secret domain of classified research, and academics do not have access to the tools and secret knowledge that may be hidden in the classified world. On the other hand, government researchers always have access to the

THE MANCHESTER GRAMMAR SCHOOL CONNECTION

Whitfield Diffie and James Ellis proposed the asymmetric cipher as a solution to the key-distribution problem, but it is not the only solution. Another approach, developed by Martin Hellman, allows Alice and Bob to securely exchange a key which can then be used to encrypt a message using a conventional encryption system. The system is commonly referred to as Diffie–Hellman–Merkle key exchange. However, this system was independently developed by GCHQ at roughly the same time as Martin Hellman made his breakthrough.

The GCHQ researcher who also developed Diffie–Hellman–Merkle key exchange was Malcolm Williamson, who, like James Ellis and Clifford Cocks, had his work classified. Williamson went to Manchester Grammar School with Cocks, and this photo shows the two of them in 1968 as part of the team representing Britain in the Mathematical Olympiad. Williamson is second from the left, and Cocks is on the extreme right. Having attended the same school, they both went to Cambridge to read mathematics. They then went their separate ways for a while, before working together at GCHQ in the 1970s.

academic literature. One might think of this flow of information in terms of a one-way function – information flows freely in one direction, but it is forbidden to send information in the opposite direction.

When Diffie told Hellman about his meeting with Ellis, Hellman's attitude was that the discoveries of the academics should be a footnote in the history of classified research, and that the discoveries at GCHQ should be a footnote in the history of academic research. However, at that stage nobody except GCHQ, NSA, Diffie and Hellman knew about the classified research, so it could not even be considered as a footnote.

By the mid-1980s, the mood at GCHQ was changing, and the management considered publicly announcing the British discovery of public-key cryptography. The mathematics of public-key cryptography was already well established in the public domain, and there seemed to be no reason to remain secretive. In fact, there would be distinct benefits if the British revealed their groundbreaking work on public-key cryptography. As Richard Walton recalls:

> We flirted with the idea of coming clean in 1984. We began to see advantages for GCHQ being more publicly acknowledged. It was a time when the government security market was expanding beyond the traditional military and diplomatic customer, and we needed to capture the confidence of those who did not traditionally deal with us. We were in the middle of Thatcherism, and we were trying to counter a sort of 'government is bad, private is good' ethos. So, we had the intention of publishing a paper, but that idea was scuppered by that blighter Peter Wright, who wrote *Spycatcher*. We were just warming up senior management to approve this release, when there was all this hoo-ha about *Spycatcher*. Then the order of the day was 'heads down, hats on'.

Peter Wright was a retired British intelligence officer, and the publication of *Spycatcher*, his memoirs, was a source of great embarrassment to the British Government. It would be another thirteen years before GCHQ reconsidered the possibility of going public. In 1997 Clifford Cocks completed some important unclassified work on RSA, which would have been of interest to the wider community, and which would not be a security risk if it were to be published. As a result, he was asked to present a paper at a conference organised by the Institute of Mathematics and its Applications to be held in Cirencester. The room would be full of cryptography experts. A handful of them would know that Cocks, who would be talking about just one aspect of RSA, was actually its unsung inventor. There was a risk that somebody might ask an embarrassing question, such as 'Did you invent RSA?' If such a question arose, what was Cocks supposed to do? According to GCHQ policy he would have to deny his role in the development of RSA, thus forcing him to lie about an issue that was totally innocuous. The situation was clearly ridiculous, and GCHQ decided that it was time to change its policy. Cocks was given permission to begin his talk by presenting a brief history of GCHQ's contribution to public-key cryptography.

On 18 December 1997 Cocks delivered his talk. After almost three decades of secrecy, Ellis and Cocks received the acknowledgement they deserved. Sadly, James Ellis had died just one month earlier, on 25 November 1997, at the age of seventy-three. Ellis joined the list of British cipher experts whose contributions would never be recognised during their lifetimes. Charles Babbage's breaking of the Vigenère cipher was never revealed during his lifetime, because it was thought that his work would be invaluable to British forces in the Crimea. Instead, credit for the work went to Friedrich Kasiski. Similarly, Alan Turing's contribution to the war effort was unparalleled, yet government secrecy demanded that his work on Enigma could not be revealed.

In 1987 Ellis wrote a document, only recently declassified, in which he recorded his contribution to public-key cryptography, including his thoughts on the secrecy that so often surrounds cryptographic work:

> Cryptography is a most unusual science. Most professional scientists aim to be the first to publish their work, because it is through dissemination that the work realises its value. In contrast, the fullest value of cryptography is realised by minimising the information available to potential adversaries. Thus professional cryptographers normally work in closed communities to provide sufficient professional interaction to ensure quality while maintaining secrecy from outsiders. Revelation of these secrets is normally only sanctioned in the interests of historical accuracy after it has been demonstrated that no further benefit can be obtained from continued secrecy.

The Politics of Privacy

J UST AS WHITFIELD DIFFIE predicted in the early 1970s, we are now entering the Information Age, a post-industrial era in which information is a valuable commodity. The exchange of digital information has become an integral part of our society. Already, tens of millions of e-mails are sent each day, and electronic mail will soon become more popular than conventional mail. The Internet, still in its infancy, has provided the infrastructure for the digital marketplace, and e-commerce is thriving. Money is flowing through cyberspace, and it is estimated that every day half the world's Gross Domestic Product travels through the Society for Worldwide Interbank Financial Telecommunications (SWIFT) network. Democracies that favour referenda will begin to have on-line voting, and governments will increasingly use the Internet to help administer their countries, offering facilities such as on-line tax declarations.

Crucially, the success of the Information Age depends on the ability to protect information as it flows around the world, and this relies on the power of cryptography. Encryption can be seen as providing the locks and keys of the Information Age. For two thousand years encryption has been of importance only to governments and the military, but today it also has a role to play in facilitating business, and tomorrow ordinary people will rely on cryptography in order to protect their privacy. Fortunately, just as the Information Age is taking off, we have access to extraordinarily strong encryption. The development of public-key cryptography, particularly the RSA cipher, has given today's cryptographers a clear advantage in their continual power struggle against cryptanalysts. If the value of N is large enough, then finding p and q takes Eve an unreasonable amount of time, and RSA encryption is therefore effectively unbreakable. Most important of all, public-key cryptography is not weakened by any key-distribution problems. In short, RSA guarantees almost unbreakable locks for our most precious pieces of information.

However, as with every technology, there is a dark side to encryption. As well as protecting the communications of law-abiding citizens, encryption also protects the communications of criminals and terrorists. Currently, police forces use wire-tapping as a way of gathering evidence to counter organised crime and terrorism, but this would be impossible if criminals used unbreakable ciphers.

In the twenty-first century, the fundamental dilemma for cryptography is to find a way of allowing the public and businesses to use encryption in order to exploit the benefits of the Information Age without allowing criminals to abuse encryption, avoid wire-taps, and evade arrest. There is currently an active and vigorous debate about the best way forward, and much of the discussion has been inspired by the story of Phil Zimmermann, an American cryptographer whose attempts to encourage the widespread use of strong encryption have panicked America's security experts, threatened the effectiveness of the billion-dollar National Security Agency, and made him the subject of a government inquiry and a grand-jury investigation.

In the late 1980s Zimmermann, who had long been a political activist, began to focus his attentions on the digital revolution and the necessity for encryption:

> Cryptography used to be an obscure science, of little relevance to everyday life. Historically, it always had a special role in military and diplomatic communications. But in the Information Age, cryptography is about political power, and in particular, about the power relationship between a government and its people. It is about the right to privacy, freedom of speech, freedom of political association, freedom of the press, freedom from unreasonable search and seizure, freedom to be left alone.

These views might seem paranoid, but according to Zimmermann there is a fundamental difference between traditional and digital communication which has important implications for security:

Phil Zimmermann

In the past, if the government wanted to violate the privacy of ordinary citizens, it had to expend a certain amount of effort to intercept and steam open and read paper mail, or listen to and possibly transcribe spoken telephone conversations. This is analogous to catching fish with a hook and a line, one fish at a time. Fortunately for freedom and democracy, this kind of labour-intensive monitoring is not practical on a large scale. Today, electronic mail is gradually replacing conventional paper mail, and is soon to be the norm for everyone, not the novelty it is today. Unlike paper mail, e-mail messages are just too easy to intercept and scan for interesting keywords. This can be done easily, routinely, automatically, and undetectably on a grand scale. This is analogous to driftnet fishing — making a quantitative and qualitative Orwellian difference to the health of democracy.

The difference between ordinary and digital mail can be illustrated by imagining that Alice wants to send out invitations to her birthday party, and that Eve, who has not been invited, wants to know the time and place of the party. If Alice uses the traditional method of posting letters, then it is very difficult for Eve to intercept one of the invitations. To start with, Eve does not know where Alice's invitations entered the postal system, because Alice could use any postbox in the city. Her only hope for intercepting one of the invitations is to somehow identify the address of one of Alice's friends, and infiltrate the local sorting office. She then has to check each and every letter manually. If she does manage to find a letter from Alice, she will have to steam it open in order to get the information she wants, and then return it to its original condition to avoid any suspicion of tampering.

In comparison, Eve's task is made considerably easier if Alice sends her invitations by e-mail. As the messages leave Alice's computer, they will go to a local server, a main entry point to the Internet; if Eve is clever enough she can hack into that local server without leaving her home. The invitations will carry Alice's e-mail address, and it would be a trivial matter to set up an electronic filter that looks for e-mails containing this address. Once an invitation has been found, there is no envelope to open, and so no problem in reading it. Furthermore, the invitation can be sent on its way without it showing any sign of having been intercepted. Alice would be oblivious to what was going on. However, there is a way to prevent Eve from reading Alice's e-mails, namely encryption.

More than a hundred million e-mails are sent around the world each day, and they are all vulnerable to interception. Digital technology has aided communication, but it has also given rise to the possibility of those communications being monitored. According to Zimmermann, cryptographers have a duty to encourage the use of encryption and thereby protect the privacy of the individual:

> A future government could inherit a technology infrastructure that's optimized for surveillance, where they can watch the movements of their political opposition, every financial transaction, every communication, every bit of e-mail, every phone call. Everything could be filtered and scanned and automatically recognized by voice recognition technology and transcribed. It's time for cryptography to step out of the shadows of spies and the military, and step into the sunshine and be embraced by the rest of us.

In theory, when RSA was invented in 1977 it offered an antidote to the Big Brother scenario because individuals were able to create their own public- and private-keys, and thereafter send and receive perfectly secure messages. However, in practice there was a major problem because the actual process of RSA encryption required substantial computing resources. Consequently, in the 1980s it was only governments, the military and large businesses that owned computers powerful enough to run the RSA encryption system. Not surprisingly, RSA Data Security, Inc., the company set up to commercialise RSA, developed their encryption products with only these markets in mind.

In contrast, Zimmermann believed that everybody deserved the right to the privacy that was offered by RSA encryption, and he directed his political zeal towards developing an RSA encryption product for the masses. He intended to draw upon his background in computer science to design a product with economy and efficiency in mind, thus not overloading the capacity of an ordinary personal computer. He also wanted his version of RSA to have a particularly friendly interface so that the user did not have to be an expert in cryptography to operate it. He called his project Pretty Good Privacy, or PGP for short. The name was inspired by Ralph's Pretty Good Groceries, a sponsor of Garrison Keillor's *Prairie Home Companion*, one of Zimmermann's favourite radio shows.

During the late 1980s, working from his home in Boulder, Colorado, Zimmermann gradually pieced together his scrambling software package. His main goal was to speed up RSA encryption. Ordinarily, if Alice wants to use RSA to encrypt a message to Bob, she looks up his public-key and then applies RSA's one-way function to the message. Conversely, Bob decrypts the ciphertext by using his private-key to reverse RSA's one-way function. Both processes require considerable mathematical manipulation, so encryption and decryption can, if the message is long, take several minutes on a personal computer. If Alice is sending a hundred messages a day she cannot afford to spend several minutes encrypting each one. To speed up encryption and decryption, Zimmermann employed a neat trick that used asymmetric RSA encryption in tandem with old-fashioned symmetric encryption. Traditional symmetric encryption can be just as secure as asymmetric encryption, and it is much quicker to perform, but symmetric encryption suffers from the problem of having to distribute the key, which has to be securely transported from the sender to the receiver. This is where RSA comes to the rescue, because RSA can be used to encrypt the symmetric key.

Zimmermann pictured the following scenario. If Alice wants to send an encrypted message to Bob, she begins by encrypting it with a symmetric cipher. Zimmermann suggested using a cipher known as IDEA. The precise details of IDEA are not important; the main point is that, to encrypt with IDEA, Alice needs to choose a key, but for Bob to decrypt the message Alice somehow has to get the key to Bob. Alice overcomes this problem by looking up Bob's RSA public-key, and then uses it to encrypt the IDEA key. So, Alice ends up sending two things to Bob: the message encrypted with the symmetric IDEA cipher and the IDEA key encrypted with the asymmetric RSA cipher. At the other end, Bob uses his RSA private-key to decrypt the IDEA key, and then uses the IDEA key to decrypt the message. This might seem convoluted, but the advantage is that the message, which might contain a large amount of information, is being encrypted with a quick symmetric cipher, and only the symmetric IDEA key, which consists of a relatively small amount of information, is being encrypted with a slow asymmetric cipher. Zimmermann planned to have this combination of RSA and IDEA within the PGP product, while the user-friendly interface would mean that neither Alice nor Bob would have to get involved in the nuts and bolts of what was going on.

By the summer of 1991, Zimmermann was well on the way to turning PGP into a polished product. Only one problem remained. The U.S. Senate's 1991 omnibus anti-crime bill contained the following clause: 'It is the sense of Congress that providers of electronic communications services and manufacturers of electronic communications service equipment shall ensure that communications systems permit the government to obtain the plaintext contents of voice, data, and other communications when appropriately authorized by law.' The Senate was concerned that developments in digital technology, such as cellular telephones, might prevent law enforcers from performing effective wire-taps.

However, as well as forcing companies to guarantee the possibility of wire-tapping, the bill also seemed to threaten all forms of secure encryption.

A concerted effort by RSA Data Security, Inc., the communications industry and civil liberty groups forced the clause to be dropped, but the consensus was that this was only a temporary reprieve. Zimmermann was fearful that sooner or later the U.S. Government would again try to bring in legislation that would effectively outlaw encryption, including PGP. He had always intended to sell PGP, but now he reconsidered his options. Rather than waiting and risk PGP being banned by the government, he decided that it was more important for it to be available to everybody before it was too late. In June 1991 he took the drastic step of asking a friend to post PGP on a Usenet bulletin board. PGP is just a piece of software, so from the bulletin board it could be downloaded by anyone for free. PGP was now loose on the Internet.

Initially, PGP caused a buzz only among aficionados of cryptography. Later it was downloaded by a wider range of Internet enthusiasts. Next, computer magazines ran brief reports and then full-page articles on the PGP phenomenon. Gradually PGP began to permeate to the most remote corners of the digital community. For example, human rights groups around the world started to use PGP to encrypt their documents, to prevent the information from falling into the hands of the regimes that were being accused of human-rights abuses. Zimmermann began to receive e-mails praising him for his creation. 'There are resistance groups in Burma', says Zimmermann, 'who are using it in jungle training camps. They've said that it's helped morale there, because before PGP was introduced, captured documents would lead to the arrest, torture and execution of entire families.' In 1991, on the day that Boris Yeltsin was shelling Moscow's Parliament building, Zimmermann received this e-mail via someone in Latvia: 'Phil, I wish you to know: let it never be, but if dictatorship takes over Russia, your PGP is widespread from Baltic to Far East now and will help democratic people if necessary. Thanks.'

While Zimmermann was gaining fans around the world, back home in America he was less popular. In February 1993 two government investigators paid Zimmermann a visit on the grounds that the U.S. Government included encryption software within its definition of munitions, along with missiles, mortars and machine guns. Therefore PGP could not be exported without a licence from the State Department. In other words, Zimmermann was accused of being an arms dealer because he had exported PGP via the Internet. Over the next three years Zimmermann became the subject of a grand-jury investigation and found himself pursued by the FBI.

The investigation into Phil Zimmermann and PGP ignited a debate about the positive and negative effects of encryption in the Information Age. The spread of PGP galvanised cryptographers, politicians, civil libertarians and law enforcers into thinking about the implications of widespread encryption. There were those, like Zimmermann, who believed that the widespread use of secure encryption would be a boon to society, providing individuals with privacy for their digital communications. Ranged against them were those who believed that encryption was a threat to society, because criminals and terrorists would be able to communicate in secret, safe from police wire-taps.

The debate continued throughout the 1990s, and is currently as contentious as ever. The fundamental question is whether or not governments should legislate against cryptography. Cryptographic freedom would allow everyone, including criminals, to be confident that their e-mails are secure. On the other hand, restricting the use of cryptography would allow the police to spy on criminals, but it might also allow the police and everybody else to spy on the average citizen. Ultimately, we, through the governments we elect, will decide the future role of cryptography.

The case against the widespread use of encryption, as argued by law enforcers, centres on the desire to maintain the status quo. For decades, police around the world have conducted legal wire-taps in order to catch criminals. For example, in America in 1918, wire-taps were used to counteract the presence of wartime spies, and in the 1920s they proved especially effective in convicting bootleggers. The view that wire-tapping was a necessary tool of law enforcement became firmly established in the late 1960s, when the FBI realised that organised crime was becoming a growing threat to the nation. Law enforcers were having great difficulty convicting suspects because the mob made threats against anyone who might consider testifying against them, and there was also the code of *omertà*, or silence. The police felt that their only hope was to gather evidence via wire-taps, and the Supreme Court was sympathetic to this argument. In 1967 it ruled that the police could employ wire-taps as long as they had first obtained a court authorisation.

Over thirty years later, the FBI still maintains that 'court ordered wire-tapping is the single most effective investigative technique used by law enforcement to combat illegal drugs, terrorism, violent crime, espionage, and organized crime'. However, police wire-taps would be useless if criminals had access to encryption. A phone call made over a digital line is nothing more than a stream of numbers, and can be encrypted according to the same techniques used to encrypt e-mails. PGPfone, for example, is one of several products capable of encrypting voice communications made over the Internet.

Law enforcers argue that effective wire-tapping is necessary to maintain law and order, and that encryption should be restricted so that they can continue with their interceptions. The police have already encountered criminals using strong encryption to protect themselves. A German legal expert said that 'hot businesses such as the arms and drug trades are no longer done by phone, but are being settled in encrypted form on the worldwide data networks'. A White House official indicated a similarly worrying trend in America, claiming that 'organized crime members are some of the most advanced users of computer systems and of strong encryption'. For instance, the Cali cartel arranges its drug deals via encrypted communications. Law enforcers fear that the Internet coupled with cryptography will help criminals to communicate and coordinate their efforts, and they are particularly concerned about the so-called Four Horsemen of the Infocalypse – drug dealers, organised crime, terrorists and paedophiles – the illegal groups who will benefit most from encryption.

As well as encrypting communications, criminals and terrorists are also encrypting their plans and records, hindering the recovery of evidence. The Aum Shinrikyo sect, responsible for the gas attacks on the Tokyo subway in 1995, were found to have encrypted some of their documents using RSA. Ramsey Yousef, one of the terrorists involved in the World Trade Center bombing, kept plans for future terrorist acts encrypted on his laptop. Besides international terrorist organisations, more run-of-the-mill criminals also benefit from encryption. An illegal gambling syndicate in America, for example, encrypted its accounts for four years. A study by Dorothy Denning and William Baugh commissioned in 1997 by the National Strategy Information Center's U.S. Working Group on Organized Crime estimated that there were five hundred criminal cases worldwide involving encryption and predicted that this number would roughly double each year.

In addition to domestic policing, there are also issues of national security. America's National Security Agency is responsible for gathering intelligence on the nation's enemies by deciphering their communications. The NSA operates a world-wide network of listening stations, in cooperation with Britain, Australia, Canada and New Zealand, who all gather and share information. The network includes sites such as the Menwith Hill Signals Intelligence Base in Yorkshire, the world's largest spy station. Part of Menwith Hill's work involves the Echelon system, which is capable of scanning e-mails, faxes, telexes and telephone calls, searching for particular words. Echelon operates according to a dictionary of suspicious words, such as 'Hezbollah', 'assassin' and 'Clinton', and the system is smart enough to recognise these words in real time. Echelon can earmark questionable messages for further examination, enabling it to monitor communications from particular political groups or terrorist organisations. However, Echelon would effectively be useless if all messages were strongly encrypted. Each of the nations participating in Echelon would lose valuable intelligence on political plotting and terrorist attacks.

On the other side of the debate are the civil libertarians, including groups such as the Center for Democracy and Technology and the Electronic Frontier Foundation. The pro-encryption case is based on the belief that privacy is a fundamental human right, as recognised by Article 12 of the Universal Declaration of Human Rights: 'No one shall be subjected to arbitrary interference with his privacy, family, home or correspondence, nor to attacks upon his honour and reputation. Everyone has the right to the protection of the law against such interference or attacks.'

Civil libertarians argue that the widespread use of encryption is essential for guaranteeing the right to privacy. Otherwise, they fear that the advent of digital technology, which makes monitoring so much easier, will herald a new era of wire-tapping and that abuses will inevitably follow. In the past, governments have frequently used their power in order to conduct wire-taps on innocent citizens. Presidents Lyndon B. Johnson and Richard Nixon were guilty of unjustified wire-taps, and President John F. Kennedy conducted dubious wire-taps in the first month of his presidency. In the run-up to a bill concerning Dominican sugar imports, Kennedy asked for wire-taps to be placed on several congressmen. His justification was that he believed that they were being bribed, a seemingly valid national-security concern. However, no evidence of bribery was ever found, and the wire-taps merely provided Kennedy with valuable political information which helped the administration to win the bill.

One of the best-known victims of continuous unjustified wire-tapping was Martin Luther King Jr, whose telephone conversations were monitored for several years. For example, in 1963 the FBI obtained information on King via a wire-tap and fed it to Senator James Eastland in order to help him in debates on a civil-rights bill. More generally, the FBI gathered details about King's personal life which were used to discredit him. Recordings of King telling bawdy stories were sent to his wife and played in front of President Johnson. Then, following King's award of the Nobel Peace Prize in 1964, embarrassing details about King's life were passed to any organisation that was considering conferring an honour upon him.

Other governments are equally guilty of abusing wire-taps. The Commission Nationale de Contrôle des Interceptions de Securité estimates that there are roughly 100,000 illegal wire-taps conducted in France each year. Possibly the greatest infringement of everybody's privacy is the international Echelon programme. Echelon does not have to justify its interceptions, and it does not focus on particular individuals. Instead, it indiscriminately harvests information, using receivers that detect the telecommunications that bounce off satellites. If Alice sends a harmless transatlantic message to Bob, then it will certainly be intercepted by Echelon, and if the message happens to contain a few words that appear in the Echelon dictionary, then it would be earmarked for further examination, alongside messages from extreme political groups and terrorist gangs. Whereas law enforcers argue that encryption should be banned because it would make Echelon ineffective, the civil libertarians argue that encryption is necessary exactly because it would make Echelon ineffective.

When law enforcers argue that strong encryption will reduce criminal convictions, civil libertarians reply that the issue of privacy is more important. In any case, civil libertarians insist that encryption would not be an enormous barrier to law enforcement because wire-taps are not a crucial element in most cases. For example, in America in 1994 there were roughly a thousand court-sanctioned wire-taps, compared with a quarter of a million federal cases.

Not surprisingly, among the advocates of cryptographic freedom are some of the inventors of public-key cryptography. Whitfield Diffie states that individuals have enjoyed complete privacy for most of history:

> In the 1790s, when the Bill of Rights was ratified, any two people could have a private conversation – with a certainty no one in the world enjoys today – by walking a few meters down the road and looking to see no one was hiding in the bushes. There were no recording devices, parabolic microphones, or laser interferometers bouncing off their eyeglasses. You will note that civilization survived. Many of us regard that period as a golden age in American political culture.

Ron Rivest, one of the inventors of RSA, thinks that restricting cryptography would be foolhardy:

> It is poor policy to clamp down indiscriminately on a technology just because some criminals might be able to use it to their advantage. For example, any U.S. citizen can freely buy a pair of gloves, even though a burglar might use them to ransack a house without leaving fingerprints.

Cryptography is a data-protection technology, just as gloves are a hand-protection technology. Cryptography protects data from hackers, corporate spies, and con artists, whereas gloves protect hands from cuts, scrapes, heat, cold, and infection. The former can frustrate FBI wiretapping, and the latter can thwart FBI fingerprint analysis. Cryptography and gloves are both dirt-cheap and widely available. In fact, you can download good cryptographic software from the Internet for less than the price of a good pair of gloves.

Possibly the greatest allies of the civil-libertarian cause are the big corporations. Internet commerce is still in its infancy, but sales are growing rapidly, with retailers of books, music CDs and computer software leading the way, and with supermarkets, travel companies and other businesses following in their wake. In 1998 a million Britons used the Internet to buy products worth £400 million, a figure that quadrupled in 1999. In just a few years from now Internet commerce could dominate the marketplace, but only if businesses can address the issues of security and trust. A business must be able to guarantee the privacy and security of financial transactions, and the only way to do this is to employ strong encryption.

At the moment, a purchase on the Internet can be secured by public-key cryptography. Alice visits a company's Website and selects an item. Next, she fills in an order form which asks her for her name, address and credit-card details. Alice then uses the company's public-key to encrypt the order form. The encrypted order form is transmitted to the company, who are the only people able to decrypt it, because only they have the private-key necessary for decryption. All of this is done automatically by Alice's browser (e.g. Netscape or Explorer) in conjunction with the company's computer. The transaction is safe because of encryption.

Businesses also desire strong encryption for another reason. Corporations store vast amounts of information on computer databases, including product descriptions, customer details and business accounts. Naturally, corporations want to protect this information from hackers who might infiltrate the computer and steal the information. This protection can be achieved by encrypting stored information to make it accessible only to employees who have the decryption key.

To summarise the situation, it is clear that the debate is between two camps: civil libertarians and businesses are in favour of strong encryption, while law enforcers are in favour of severe restrictions. In general, popular opinion appears to be swinging behind the pro-encryption alliance, who have been helped by a sympathetic media and a couple of Hollywood films. In early 1998, *Mercury Rising* told the story of a new, supposedly unbreakable NSA cipher which is inadvertently deciphered by a nine-year-old autistic savant. Alec Baldwin, an NSA agent, sets out to assassinate the boy, who is perceived as a threat to national security. Luckily, the boy has Bruce Willis to protect him. Also in 1998, Hollywood released *Enemy of the State*, which dealt with an NSA plot to murder a politician who supports a bill in favour of strong encryption. The politician is killed, but a lawyer played by Will Smith and an NSA rebel played by Gene Hackman eventually bring the NSA assassins to justice. Both films depict the NSA as more sinister than the CIA, and in many ways the NSA has taken over the role of establishment menace.

While the pro-encryption lobby argues for cryptographic freedom, and the anti-encryption lobby for cryptographic restrictions, there is a 'third way' that might offer a compromise. Over the last decade, cryptographers and policy-makers have been investigating the pros and cons of a scheme known as *key escrow*. The term 'escrow' usually relates to an arrangement in which someone gives a sum of money to a third party, who can then deliver the money to a second party under certain circumstances. For example, a tenant might lodge a deposit with a solicitor, who can then deliver it to a landlord in the event of damage to the property. In terms of cryptography, escrow means that Alice would give a copy of her private-key to an escrow agent — an independent, reliable middleman who is empowered to deliver the private-key to the police if ever there was sufficient evidence to suggest that Alice was involved in crime.

The most famous trial of cryptographic key escrow was the American Escrowed Encryption Standard, adopted in 1994. The aim was to encourage the adoption of two encryption systems, called *clipper* and *capstone*, to be used for telephone communication and computer communication, respectively. To use clipper encryption, Alice would buy a phone with a pre-installed chip which would hold her secret private-key information. At the very moment she bought the clipper phone, a copy of the private-key in the chip would be split into two halves, and each half would be sent to two separate Federal authorities for storage. The U.S. Government argued that Alice would have access to secure encryption, and her privacy would be broken only if law enforcers could persuade both Federal authorities that there was a case for obtaining her escrowed private-key.

The U.S. Government employed clipper and capstone for its own communications, and made it obligatory for companies involved in government business to adopt the American Escrowed Encryption Standard. Other businesses and individuals were free to use other forms of encryption, but the government hoped that clipper and cap-stone would gradually become the nation's favourite form of encryption. However, the policy did not work. The idea of key escrow won few supporters outside government. Civil libertarians did not like the idea of Federal authorities having possession of everybody's keys – they drew an analogy with real keys, and asked how people would feel if the government had the keys to all our houses. Cryptographic experts pointed out that just one crooked employee could undermine the whole system by selling escrowed keys to the highest bidder. And businesses were worried about confidentiality. For example, a European business in America might fear that its messages were being intercepted by American trade officials in an attempt to obtain secrets that might give American rivals a competitive edge.

Despite the failure of clipper and capstone, many governments remain convinced that key escrow can be made to work, as long as the keys are sufficiently well protected from criminals and as long as there are safeguards to reassure the public that the system is not open to government abuse. Louis J. Freeh, Director of the FBI, said in 1996:

> The law enforcement community fully supports a balanced encryption policy . . . Key
> escrow is not just the only solution; it is, in fact, a very good solution because it effectively
> balances fundamental societal concerns involving privacy, information security, electronic
> commerce, public safety, and national security.

Although the U.S. Government has backtracked on its escrow proposals, many suspect that it will attempt to reintroduce an alternative form of key escrow at some time in the future. Having witnessed the failure of optional escrow, governments might even consider compulsory escrow. Meanwhile, the pro-encryption lobby continues to argue against key escrow. Kenneth Neil Cukier, a technology journalist, has written that, 'The people involved in the crypto debate are all intelligent, honorable and pro-escrow, but they never possess more than two of these qualities at once.'

There are various other options that governments could choose to implement in order to try to balance the concerns of civil libertarians, business and law enforcement. It is far from clear which will be the preferred option, because at present cryptographic policy is in a state of flux. By the time you read this there will have been several more twists and turns in the debate on cryptographic policy.

Nobody can predict with certainty the shape of cryptographic policy ten years from now. Personally, I suspect that in the near future the pro-encryption lobby will initially win the argument, mainly because no country will want to have encryption laws that prohibit e-commerce. If this policy does turn out to be a mistake then the consequences would not necessarily lead to long-term disaster because it will always be possible to reverse the laws. If there were to be a series of terrorist atrocities, and law enforcers could show that wire-taps would have prevented them, then governments would rapidly gain sympathy for a policy of key escrow. All users of strong encryption would be forced to deposit their keys with a key-escrow agent, and thereafter anybody who sent an encrypted message with a non-escrowed key would be breaking the law. If the penalty for non-escrowed encryption were sufficiently severe, law enforcers could regain control. Later, if governments were to abuse the trust associated with a system of key escrow, the public would call for a return to cryptographic freedom, and the pendulum would swing back. In short, there is no reason why we cannot change our policy to suit the political, economic and social climate. The deciding factor will be whom the public fears most — the criminals or the government.

The Future of Cryptography

Back in 1993, Phil Zimmermann had become the subject of a grand-jury investigation. According to the FBI he had exported a munition because he was supplying hostile nations and terrorists with the tools they needed to protect themselves against eavesdropping by the U.S. Government. As the investigation dragged on, more and more cryptographers and civil libertarians rushed to support Zimmermann, establishing an international fund to finance his legal defence. At the same time, the kudos of being the subject of an FBI inquiry boosted the reputation of PGP, and Zimmermann's creation spread via the Internet even more quickly — after all, this was the encryption software that was so secure that it frightened the Feds.

Pretty Good Privacy had initially been released in haste, and as a result the product was not as polished as it could have been. Soon there was a clamour to develop a revised version of PGP, but clearly Zimmermann was not in a position to continue working on the product. Instead, software engineers in Europe began to rebuild PGP. In general, European attitudes towards encryption were, and still are, more liberal, and there would be no restrictions on exporting a European version of PGP around the world.

After three years the grand-jury investigation had still not brought Zimmermann to trial. The case was complicated by the nature of PGP and the way it had been distributed. If Zimmermann had loaded PGP onto a computer and then shipped it to a hostile regime, the case against him would have been straightforward because clearly he would have been guilty of exporting a complete working encryption system. Similarly, if he had exported a disk containing the PGP program, then the physical object could have been interpreted as a cryptographic device, and once again the case against Zimmermann would have been fairly solid. On the other hand, if he had printed the computer program and exported it as a book, the case against him would no longer be clear cut because he would then be considered to have exported knowledge rather than a cryptographic device. However, printed matter can easily be scanned electronically and the information can be fed directly into a computer, which means that a book is as dangerous as a disk. What actually occurred was that Zimmermann gave a copy of PGP to 'a friend', who simply installed it on an American computer, which happened to be connected to the Internet. After that, a hostile regime may or may not have downloaded it. Was Zimmermann really guilty of exporting PGP? Even today, the legal issues surrounding the Internet are subject to debate and interpretation. Back in the early 1990s the situation was vague in the extreme.

In 1996, after three years of investigation, the U.S. Attorney General's Office dropped its case against Zimmermann. The FBI realised that it was too late – PGP had escaped onto the Internet, and prosecuting Zimmermann would achieve nothing. There was the additional problem that Zimmermann was being supported by major institutions, such as the Massachusetts Institute of Technology Press, which had published PGP in a 600-page book. The book was being distributed around the world, so prosecuting Zimmermann would have meant prosecuting the MIT Press. The FBI was also reluctant to pursue a prosecution because there was a significant chance that Zimmermann would not be convicted. An FBI trial might achieve nothing more than an embarrassing constitutional debate about the right to privacy, thereby stirring up yet more public sympathy in favour of widespread encryption.

At last, PGP was a legitimate product and Zimmermann was a free man. The investigation had turned him into a cryptographic crusader, and every marketing manager in the world must have envied the notoriety and free publicity that the case gave to PGP. At the end of 1997 Zimmermann sold PGP to Network Associates and became one of their senior fellows. Although PGP is now sold to businesses, it is still freely available to individuals who do not intend to use it for any commercial purpose. In other words, individuals who merely wish to exercise their right to privacy can still download PGP from the Internet without paying for it.

If you would like to obtain a copy of PGP, there are many sites on the Internet that offer it, and you should be able to find them fairly easily. Probably the most reliable source is at http://www.pgpi.com/, the International PGP Home Page, from where you can download the American and international versions of PGP. At this point I would like to absolve myself of any responsibility – if you do choose to install PGP, it is up to you check that your computer is capable of running it, that the software is not infected with a virus, and so on. Also, you should check that you are in a country that permits the use of strong encryption. Finally, it is worth noting that towards the end of 1999 the U.S. Government showed signs of relaxing its restrictions on the export of PGP and other forms of strong encryption. Nevertheless, policies do change, so I would recommend downloading the international version of PGP, which has never suffered from export restrictions.

I still remember the Sunday afternoon when I first downloaded a copy of PGP from the Internet. Ever since, I have been able to guarantee my e-mails against being intercepted and read, because I can now encrypt sensitive material to Alice, Bob and anybody else who possesses PGP software. My laptop and its PGP software provide me with a level of security that is beyond the combined efforts of all the world's codebreaking establishments.

The invention of public-key cryptography and the political debate that surrounds the use of strong cryptography bring us up to the present day, and it is clear that the cryptographers are winning the information war. According to Phil Zimmermann, we live in a golden age of cryptography: 'It is now possible to make ciphers in modern cryptography that are really, really out of reach of all known forms of cryptanalysis. And I think it's going to stay that way.' Zimmermann's view is supported by William Crowell, Deputy Director of the NSA: 'If all the personal computers in the world – approximately 260 million computers – were to be put to work on a single PGP encrypted message, it would take on average an estimated 12 million times the age of the universe to break a single message.'

Previous experience, however, tells us that every so-called unbreakable cipher has sooner or later succumbed to cryptanalysis. The Vigenère cipher was called *le chiffre indéchiffrable*, but Babbage broke it; Enigma was considered invulnerable until the Allies revealed its weaknesses. So, are cryptanalysts on the verge of another breakthrough, or is Zimmermann right? Predicting future developments in any technology is always a precarious task, but with ciphers it is particularly risky. Not only do we have to guess which discoveries lie in the future, but we also have to guess which discoveries lie in the present. The tale of James Ellis and GCHQ warns us that there may already be remarkable breakthroughs hidden behind the veil of government secrecy.

One unclassified development already offers hope for secure encryption if or when RSA is cracked. In 1984, Charles Bennett, a research fellow at IBM's Thomas J. Watson Laboratories in New York, developed the idea of quantum cryptography, an encryption system that is absolutely unbreakable. Quantum cryptography is based on quantum physics, a theory that explains how the universe operates at the most fundamental level. In particular, Bennett's idea exploits an aspect of quantum physics known as Heisenberg's uncertainty principle, which states that it is impossible to measure something with perfect accuracy because the act of measurement alters the object being measured.

Charles Bennett

For example, in order to measure the length of my hand, I must be able to see it and therefore I must have a source of light, whether it is the sun or a light bulb. The waves of light stream onto my hand and are then reflected towards my eye. First, the wavelength of the light limits the accuracy of any length measurement. Worse still, the impact of light waves on my hand will actually change it, just like sea waves lapping against a cliff. As in the case of sea waves, the effect of the light waves is minuscule and is imperceptible at an everyday level. Hence, an engineer trying to measure a bolt to a high precision is limited by the quality of even the best measuring apparatus long before he runs into the limitations resulting from the uncertainty principle. In contrast, at the microscopic level, the uncertainty principle is a serious problem. At the scale of atoms, protons and electrons, inaccuracies in measurement can become comparable to the size of objects, and the impact of light can significantly alter the tiny particles being observed.

Bennett came up with the idea of sending messages using fundamental particles so tiny that if Eve tried to intercept or measure them then she would mismeasure and alter them. In short, it becomes impossible for Eve to accurately intercept a communication, and even if she attempts to do this then her impact on the communication will betray her presence to Alice and Bob, who will know that she is listening and will halt their correspondence.

You might wonder about the following problem: if Alice sends Bob a quantum cryptographic communication, and Eve cannot read it because of the uncertainty principle, then how can Bob read it? Isn't he also stymied by the uncertainty principle? The solution is that Bob needs to send a message back to Alice to confirm what he has received. Because Alice knows what she originally sent to Bob, this second message can be used to remove any ambiguity between Alice and Bob, while still leaving Eve in the dark. At the end of this double exchange Alice and Bob are in a position to enjoy absolutely secure communication.

The whole idea of quantum cryptography sounds preposterous, but in 1988 Bennett successfully demonstrated secure communication between two computers (Alice and Bob) across a distance of 30 cm. Long-distance messages are problematic, because the message is being conveyed by individual particles which are more likely to be corrupted the farther they have to travel. So, ever since Bennett's experiment, the challenge has been to build a quantum cryptographic system that operates over useful distances. Universities, companies and governments, including groups at Oxford University, the Defence Evaluation Research Agency at Malvern, the Los Alamos National Laboratory and British Telecom, are all pushing the limits of this technology. In 1995, researchers at the University of Geneva succeeded in implementing quantum cryptography across 23 km from Geneva to the town of Nyon.

Security experts are now wondering how long it will be before quantum cryptography becomes a practical technology. At the moment there is no advantage in having quantum cryptography, because the RSA cipher already gives us access to effectively unbreakable encryption. However, if a codebreaker found a flaw in RSA then quantum cryptography would become a necessity. So the race is on. The Swiss experiment already demonstrates that it would be feasible to build a system that permits secure communication between financial institutions within a single city. Indeed, it is currently possible to build a quantum cryptography link between the White House and the Pentagon. Perhaps there already is one.

Quantum cryptography would mark the end of the battle between codemakers and codebreakers, the codemakers emerging victorious. Quantum cryptography is an unbreakable system of encryption. This may seem a rather exaggerated assertion, particularly in the light of previous similar claims. At different times over the last two thousand years cryptographers have believed that the monoalphabetic cipher, the polyalphabetic cipher and machine ciphers such as Enigma were all unbreakable. In each of these cases the cryptographers were eventually proved wrong because their claims were based merely on the fact that the complexity of the ciphers outstripped the ingenuity and technology of cryptanalysts at one point in history. With hindsight, we can see that the cryptanalysts would inevitably figure out a way of breaking each cipher, or developing technology that would break it for them.

However, the claim that quantum cryptography is secure is qualitatively different from all previous claims. Quantum cryptography is not just effectively unbreakable, it is absolutely unbreakable. Quantum theory, the most successful theory in the history of physics, means that it is impossible for Eve to intercept accurately any communication between Alice and Bob. Eve cannot even attempt to intercept anything without Alice and Bob being warned of her eavesdropping. Indeed, if a message protected by quantum cryptography were ever to be deciphered, it would mean that quantum theory is flawed, which would have devastating implications for physicists – they would be forced to reconsider their understanding of how the universe operates at the most fundamental level.

If quantum cryptography systems can be engineered to operate over long distances, the evolution of ciphers will stop. The quest for privacy will have come to an end. The technology will be available to guarantee secure communications. The only question remaining would be whether or not governments would allow us to use the technology.

THE MINI CIPHER CHALLENGE

When I published my first book on cryptography, *The Code Book*, in September 1999, it included a Cipher Challenge. This was a series of ten encrypted messages with a prize of £10,000 for the first person to crack all of them. In this book I thought that I would offer a somewhat less serious Mini Cipher Challenge, without a prize but still an opportunity for readers to test their codebreaking skills.

The Mini Cipher Challenge contains just five cryptograms, based partly on stages in the original challenge. Each cryptogram is supposed to be tougher than the previous one, but please move on if you get stuck. I do not expect you to crack all five stages, but I hope you will derive some satisfaction from deciphering perhaps just one or two of the cryptograms.

Please note that the solutions to the encrypted texts are not printed anywhere, so the only way for you to crack the message is to use your ingenuity and determination. The methods for analysing each cryptogram are outlined in chapters 1 and 2 of this book. Good luck, and happy cracking!

Cryptogram 1: Caesar Shift Cipher (easy)

BZDRZQ'R VHED LTRS AD ZANUD RTROHBHNM

Cryptogram 2: Caesar Shift Cipher (harder)

MHILY LZA ZBHL XBPZXBL MVYABUHL HWWPBZ
JSHBKPBZ JHLJBZ

Cryptogram 3: Simple Monoalphabetic Substitution Cipher

BT JPX RMLX PCUV AMLX ICVJP IBTWXVR CI M
LMT'R PMTN, MTN YVCJX CDXV MWMBTRJ JPX
AMTNGXRJBAH UQCT JPX QGMRJXV CI JPX YMGG CI
JPX HBTW'R QMGMAX; MTN JPX HBTW RMY JPX QMVJ
CI JPX PMTN JPMJ YVCJX. JPXT JPX HBTW'R
ACUTJXTMTAX YMR APMTWXN, MTN PBR JPCUWPJR
JVCUFGXN PBL, RC JPMJ JPX SCBTJR CI PBR GCBTR
YXVX GCCRXN, MTN PBR HTXXR RLCJX CTX MWMBTRJ
MTCJPXV. JPX HBTW AVBXN MGCUN JC FVBTW BT JPX
MRJVCGCWXVR, JPX APMGNXMTR, MTN JPX
RCCJPRMEXVR. MTN JPX HBTW RQMHX, MTN RMBN JC
JPX YBRX LXT CI FMFEGCT, YPCRCXDXV RPMGG VXMN
JPBR YVBJBTW, MTN RPCY LX JPX BTJXVQVXJMJBCT
JPXVXCI, RPMGG FX AGCJPXN YBJP RAMVGXJ, MTN
PMDX M APMBT CI WCGN MFCUJ PBR TXAH, MTN
RPMGG FX JPX JPBVN VUGXV BT JPX HBTWNCL. JPXT
AMLX BT MGG JPX HBTW'R YBRX LXT; FUJ JPXE
ACUGN TCJ VXMN JPX YVBJBTW, TCV LMHX HTCYT JC
JPX HBTW JPX BTJXVQVXJMJBCT JPXVXCI. JPXT YMR
HBTW FXGRPMOOMV WVXMJGE JVCUFGXN, MTN PBR
ACUTJXTMTAX YMR APMTWXN BT PBL, MTN PBR GCVNR
YXVX MRJCTBRPXN. TCY JPX KUXXT, FE VXMRCT CI
JPX YCVNR CI JPX HBTW MTN PBR GCVNR, AMLX
BTJC JPX FMTKUXJ PCURX; MTN JPX KUXXT RQMHX
MTN RMBN, C HBTW, GBDX ICVXDXV; GXJ TCJ JPE
JPCUWPJR JVCUFGX JPXX, TCV GXJ JPE
ACUTJXTMTAX FX APMTWXN; JPXVX BR M LMT BT JPE
HBTWNCL, BT YPCL BR JPX RQBVBJ CI JPX PCGE
WCNR; MTN BT JPX NMER CI JPE IMJPXV GBWPJ MTN
UTNXVRJMTNBTW MTN YBRNCL, GBHX JPX YBRNCL CI
JPX WCNR, YMR ICUTN BT PBL; YPCL JPX HBTW
TXFUAPMNTXOOMV JPE IMJPXV, JPX HBTW, B RME,

JPE IMJPXV, LMNX LMRJXV CI JPX LMWBABMTR,
MRJVCGCWXVR, APMGNXMTR, MTN RCCJPRMEXVR;
ICVMRLUAP MR MT XZAXGGXTJ RQBVBJ, MTN
HTCYGXNWX, MTN UTNXVRJMTNBTW, BTJXVQVXJBTW CI
NVXMLR, MTN RPCYBTW CI PMVN RXTJXTAXR, MTN
NBRRCGDBTW CI NCUFJR, YXVX ICUTN BT JPX RMLX
NMTBXG, YPCL JPX HBTW TMLXN FXGJXRPMOOMV; TCY
GXJ NMTBXG FX AMGGXN, MTN PX YBGG RPCY JPX
BTJXVQVXJMJBCT.

Cryptogram 4: Monoalphabetic Cipher (no word breaks)

QWNQJDLKNCHQLWNQMYICGEKWNLKQUMLQEYQEUELKQEKS
QKNMKWNMNNEKNMNYQKQSSMIYYDPSNQELWQJNEONEKSNR
QEHWGLNPSNQMNDNLQEYXSGMUYFWNNTLKGSYGXQSUXNSN
YXQMXMGRKWNXGOLGXZQTNMLKMNNKWNLNNKNYKGZMUEOQ
HWUXXGXWULLKMGEOXMNLWZMQPUEONQLKPGQLKQUMHUKW
WURQLWNNEKNMNYWQJUEOLWQTNEWQEYLHUKWNQPWGXILW
NHQLQZGIKKGLUKYGHEHWNEWULNDNLMNLKNYICGEKWNCQ
CNMHUKWKWNPIMUGILRQMTUEOLHWUPWUWQYVILKNFQRUE
NYQEYSNXKICGEKWNKQZSNKWNQYJNEKIMNGXKWNYQEPUE
ORNEZDLUMQMKWIMPGEQEYGDSN

Cryptogram 5: Vigenère Cipher

FHYULCVBYEBYJEUDSYQEAFELWRGFGCQ
ISVBCVTIQOUQFMUDCYEJRPGQGRKEZOU
CSRGOTDRRRKEKRDCUNARMNXTCUHCZAQ
WHCVOLRFZHNHDMGQBYEBYJEYZEYOTFB
LMQDMQBYQKCUHCDPNOICGHGVGCQISVT
MPALBPPRBJHMQKIQLNTHNRLOLVILFLS
GERKEQSECGOKHTCU

GLOSSARY

ASCII American Standard Code for Information Interchange, a standard for turning alphabetic and other characters into numbers.

asymmetric-key cryptography A form of cryptography in which the key required for encrypting is not the same as the key required for decrypting. Describes public-key cryptography systems, such as RSA.

Caesar-shift substitution cipher Originally a cipher in which each letter in the message is replaced with the letter three places further on in the alphabet. More generally, it is a cipher in which each letter in the message is replaced with the letter x places further on in the alphabet, where x is a number between 1 and 25.

cipher Any general system for hiding the meaning of a message by replacing each letter in the original message with another letter. The system should have some built-in flexibility, known as the key.

cipher alphabet The rearrangement of the ordinary (or plain) alphabet, which then determines how each letter in the original message is enciphered. The cipher alphabet can also consist of numbers or any other characters, but in all cases it dictates the replacements for letters in the original message.

ciphertext The message (or plaintext) after encipherment.

code A system for hiding the meaning of a message by replacing each word or phrase in the original message with another character or set of characters. The list of replacements is contained in a codebook. (An alternative definition of a code is any form of encryption which has no built-in flexibility, i.e. there is only one key, namely the codebook.)

codebook A list of replacements for words or phrases in the original message.

cryptanalysis The science of deducing the plaintext from a ciphertext, without knowledge of the key.

cryptography The science of encrypting a message, or the science of concealing the meaning of a message. Sometimes the term is used more generally to mean the science of anything connected with ciphers, and is an alternative to the term cryptology.

cryptology The science of secret writing in all its forms, covering both cryptography and cryptanalysis.

decipher To turn an enciphered message back into the original message. Formally, the term refers only to the intended receiver who knows the key required to obtain the plaintext, but informally it also refers to the process of cryptanalysis, in which the decipherment is performed by an enemy interceptor.

decode To turn an encoded message back into the original message.

decrypt To decipher or to decode.

DES Data Encryption Standard, developed by IBM and adopted in 1976.

Diffie–Hellman–Merkle key exchange A process by which a sender and receiver can establish a secret key via public discussion. Once the key has been agreed, the sender can use a cipher such as DES to encrypt a message.

digital signature A method for proving the authorship of an electronic document. Often this is generated by the author encrypting the document with his or her private-key.

encipher To turn the original message into the enciphered message.

encode To turn the original message into the encoded message.

encrypt To encipher or encode.

encryption algorithm Any general encryption process which can be specified exactly by choosing a key.

homophonic substitution cipher A cipher in which there are several potential substitutions for each plaintext letter. Crucially, if there are, say, six potential substitutions for the plaintext letter **a**, then these six characters can only represent the letter **a**. This is a type of monoalphabetic substitution cipher.

key The element that turns the general encryption algorithm into a specific method for encryption. In general, the enemy may be aware of the encryption algorithm being used by the sender and receiver, but the enemy must not be allowed to know the key.

key distribution The process of ensuring that both sender and receiver have access to the key required to encrypt and decrypt a message, while making sure that the key does not fall into enemy hands. Key distribution was a major problem in terms of logistics and security before the invention of public-key cryptography.

key escrow A scheme in which users lodge copies of their secret keys with a trusted third party, the escrow agent, who will pass on keys to law enforcers only under certain circumstances, for example if a court order is issued.

key length Computer encryption involves keys which are numbers. The key length refers to the number of digits or bits in the key, and thus indicates the biggest number that can be used as a key, thereby defining the number of possible keys. The longer the key length (or the greater the number of possible keys), the longer it will take a cryptanalyst to test all the keys.

monoalphabetic substitution cipher A substitution cipher in which the cipher alphabet is fixed throughout encryption.

National Security Agency (NSA) A branch of the U.S. Department of Defense, responsible for ensuring the security of American communications and for breaking into the communications of other countries.

one-time pad The only known form of encryption that is unbreakable. It relies on a random key that is the same length as the message. Each key can be used once and only once.

plaintext The original message before encryption.

polyalphabetic substitution cipher A substitution cipher in which the cipher alphabet changes during the encryption, for example the Vigenère cipher. The change is defined by a key.

Pretty Good Privacy (PGP) A computer encryption algorithm developed by Phil Zimmermann, based on RSA.

private-key The key used by the receiver to decrypt messages in a system of public-key cryptography. The private-key must be kept secret.

public-key The key used by the sender to encrypt messages in a system of public-key cryptography. The public-key is available to the public.

public-key cryptography A system of cryptography which overcomes the problems of key distribution. Public-key cryptography requires an asymmetric cipher, so that each user can create a public encryption key and a private decryption key.

quantum cryptography An unbreakable form of cryptography that exploits quantum theory, in particular the uncertainty principle – which states that it is impossible to measure all aspects of an object with absolute certainty. Quantum cryptography guarantees the secure exchange of a random series of bits, which is then used as the basis for a one-time pad cipher.

RSA The first system that fitted the requirements of public-key cryptography, invented by Ron Rivest, Adi Shamir and Leonard Adleman in 1977.

steganography The science of hiding the existence of a message, as opposed to cryptography, which is the science of hiding the meaning of a message.

substitution cipher A system of encryption in which each letter of a message is replaced with another character, but retains its position within the message.

symmetric-key cryptography A form of cryptography in which the key required for encrypting is the same as the key required for decrypting. The term describes all traditional forms of encryption, i.e. those in use before the 1970s.

transposition cipher A system of encryption in which each letter of a message changes its position within the message, but retains its identity.

Vigenère cipher A polyalphabetic cipher which was developed around 1500. The Vigenère square contains 26 separate cipher alphabets, each one a Caesar-shifted alphabet, and a keyword defines which cipher alphabet should be used to encrypt each letter of a message.

ACKNOWLEDGEMENTS

While working in the TV series and writing this book I have had the privilege of meeting some of the world's greatest living codemakers and codebreakers, ranging from those who worked at Bletchley Park to those who are developing the ciphers that will enrich the Information Age. I would like to thank Whitfield Diffie and Martin Hellman, who took the time to describe their work to me while I was in sunny California. Similarly, Clifford Cocks, Malcolm Williamson and Richard Walton were enormously helpful during my visit to cloudy Cheltenham. In particular, I am grateful to Professor Fred Piper of the Information Security Group at Royal Holloway College, London, who allowed me to attend the M.Sc. course on information security.

I would also like to thank Leonard Adleman, Ole Franksen, Mitchel Leaman, Rosemary North, Michael Parish, Richard Parkinson, Doron Swade, David Kahn, Jenny Wormald and Philip Zimmermann, who all gave up their valuable time to be filmed and interviewed for the television series. Most of all, thanks go to Bill Manley, who accompanied us on our filming trip to Egypt and provided us with great insights into the monuments we visited.

Dr Mohammed Mrayati and Dr Ibrahim Kadi have been involved in revealing some of the early breakthroughs in Arab cryptanalysis, and were kind enough to send me relevant documents and to help during filming in Istanbul. The periodical *Cryptologia* has carried articles about Arabian cryptanalysis, as well as many other cryptographic subjects, and I would like to thank Brian Winkel for sending me back issues.

I would encourage readers to visit the National Cryptologic Museum near Washington, D.C. and the Cabinet War Rooms in London, and I hope that you will be as fascinated as I was during my visits. Thank you to the curators and librarians of these museums for helping me with my research.

As well as interviewing experts, I have also depended on numerous books and articles. The list of further reading contains some of my sources, but it is neither a complete bibliography nor a definitive reference list. Instead, it merely includes material that may be of interest to the general reader. Of all the books I have come across during my research, I would like to single out one in particular: *The Codebreakers* by David Kahn. This book documents almost every cryptographic episode in history, and as such it is an invaluable resource.

Various libraries, institutions and individuals have provided me with photographs. All the sources are listed in the picture credits, but particular thanks go to Professor Eva Brann, for discovering the only known photograph of Alice Kober; Joan Chadwick, for sending me a photograph of John Chadwick; and Brenda Ellis, for allowing me to borrow photographs of James Ellis. These images and all the others in the book were incorporated into the text by Robert Updegraff, who did an excellent job of designing this book.

Finally, I was fortunate to receive a tremendous amount of help from the people at Channel 4 and Diverse Productions who commissioned and made the television series. Barbara Altounyan and Charles Furneaux spotted the potential of the series; Polly Williams, Mike Duxbury and Tim Copestake directed the series; Kate Smith and Dan Leon researched many aspects of it; Chris Merry and Adam Scourfield were respectively cameraman and soundman; Janet Smyth and Vanessa Myrie oversaw the whole project and ensured that everything went relatively smoothly. Without the enormous contribution of these people, the television series would not have been made and this book would not have been written. Above all, Paul Sen, the series producer, provided constant support and enthusiasm.

Patrick Walsh is an agent with a love of science, a concern for his authors and boundless energy. He has put me in touch with the kindest and most capable publishers, most notably Fourth Estate, whose staff continue to endure my constant stream of queries with great spirit. Last, but certainly not least, I thank my editors: Christopher Potter and Leo Hollis at Fourth Estate; and John Woodruff, whose input has been invaluable and who contributed material for the boxes that appear throughout this book. As all good editors should, they have helped the author to steer a clear path through his subject, in my case one that twists and turns its way across three thousand years. For that I am tremendously grateful.

FURTHER READING

The following is a list of books aimed at the general reader. I have avoided giving more detailed technical references, but several of the texts listed contain a detailed bibliography.

There is a great deal of interesting material on the Internet relating to codes and ciphers. In addition to the books, I have therefore listed a few of the websites that are worth visiting.

General

Kahn, David, *The Codebreakers* (New York: Scribner, 1996).
  A 1,200-page history of ciphers. The definitive story of cryptography from ancient times to the 1950s.
Newton, David E., *Encyclopedia of Cryptology* (Santa Barbara, CA: ABC-Clio, 1997).
  A useful reference, with clear, concise explanations of most aspects of ancient and modern cryptology.
Smith, Lawrence Dwight, *Cryptography* (New York: Dover, 1943).
  An excellent elementary introduction to cryptography with more than 150 problems. Dover publishes many books on the subject of codes and ciphers.
Beutelspacher, Albrecht, *Cryptology* (Washington, D.C.: Mathematical Association of America, 1994).
  An excellent overview of the subject, from the Caesar cipher to public-key cryptography, concentrating on the mathematics rather than the history. It is also the cryptography book with the best subtitle: *An Introduction to the Art and Science of Enciphering, Encrypting, Concealing, Hiding, and Safeguarding, Described Without any Arcane Skullduggery but not Without Cunning Waggery for the Delectation and Instruction of the General Public.*

Chapter 1

Gaines, Helen Fouché, *Cryptanalysis* (New York: Dover, 1956).
  A study of ciphers and their solution. An excellent introduction to cryptanalysis, with many useful frequency tables in the appendix.
Al-Kadi, Ibraham A., 'The origins of cryptology: The Arab contributions', *Cryptologia*, vol. 16, no. 2 (April 1992), pp. 97–126.
  A discussion of recently discovered Arab manuscripts and the work of al-Kindī.
Fraser, Lady Antonia, *Mary Queen of Scots* (London: Random House, 1989).
  A highly readable account of the life of Mary Queen of Scots.

Chapter 2

Standage, Tom, *The Victorian Internet* (London: Weidenfeld & Nicolson, 1998).
  The remarkable story of the development of the electric telegraph.
Swade, Doron, *The Cogwheel Brain* (London: Little Brown, 2000).
  A fascinating biography of Charles Babbage, focusing on his struggle to design and build his calculating and computing engines.

Chapter 3

Pope, Maurice, *The Story of Decipherment* (London: Thames & Hudson, 1975).
  A description of various decipherments, from Hittite hieroglyphs to the Ugaritic alphabet, aimed at the layperson.
Davies, W.V., *Reading the Past: Egyptian Hieroglyphs* (London: British Museum Press, 1997).
  Part of an excellent series of introductory texts published by the British Museum. Other authors in the series have written books on cuneiform, Etruscan, Greek inscriptions, Linear B, Maya glyphs and runes.
Chadwick, John, *The Decipherment of Linear B* (Cambridge: C.U.P., 1987).
  A brilliant description of the decipherment.
Collier, Mark and Manley, Bill, *How to Read Egyptian Hieroglyphs* (London: British Museum Press, 1998).
  An excellent book for beginners who want to learn about the script of the ancient Egyptians.

Parkinson, Richard, *Cracking Codes: The Rosetta Stone and Decipherment* (London: British Museum Press, 1999).

An authoritative account of the story of the Rosetta Stone, lavishly illustrated, and published to accompany an exhibition celebrating the two hundredth anniversary of the Stone's discovery.

Chapter 4

Tuchman, Barbara W., *The Zimmermann Telegram* (New York: Ballantine, 1994).

A highly readable account of the most influential decipherment in the First World War.

Kahn, David, *Seizing the Enigma* (London: Arrow Books, 1996).

The story of the cracking of the Enigma cipher, focusing particularly on Bletchley Park's contribution to the Battle of the Atlantic.

Chapter 5

Gardner, Martin, 'A new kind of cipher that would take millions of years to break', *Scientific American*, vol. 237 (August 1977), pp. 120–24.

The article that introduced RSA to the world.

Hellman, M.E., 'The mathematics of public-key cryptography', *Scientific American*, vol. 241 (August 1979), pp. 130–39.

An excellent overview of the various forms of public-key cryptography.

Schneier, Bruce, *Applied Cryptography* (New York: John Wiley & Sons, 1996).

An excellent survey of modern cryptography. A definitive, comprehensive and authoritative introduction to the subject.

Epilogue

Zimmermann, Philip R., *The Official PGP User's Guide* (Cambridge, MA: MIT Press, 1996).

A friendly overview of PGP, written by the man who developed it.

Garfinkel, S., *PGP: Pretty Good Privacy* (Sebastopol, CA: O'Reilly & Associates, 1995).

An excellent introduction to PGP and the issues surrounding modern cryptography.

Bamford, James, *The Puzzle Palace* (London: Penguin, 1983).
> Inside the National Security Agency, America's most secret intelligence organisation.

Diffie, Whitfield, and Landau, Susan, *Privacy on the Line* (Cambridge, MA: MIT Press, 1998).
> The politics of wire-tapping and encryption.

INTERNET SITES

Bletchley Park

http://www.cranfield.ac.uk/ccc/bpark/

The official website, which includes opening times and directions.

The Alan Turing Homepage

http://www.turing.org.uk/turing/

Enigma emulator

http://www.attlabs.att.co.uk/andyc/enigma/enigma_j.html

An excellent emulator that shows how the Enigma cipher machine works. It allows you to alter the machine settings and encrypt messages.

Phil Zimmermann and PGP

http://www.pgp.com/phil/phil.asp

Electronic Frontier Foundation

http://www.eff.org/

An organisation devoted to protecting rights and promoting freedom on the Internet.

Information Security Group, Royal Holloway College

http://isg.rhbnc.ac.uk/

National Cryptologic Museum

http://www.nsa.gov/museum/index.html

American Cryptogram Association (ACA)

http://www.und.nodak.edu/org/crypto/crypto/

An association which specialises in setting and solving cipher puzzles.

Cryptologia

http://www.dean.usma.edu/math/resource/pubs/cryptolo/index.htm

A quarterly journal devoted to all aspects of cryptology.

RSA Laboratories' Frequently Asked Questions About Cryptography
http://www.rsasecurity.com/rsalabs/faq/
Yahoo! Security and Encryption Page
http://uk.dir.yahoo.com/Computers_and_Internet/
Security_and_Encryption/

PICTURE CREDITS

INDEX